The Elephant in the Room
by
Eamonn Hamilton

The Elephant in the Room

An Evidence-Based Study of Government Waste, Error and Inefficiency

by

Eamonn Hamilton

Copyright © Eamonn Hamilton 2015

All rights reserved. No part of this publication may be reproduced, stored in a retrieval system or transmitted in any form or by any means electronic, mechanical, audio, visual or otherwise, without prior permission of the copyright owner. Nor can it be circulated in any form of binding or cover other than that in which it is published and without similar conditions including this condition being imposed on the subsequent purchaser.

ISBN: 978-0-9571084-2-4

Published by Evae Publishing in conjunction with Writersworld. This book is produced entirely in the UK. It is available to order from most book shops in the United Kingdom, and is also globally available via UK-based Internet book retailers.

Copy edited by Ian Large

Cover design by David Anderson and Jag Lall

www.writersworld.co.uk

WRITERSWORLD
2 Bear Close Flats
Bear Close
Woodstock
Oxfordshire, OX20 1JX
England

☎ 01993 812500
☎ +44 1993 812500

The text pages of this book are produced via an independent certification process that ensures the trees from which the paper is produced come from well-managed sources that exclude the risk of using illegally logged timber while leaving options to use post-consumer recycled paper as well.

To my late wife Cathy and my wife Sarah who allowed me the scope to develop my ambitions. And to the 632 brave British and Commonwealth individuals who died in the Iraq and Afghanistan wars.

THANKS

To Dominic Bell who introduced me to Dragon voice recognition system; to David Anderson of Graphic-Ads (www.graphic-ad.com) who originated the front cover and created the newsletter; to David Hearn of DMH Web Design (www.dmhwebdesign) who conceived and activated the website; to Graham Cook and his team at Writersworld (www.writersworld.co.uk) – Ian Large had the unenviable task of copy editing the missive and Jag Lall (www.jaglallart.com) creatively organised the front and back covers; to those at the National Audit Office who answered my sometimes naive questions; to Chris Connor, Managing Partner of Robson Rhodes until 2007 who helped me understand the complexity of procurement in the public sector; and to my family and friends whose eyes would understandably glaze over when I mentioned the project. The errors and omissions are my responsibility but I have the opportunity of correcting them in future volumes and indeed, I welcome constructive comments which will allow me to do so.

www.governmentwaste.info

FOREWORD

The TaxPayers' Alliance has been fighting for lower taxes and more efficient government spending for over ten years. With public sector debt rising to nearly £1.5 trillion, the fight to protect taxpayers is more urgent than ever.

Public spending must come down so it is affordable, and that would leave room for tax cuts. People should keep more money to spend on their own families and priorities. Lower taxes will also see businesses flourish, creating jobs and prosperity.

But the reality is that the coalition government has failed to get spending under control and the deficit, despite recent falls, is still forecast to be £91 billion in 2014/15. Every pound we borrow to pay for something politicians want today has to be paid back. But that is a bill for our children and grandchildren to pay for in higher taxes, not us.

The easiest way for politicians to get control of spending is to cut out the waste: and our latest *Bumper Book of Government Waste* found £120 billion worth in just a year.

Highlighting examples of waste at national and local government level – from Porsches for local councillors to £6 million blown on military earplugs that were not fit for use – the TPA has demonstrated the need for transparency and accountability in the public sector that will help bring spending down.

The Elephant in the Room is an extremely valuable contribution to the ongoing debate about the future of the public finances in the UK. Demonstrating the levels of waste and inefficiency in the system in a clear and uncompromising way, this book makes a decisive case for an efficient small state.

Politicians and bureaucrats should be held accountable for how they spend our money and Eamonn Hamilton's book will serve as a key part of the taxpayers' arsenal in the years ahead. It is a great shame that many of those in charge of our money do not have the same forensic attention to detail as the author of this impressive work.

Matthew Elliott
Founder, The TaxPayers' Alliance

"One of the causes of the downfall of Rome was that people, being fed by the State... ceased to have any responsibility for themselves or their children, and consequently became a nation of unemployed wasters. They frequented the circuses, where paid performers appeared before them in the arena, much as we see the crowds now flocking to look on at paid players playing football... thousands of boys and young men, pale, narrow-chested, hunched-up, miserable specimens, smoking endless cigarettes, numbers of them betting, all of them learning to be hysterical as they groan or cheer in panic unison with their neighbours – the worst sound of all being the hysterical scream of laughter that greets any little trip or fall of a player. One wonders whether this can be the same nation which had gained for itself the reputation of being a stolid, pipe-sucking manhood, unmoved by panic or excitement, and reliable in the tightest of places.

Get the lads away from this – teach them to be manly..."

Baden-Powell, R, *Scouting for Boys*, 1908

INTRODUCTION

Between 2000 and 2005 the UK Government wasted over £230 billion because of fraud, error and inefficiency. Instead of correcting the problem, government consistently introduces new taxes, adding to the burdens of an already heavily-taxed population. The growth of *Tolley's Tax Annual* since 2000 supports the hypothesis that government regards the imposition of new taxes as a more attractive option than solving the issue of waste. This evidence-based book quantifies waste by examining government documents and identifies a scenario which sadly does not seem to have altered in the last 15 years. The 2014 Budget disclosed that the National Debt of £1.304 trillion will reach £1.57 trillion by 2017 and that the interest charges alone on the debt will be more than £62 billion per annum (Note 1). As a nation we currently add to this debt at the rate of £93.7 billion a year, i.e. the amount that government spends in excess of income. The pressure to reduce the annual overspend and to eventually reduce this massive debt should be motivation enough for the Treasury to identify and then correct the problems of fraud, error or inefficiency.

This book identifies a number of waste issues which could reduce the tax burden or at least slow down the rate of increase. All analysis is evidence-based using Public Accounts Committee (PAC), National Audit Office (NAO) and other Select Committee reports for the period. Many books have been written about the subject, some excellent, some uninspiring, some bad. In most cases these books have concentrated on a specific subject, a specific Department of State or a specific industry. Everyone is aware of waste by government but most people are only conscious about a subject which relates to their own interest. Stories are numerous about waste whether anecdotal or factual. People are aware that we lost a lot of money when we sold our gold reserves but are unsure about the detail. People are aware that the directors of MG Rover managed to acquire £40 million before the company collapsed with the loss of 6,000 jobs, but do not understand how. People believe that benefit claimants are paid sizeable sums (Note 2). People are aware that government IT schemes always appear to be delivered way above the initially quoted costs and are usually late. Most people have their favourite 'waste' story. These stories confirm to people that the tax they pay to central government is not used as efficiently as it should be. The knowledge of specific employees may be restricted to their own areas of expertise: medical practitioners wax lyrical about waste in the NHS, soldiers list many of the examples of waste in the Ministry of Defence and fire fighters are knowledgeable about the fiasco of the FiReControl project.

Interest in the subject of government waste was ignited for the writer by a very public spat between John Prescott, former Deputy Prime Minister, and his civil servants with input from the Fire Brigades Union (FBU) about who was responsible for the FiReControl fiasco. The project was budgeted at £120 million, cost £635 million and has never been used, and there remains a commitment of between £247 and £431 million until the lease terminates in 2036. The FBU said, "The central failing of FiReControl was political. Prescott was the prime mover and the Secretary of State who could have ended the project at any point. The FBU was the only organisation to have warned from the beginning that the project was flawed" (Note 3), whilst Lord Prescott laid the blame at the door of Sir John Housden, who was Permanent Secretary at the Department for Communities and Local Government. A spokesman for Sir John, who later became Permanent Secretary for Scotland, said, "As already made clear to parliament, the Permanent Secretary joined the department responsible for fire control in late October 2005 by which time all the key decisions on the design and procurement had been made" (Note 4). The inability of anyone to take responsibility for this gigantic fiasco, which could potentially cost £1 billion, was serious enough, but as always the jobs and pensions of those connected with this project have been protected. The normal procedure for investigating such a fiasco is that reports are meticulously assembled and published, which sometimes result in an appearance by the major players involved in the drama before a government committee, after which the reports are suitably filed without any appropriate lessons being absorbed and with the major players congratulating themselves on a job well done.

One of the problems about this subject is its sheer size. Despite claims about austerity we continue to spend more than we earn, and in 2014 government is expected to spend £734 billion, although only £648 billion will have been generated by taxes and other means, with the remainder borrowed. Public spending in the UK was £341 billion in 2000, had more than doubled to £692 billion by 2010 and is projected in 2015 to increase to £734 billion. Despite the rhetoric about austerity and the need to adjust to more efficient smaller government, it would appear that the opposite is the norm as we continue to spend more than we accrue. Government talks about "our place in the world" and indeed that is something which needs redefinition. José

Manuel Barroso, the former non-elected leader of the EU, suggested that the UK was in danger of being compared with Norway and Switzerland and losing its place at the top table of nations should it decide to operate outside membership of the EU (Note 5). Norway enjoys a deficit of less than 1% of GDP and Switzerland has been mandated by voters to produce structurally balanced budgets each year, so both seem ideal role models for the UK – unlike most members of the EU.

Most taxpayers pay their taxes because they have to and the 25 million who pay tax through the PAYE system do so because they have no choice. In addition there are over 4.5 million companies which fall within the European Commission classification of Small Business Enterprise (SME), of which 4.3 million employ between one and nine people. The remaining 200,000 SME companies employ between 10 and 249 people. These SME enterprises generally use an outside agency to monitor their tax affairs and, like PAYE individuals, accept that the payment of tax is an integral part of running a small business. SMEs generally do not get involved in fancy legal footwork using expensive lawyers and accountants to shirk their responsibility for tax. Like PAYE employees they are part of the backbone of the tax system. Like PAYE employees, SME owners are part of the very squeezed middle in the UK tax structure and meet Leona Helmsley's (owner of the Helmsley Hotel group who went to jail for tax evasion) definition: "We don't pay taxes. Only the little people pay taxes." (Note 6).

Times writer William Rees-Mogg suggests that amongst the current difficulties facing SME owners is a decrease in reserves and an inability to borrow money, so the SME is generally in the art of survival rather than the process of expansion, and naturally would like to reduce their tax commitment. Rees-Mogg also argues that Britain is an overtaxed country, that there is a correlation between high government expenditure, declining competitiveness and the loss of business confidence, which has led to a widespread loss of belief in the equity or efficiency of the tax system (Note 7).

The TaxPayers' Alliance (Note 8) has produced four editions of the *Bumper Book of Government Waste*, which highlights some of the most obvious examples of waste. This book sets out to complement the *Bumper Book* and a number of other books, and in the process examined over 1,000 government reports for the period 2000 to 2005, which identify and report on issues of waste across all Departments of State, and in doing so have confirmed that at least £230 billion has been wasted. Each statement about waste is supported by a specific report, generally audited, without resort to hyperbole. Errors may be made in the interpretation of such reports but the overall figure for waste is so enormous that such errors, although important, become statistically insignificant. Sadly, the book cannot claim to be finite, and indeed it is the author's opinion that the overall figure of £230 billion is understated because of the sheer scale and complexity of the subject. For example, a particular project may only be examined by the PAC or NAO once in the five-year period and recorded as such, but the error may occur in the other four years with the same amount of waste but without evidence to support. It would be improper to suggest that major government departments are economical with the truth but the example of the introduction of various Tax Credits in 1999 does not help their case. For 3½ years the Inland Revenue advised the NAO that losses due to fraud and error in the distribution of Tax Credits was within the order of £13-£22 million a year. When the scheme was closed in 2003, and a new scheme introduced, the department delivered an analysis, based on 2001 but delivered some five months after the previous scheme had finished, which showed that the level of fraud and error was between £510 and £710 million a year.

This book is an attempt to pull together a record for the period and hopefully create a basis for debate about how waste can be eradicated from the government psyche. Reports by newspapers about government waste are usually ephemeral and are quickly forgotten – the subject is dull and unexciting except to those involved. Television news channels occasionally mention a specific cause of waste – that too is ephemeral and initial interest soon evaporates. One of the more effective campaigners about government waste is the satirical magazine *Private Eye* which has mounted relentless campaigns against many issues of waste but who, by the very nature of their fortnightly publication and space restrictions, cannot give as much weight to the subjects as they would possibly like. However, *Private Eye* has been a source of inspiration to many journalists, MPs and writers who suddenly identify an interest in a particular area of government waste and has been a rich source of information for this writer.

We all know what waste is – or do we? We buy food, leave it in the fridge and let it run past its 'use by' date. Food is wasted and the solution is very simple – the waste is dumped. Government waste is similar – government buys goods and services that are not really needed and when those goods go beyond their 'sell by' date they are also dumped. Government is in the habit of buying goods at agreed prices but finding that when the goods or contractors are in place the contract suddenly needs to be reviewed, recosted, revised or reallocated. It will not come as a surprise to observers that suppliers to government feel they can change the rules once they have been appointed. Government itself has redefined the meaning of the word 'budget' and believes that budgets and tenders are an expression of intent rather than the creation of a fixed-price contract. The chapters of this book are littered with examples of companies who have tendered, won, and then successfully renegotiated contracts, and it will come as no surprise to the reader that the re-negotiations have generally been upwards. But government waste is not just about tenders and big business. It is also about the amount of fraud, error and inefficiency identified in areas where the government is paymaster.

In examining the reports a decision was necessary about how to handle inflation, changes in regulation, and changes in responsibility, amongst other matters, and it was decided to use figures on both a real-time and inflation-added basis, i.e. a project examined in 2000 would show the waste associated with the project as it was at 2000 but would be extrapolated to 2014 figures at the end of the book.

The period chosen was arbitrary but it did seem that the arrival of the New Labour Government in 1997 had created an era of reform and transparency and that access to records and figures would be easier from 2000 onwards. Most of the projects examined were therefore approved by New Labour, although some of the projects had their genesis with the previous Conservative Government, e.g. The Millennium Dome. It is acknowledged that reporting by government improved as the decade progressed, with more transparency and more meaningful information. Mention of the New Labour ambition to reform should not be seen as an indication of any type of political bias. The book is apolitical, although having studied 1,000 Civil Service type reports it has to be acknowledged that politicians are entitled to some sympathy. They are for five years the temporary custodians of the decision-making process of which the first 30 months are spent getting to grips with the running of the nation whilst the second 30 months are spent with an eye to their reappointment as Minister, MP or whatever. They may be the masters of strategy but the Civil Service/Establishment make or break that strategy.

The book looks at projects which have been measured and reported upon officially and, for that reason, subjective projects such as the UK's involvement in the wars in Iraq and Afghanistan (£20 billion and rising) or our membership of the European Union (£15 billion a year and rising) (Note 9), are not considered. What is considered are projects which have been examined and where reports exist, which have been compiled by the Public Accounts Committee, the National Audit Office, other Select Committees as well as statutory reports from specific departments. Standard Notes for MPs have also been accepted as primary sources (Note 10).

The PAC and NAO have wide-ranging powers to examine projects that they identify and for the purpose of this exercise the date of the PAC report determines where the chosen report fits within the book, i.e. a project in 2002 which was reported upon by the PAC in 2004 will be found in the 2004 section of the book. Should the PAC not issue a report then the date of the NAO report will decide which year the project is considered. Similarly, should neither a PAC nor a NAO report exist other Select Committees' reports as well as Standard Notes will become the primary source and will be dealt with in the year in which they were published.

The PAC is currently chaired by Margaret Hodge, MP for Barking, and a former New Labour Minister, who not only conducts her committee witness sessions with energy and commitment, but also rises above politics in her interviews of departmental heads and businessmen called before her committee. She has an ability to frame suitable quotes for newspapers and TV and has increased PAC visibility nationwide. The Committee for Public Accounts, to give it its correct title, was established in 1862 under Standing Order 148, "for the examination of the accounts showing the appropriation of the sums granted by Parliament to meet the public expenditure and [since 1934] of such other accounts laid before Parliament as the Committee may think fit". In 2007 the committee celebrated the 150th anniversary of its inception. Following the 1983 National Audit Act, the main work of the committee has been examination of the reports compiled by the Comptroller and Auditor General of the NAO on his value for money (VFM) studies of the economy and the efficiency and effectiveness with which government departments and other bodies have used their resources to further their objectives. There are about 60 of these reports in a year and about two thirds are investigated by the committee by either taking oral evidence or submitting written questions to the department concerned. It focuses on the VFM aspect of the report and decides whether the project was handled in line with its objectives. It does not have the power to consider the formulation or merit of policy. The composition of the committee is synchronised with the political make-up in parliament and there are 16 members, with the quorum needed being four. Members are nominated at the beginning of parliament and changes may occur during parliament due to members becoming Ministers or front bench opposition spokespersons, or from death or resignation. For the 2010 to 2015 parliament there are eight Conservatives, five Labour and two Liberal Democrat members plus the Chairperson.

NAO reports are generally published before the appropriate PAC or Select Committee report. The NAO pride themselves on their independence and indeed preface the introduction to every report with a statement emphasising that the NAO employ 800 staff and are totally independent of government. No one, however, is ever totally independent of their paymaster and every Comptroller and Auditor General has been a Treasury ex-employee. Senior staff at the NAO no doubt have attended the Civil Service management college together with other contemporaries now working in different departments and may indeed have moved around themselves within those departments. The NAO reports studied for this book have generally been well written and, whilst offering advice and direction to the department upon which they are reporting, have never allowed themselves to be critical of the actions of a fellow civil servant. They can be critical of outside bodies and departments but never identify accountability to an individual. They issue a number of reports: statutory ones which affect the accounts of all government departments as well as a wide range of other public sector bodies and as already mentioned issue Value for Money reports, usually commissioned by a department, the PAC, other Select Committees or indeed a self-initiated report. The reports used in this evaluation have been a mixture of types.

The NAO and PAC investigate all departments but it is noticeable that the big beast departments, i.e. the Foreign Office, the Home Office and the Treasury do not attract as much attention from these bodies as other departments. The Foreign Office does not feature in our analysis and the Treasury only featured twice – once in a self-congratulatory report about the sale of the gold reserves – a document which they no doubt now hope will never again see the light of day. Attempts are made in all cases to use primary sources but in situations where information is obtained from secondary sources, i.e. the Political Cleanup campaign, *Computer Weekly* magazine etc., those sources will be acknowledged.

Public Private Partnerships (PPP) are mentioned frequently in the projects featured in this book. Essentially, a PPP is a venture between a government service and private business which is funded and operated through a partnership. The initial philosophy of PPP was that the private company would assume substantial financial, technical and/or operational risk in projects. The PPP was usually structured so that the public sector body does not incur any borrowing and that the private sector incurs the financial obligation of the project. A derivative of the PPP is the Private Finance Initiative (PFI) under which the contractor pays for the construction costs of the project and rents the finished project back to the public sector. The PFI initiative has been written about widely and now faces closer examination, as the schemes originally launched in a mood of all-round bonhomie have become mature projects with financial obligations sometimes beyond the capacity of the host, whether NHS Trust, Prison Service or Highway Agency. John Major's Conservative Government introduced, on a relatively small scale, the concept of PFI, which offered the attraction of the transfer of risk from the public sector to the private sector and also had the attraction of funding major investments, such as hospitals, schools, libraries, police headquarters, army barracks and other individual projects, off the State balance sheet. When first introduced Labour was vehemently opposed and early critics of the philosophy were Alistair Darling, later Chancellor of the Exchequer, and Patricia Hewitt. However, the real users of the PFI concept were the Blair and Brown governments, who between them, by 2009, had activated some 920 projects using PFI. The concept continued with the Coalition Government from 2010 when George Osborne, then Chancellor of the Exchequer, authorised 61 projects in his first year, some of which may have been projects already committed and primed by the previous government but not finally authorised.

New Labour saw the PFI as a way of improving infrastructure without public sector financing requirements – the financing would typically be sourced by a Special Purpose Vehicle (SPV) created for the specific purpose of creating a PFI. The SPV would be owned by a number of private sector investors with usually a construction company and service provider and sometimes a bank as shareholders. The funding would be used to build the facility and to maintain the facilities for the lifetime of the contract – typically 25 to 30 years, although there are PFI contracts as short as 20 years and some as long as 40 years. During the contract, the consortium provides certain services which were previously provided by the public sector. Whilst risk was transferred, no doubt the private sector consortium quickly identified that, despite all the rhetoric, government would not allow hospitals, schools or police stations to fall into the hands of administrators, which no doubt added to their peace of mind when negotiating the contracts.

Ironically, after the 2007/08 economic crisis, government had to step in and provide some of the funding not available from banks, and in March 2009, Yvette Cooper, New Labour's Chief Secretary to the Treasury announced loans of £2 billion to private firms building schools and other projects. Mistakes were made during the early years of negotiation which were later rectified. The private sector quickly identified that refinancing could bring an instant gain to the balance sheet – capital would be cheaper after the risk period of building and opening the project had been achieved. However, the gain from refinancing went to the private sector and was not shared with government. Similarly, some investors sold shares after the project was running effectively and, again, no provision was made for the sharing of these profits with the Treasury. The mistake, which was not rectified, was that many of the investor SPVs were registered overseas for tax avoidance purposes, despite the proviso in many contracts that there would be a 'return' to the Treasury in the form of tax from profits achieved, but these returns never materialised because the profits were routed to the overseas vehicle.

One of the most extreme examples of this flaw was the sale and lease back by HMRC of a large part of their property portfolio to a company called Mapeley, which turned out to be based in Bermuda. It is worth noting that the Board of HMRC was unaware of the offshore nature of the company until just before the contract was signed. All properties occupied by HMRC managed by Mapeley make little contribution to the Treasury 'pot'. Edward Leigh, MP, then Chairman of the PAC, said it was incredible that the Inland Revenue, of all departments, did not, during contract negotiations find out more about Mapeley's structure. Gordon Brown perhaps provides some clues about why his government were so keen on PFI, when in answer to a question from Allyson Pollock (Note 11) about the rationale for PFI replied, that "the public sector is bad at management, and that only the private sector is efficient and can manage services well". In 2010, the UK Government released spending figures showing that the total financial obligation for PFI contracts in the UK was £267 billion. It is off the national balance sheet but is it really a liability of the private sector?

Not normally associated with waste, the National Lottery features in the section about the Millennium Dome and no doubt will feature in a future section about the 2012 Olympics, but is mentioned here to allow some background information. Created by John Major's government, the National Lottery began life in 1994 and since then has distributed many billions of pounds to worthy causes throughout the UK. The charter for distribution says that grants are awarded to organisations whose activities reach out across the whole of the UK rather than just a specific region of the country, yet on at least two occasions Lottery Funds have been used to support projects which, it is assumed, would not have been financed by any other Department of State. The story of the Millennium Dome identifies that £688 million of Lottery Funds found its way to support a project which was doomed to failure before it even opened, and this money was thereby lost for the purposes intended. The Millennium Dome was London-centric and, apart from the hilarity it caused in the regions, had a nominal effect outside the capital. Lottery Funding was misused and wasted. The 2012 Olympics will also be seen as a London-centric event which absorbed huge amounts of lottery cash. The Big Lottery Fund alone allocated £638 million, with the promise that it would be paid back by 2030/31. A further £2.175 billion was raised by the creation of an Olympic Lottery Scratchcard and was used for infrastructure (£1.7 billion), held for London Organising Committee of the Olympic and Paralympic Games (LOCOG) (£66 million) and the Cultural Olympiad (£16.5 million) etc. The creation of the Scratchcard did not increase the overall market but diverted money to a cause close to government in that the £2.175 billion was devoted to the Olympics rather than the good causes envisaged by John Major's government.

Each chapter in this book deals with a specific year, beginning with 2000 and finishing with 2004. Each year has identified sections dealing with specific projects. The identification consists of six figures, e.g. 01 02 03. The first two digits refer to the year, the second two digits refer to the chapter and the third two digits refer to the section so 01 02 03 is the Year 2001, Chapter 2 and Section 3. Some projects are stand-alone, e.g. the Millennium Dome, the sale of the Gold Reserves, the cancellation of the Benefits Card Project, whilst others are recurring and feature in most chapters. At the end of each chapter there is a summary showing the monetary values of that year's waste, inefficiencies and error. At the end of the book there is a schedule showing a total for each year and also a total for the five years under review with a league table showing in monetary terms the position of each department in terms of waste. This is perhaps one league table where a government department does not wish to be at the top of the league.

The results are depressing and will continue to be so until some government introduces individual and departmental accountability and realises that the eradication of the causes of waste will more than likely lead to a resulting reduction in the number of tax rises, with appropriate appreciation from taxpayers. Government has realised that the cupboard is bare, confirmed by the absence of massive spending plans usually promised in the year preceding a General Election and the relative paucity of the offers made to the 1.5 million voters working in the NHS. However, there is a goldmine to excavate by finally solving the government error, inefficiency and waste conundrum.

NOTES

1 Holmes, Ed: *Money for Nothing: Rules to Secure the UK's Fiscal Policy*, Policy Exchange, Dec 2013

2 A large section of Middle England were incredulous when government proudly announced that they were capping welfare payments at a net level of £26,000 per household, i.e. the equivalent of a pre-tax salary of £35,000 per year. A significant number of Middle Englanders aspire to earn £26,000 gross.

3 FBU Press Release, 4 January 2005

4 Wainwright, David: *Express and Star*, Wolverhampton, 11 June 2013

5 Milliband, David: *The New Statesman: How is Britain so open to the world, but so closed to Europe?*, Interview with Jose Manuel Barroso, July 2012

6 Helmsley, Leona: *The New York Times*, 12 July 1989

7 Rees-Mogg, William: *The Times: Why Google or Tesco should collect our taxes*, 27 November 2013

8 The TaxPayers' Alliance: An independent campaigner for lower taxes. For information visit www.taxpayersalliance.com.

9 Leach, Graeme: *EU Membership – What's the Bottom Line?* IoD Policy Paper, undated.

10 Standard Notes are created to provide MPs, amongst others, with non-partisan information which is timely and appropriate to the MP's needs. They are generally short and relatively informal but are not updated as frequently as desired by the Parliament and Constitution Centre. They do, however, give the government's 'view' about the topic under review.

11 Allyson Pollock is Professor of Public Health Research at Queen Mary, University of London.

INDEX: CHAPTER ONE – 2000

00 01 00   The Home Office: The Immigration and Nationality Directorate's Casework Programme

00 01 01   The Sheep Annual Premium Scheme in England

00 01 02   NHS (England) Summarised Accounts 1997/98

00 01 03   NHS (England) Summarised Accounts 1998/99

00 01 04   The PFI Contract for the New Dartford and Gravesham Hospital

00 01 05   The Contributions Agency: The Newcastle Estate Development Project

00 01 06   Highways Agency: Getting Best Value from the Disposal of Property

00 01 07   The Passport Delays of 1999

00 01 08   Child Support Agency: Client Funds Account 1998/99

00 01 09   Child Support Agency: Client Funds Account 1999/2000

00 01 10   Ministry of Defence: Major Projects Report

00 01 11   Criminal Justice: Working Together

00 01 12   Ministry of Defence: Appropriation Accounts

00 01 13   Ministry of Defence: Major Projects Report

00 01 14   State Earnings-Related Pension Scheme: The Failure to Inform the Public about Reduced Pension Rights for Widows and Widowers

00 01 15   Ministry of Defence: Accepting Equipment Off-Contract and Into Service

00 01 16   Various

"But in this world nothing can be said to be certain, except death and taxes."

> Benjamin Franklin (1706-1790) writing to Jean Baptiste Leroy, 13 November, 1789

"My first rule – the golden rule – ensures that over the economic cycle the Government will borrow only to invest, and that current spending will be met from taxation."

> Gordon Brown (b.1951) Former Chancellor of the Exchequer and Prime Minister of the United Kingdom

00 01 00

The Home Office: The Immigration and Nationality Directorate's Casework Programme

Stephen Calvard, a Director of the Immigration and Nationality Directorate (IND) was quoted as saying, "The Casework Application was always a high-risk undertaking and in the end it proved too ambitious and complex". (Note 1) Six years after the PFI contract was awarded to Siemens Business Systems (Siemens) and a year after the Home Office rolled out interim systems across the IND, the Home Secretary, Jack Straw, announced the decision to end work on the project in an obscure Commons written answer. The cancellation of the Casework Programme was not without cost to the taxpayer.

The IND operate immigration controls at ports, and process applications from people who have already entered the United Kingdom and who wish to apply for citizenship, seek asylum or extend their stay. In 1997 the directorate handled approximately 33,000 applications for asylum and 64,000 applications for British citizenship. (Note 2) These applications were by their very nature complex and this, when combined with the directorate's predominantly paper-based system, had led to a large backlog of work. In April 1996, Siemens agreed a PFI contract, known as the Casework Programme, with the Home Office. The programme depended on new information technology which would allow the directorate to become more efficient in its operations. However, the detailed design of the IT systems, organisational structure and new business processes had not been carried out at the time the contract was let, so the directorate were not in the position to specify in full their requirements for the system. The directorate did not have enough information on the unit cost of casework, so the detailed mechanism for remunerating Siemens was negotiated after the contract was signed, reducing the directorate's and improving Siemens' negotiation position. The unit cost was agreed only in November 1997, even though implementation of the system was scheduled for 1998.

The IND business requirement took longer to finalise then expected, so Siemens started to develop the IT system for the business requirement, allowing the two strands to diverge, leading to subsequent delays with the project. The requirements analysis exercise carried out by Siemens after the contract was let identified over 100 further requirements, in addition to the 233 detailed requirements identified in the directorate's Statement of

Service Requirement, and was not finally agreed until April 1998. Siemens' position was not helped by the directorate's plans to move offices during this period, which led to severe disruption and caused an increase in the backlog totals. Siemens subcontracted the mix of off-the-shelf and bespoke software to Perot Systems Europe Ltd (Perot) but, in July 1998, Siemens decided to complete the programme alone, a decision which caused the PAC to comment, "These problems were made worse by the apparent lack of an agreed approach between the primary contractor and a subcontractor regarding the type of software to be used. Although the technical details of proposed solutions should be something for contractors to organise in privately financed projects, it is crucial that departments keep a very close eye on progress". (Note 3) The planned implementation date of October 1998 for the Casework Application Programme was scrapped and a new target date of October 1999 agreed.

NAO and PAC reports identified many of the shortcomings in the progress of the Casework Programme. There was intense pressure as the backlog for asylum seekers alone had increased from 52,000 in May 1998 to 76,000 in June 1999. (Note 4) Despite the recruitment of a new development team of 120 staff by Siemens, the October 1999 implementation date was not fulfilled, and in 2000 the Home Office rolled out an interim system, which included the installation of 3,000 terminals at 23 IND locations across the UK as well as the introduction of new databases, which presumably did not work, as the Home Office announced the decision to cancel the system. The NAO report identifies a contract value of £76.8 million, (Note 5) whilst a UNISON case study, (Note 6) suggests that the government injected an extra £120 million funding to pay for the extra Siemens staff and IT maintenance, described in a Home Office memorandum to the PAC: "The government is investing an additional £120 million in IND over the next 5 years." (Note 7) However, the PAC also suggested that the cost should be substantially higher. They reported that the majority of asylum applicants received state aid whilst their applications are processed. They established from the Home Office that the cost of support for asylum seekers falling within their budget was £375 million a year. The average processing time for an application for British citizenship in 1998/99 was 18 months, whilst 10,000 applications for asylum were over five-years old, which would suggest that the estimate by the Home Office was conservative.

A total therefore of the £76.8 million wasted due to the cancellation of the programme; the extra £120 million paid to Siemens; and a figure of £1.4

billion for state aid for people awaiting decisions for the four-year period of the contract will be added to the summary at the end of this chapter, i.e. a total of £1.597 billion.

SOURCES

PAC Report: *Improving the Delivery of Government IT Projects*, HC65, 5 January 2000

PAC Report: *The Home Office: The Immigration and Nationality Directorate's Casework Programme*, HC130, 26 January 2000

NAO Report: *The Immigration and Nationality Directorate's Casework Programme*, HC277, 24 March 1999

Pollock, Allyson; Price, David and Player, Stewart: *Public Risk for Private Gain? Case Study 8: The Immigration and Nationality Directorate's Casework Programme*, UNISON

Simons, Mike: *Computer Weekly: Home Office cancels key immigration IT system*

Private Eye, Edition 977, 28 May 1999

NOTES

1 *Computer Weekly*: www. computerweekly.com/feature/Home-Office-cancels-key-immigration-IT-system.

2 PAC Report, p2/3

3 PAC Report, p2/9

4 ibid, p2/3

5 NAO Report, p28

6 UNISON Case Study 8, p35

7 PAC Report, p3/3

00 01 01

The Sheep Annual Premium Scheme in England

The United Kingdom headed the table for both the number of animals paid for under the Common Agricultural Policy and the amount disallowed by the European Commission for less than satisfactory completion of the farmers' flock records.

The Sheep Annual Premium Scheme was introduced in the European Union to guarantee sheep producers a certain level of support. To qualify for support a farmer needed to maintain flock records which met the standards requested by the European Union. There was, however, no sanction if the farmer did not meet the requirements, whilst there was a sanction to the taxpayer if the Ministry of Agriculture, Fisheries and Food failed to monitor the scheme. The scheme was introduced in 1990 and, ten years later, in 2000, the NAO were recommending that the department should seek to clarify the European Commission's concerns "at the earliest possible opportunity"; (Note 1) the department should maintain close liaison with other agricultural departments in the United Kingdom, i.e. Wales, Scotland and Northern Ireland; the department "should make every effort to adopt the recommended standard format for the combined flock and movement record and to ensure that the farmers' compliance satisfied the Commission"; (Note 2) the department must ensure that farmers only use movement record books if they met with the department's requirements; and the department must "satisfy itself as to the inspectors' consistency in their assessment of the quality of a farmer's flock records". (Note 3)

It will not surprise the reader to find out that, having ignored the problem for ten years, £87.3 million was disallowed by the European Union for the period 1993 to 1996. The NAO note that, "Member States bear the cost of disallowance as it represents a failure on the part of administrators rather than claimants". (Note 4)

A total of £87 million has therefore been added to the summary at the end of this chapter. The total only deals with records between 1993 and 1996 so it would not be a surprise if other payments were disallowed.

SOURCES

NAO Report: *Ministry of Agriculture, Fisheries and Food – The Sheep Annual Premium Scheme in England*, HC 273, 10 March 2000

NOTES

1 NAO Report, p2
2 ibid, p2
3 ibid, p3
4 ibid, p1

Two NAO reports were filed this year: the NHS (England) Summarised Accounts for 1997/98 in January and for 1998/99 in April.

00 01 02

NHS (England) Summarised Accounts 1997/98

This report makes it clear that there were significant levels of fraud in specific areas of the NHS. What was alarming was that the NHS Executive could not offer a realistic estimate of the overall level of fraud, but having recognised the existence of fraud were taking corrective action which included the establishment of a Directorate of Counter Fraud Services; the recognition of the need to change the culture of the NHS to encourage prevention; the need to improve fraud detection; and the resolve to deal firmly with those who committed fraud.

This summarised report deals with the 100 health authorities responsible for purchasing healthcare and related services, and the 425 NHS Trusts which delivered healthcare. The figures associated with the NHS are staggering, with the health authorities spending £33.266 billion during this period and the 425 NHS Trusts spending a further £25.1 billion. In this period 19 health authorities and 50 NHS Trusts experienced serious financial problems, but the PAC report into the matter suggested that this was a "significant improvement over the position nine months earlier". (Note 1) The same report suggested that some of these difficulties were due to a lack of planning or insight on the part of the people concerned and suggested that it was therefore right that the future employment of those accountable – the Chairmen and Chief Executives of the health authorities and NHS Trusts concerned – should be reviewed. They noted that, in the previous two years, at least six Chairmen and Chief Executives had lost their jobs because of failures in financial control.

This PAC report acknowledges that the NHS Executive did not have detailed information to identify total estimated fraud, but recorded that on prescription charge evasion alone the total recorded fraud was over £150 million in England, (Note 2) and that the Audit Commission in December 1998 had reported that the level of detected fraud was only £2.6 million. The two figures were not consistent so the NHS Executive were asked why the level of detected fraud was so low and in reply highlighted that they had been tackling fraud through good systems of governance, financial control and internal audit that had a preventative impact, which could not be measured, and admitted, "They had never before tackled the issue in a concerted and rigorous way". (Note 3) Whilst a reward scheme for people who reported fraudulent activity did exist there had been very few prosecutions for fraud and only £250,000 had been recovered. The Department of Health and the Dental Practice Board had estimated the annual losses relating to fraudulent exemption claims in relation to general dental services as between £18 and £35 million. The NHS Executive also admitted that work was needed to identify fraud in the pharmaceutical, ophthalmic and general medical services areas.

In the year under review, the NHS Executive paid out a total of £79 million to settle clinical negligence claims, but what caught the PAC's interest was the likely outstanding liability for future claims, which could be as high as possibly £2.8 billion. The charity, Action for Victims of Medical Accidents, suggested that there were perhaps 80,000 cases of clinical negligence within the health services across the country. The NHS Executive acknowledged that they had 15,000 cases on their books and they suggested that the total number of clinical negligence patients cases could be somewhere between the two figures, i.e. around 47,000 cases. The PAC were appalled at the level of at least 15,000 cases of clinical medical negligence and suggested that the real issue was how to minimise the risks of negligence happening in the first place and thereby avoiding any claim – a fundamental answer to any long-term problem.

The PAC also asked the NHS about the number of patients registered for NHS treatment, and was told that in total there are some 2 million more patients registered with general practitioners than the estimated resident population and that this difference had been appearing for over 25 years. The Office of National Statistics estimated that about 1.75 million of these were people who had been issued with another NHS number, but the significance of this level of registration was that GPs earn capitation fees for the number of registered patients with their practice, i.e. whether or not the patient attends a clinic. The scale of capitation fee per patient is difficult to assess but it does seem that GPs could be paid for patients who had moved to new addresses or indeed were dead, or GPs could retain registrations for fraudulent purposes. This did not seem to be a difficulty for the NHS Executive, as in evidence to the PAC they stated, "The profession as a whole is entitled to an amount that delivers an intended average net income per GP, recommended by the Pay Review Body. Eliminating capitation payments for duplicate registrations would initially lead to a shortfall in delivery of this average income which would subsequently need to be made good. List inflation does not therefore affect the overall level of payments to GPs although it does change the distribution of payments between them. It also means that registered populations would currently be an imperfect basis for allocating health service resources to health authorities". (Note 4)

The report notes that the NHS spent £307 million to make sure that the 'Millennium Bug' did not affect their performance. As readers know, nothing extraordinary happened on 1 January 2000 and the jury is still debating about whether the extraordinary amount of money spent by governments and other organisations was money well spent.

For the purpose of this exercise the Millennium Bug costs have been ignored, as indeed has the capitation issue relating to the overstatement of registered patients, but what has been included is the £150 million lost through prescription fraud; the £26.5 million lost through dental fraud; the £79 million paid out and the £2.8 billion provision for clinical negligence, so a total of £3.055 billion has been added to the summary at the end of this section.

SOURCES

PAC Report: *NHS (England) Summarised Accounts 1997/98*, 19 January 2000

NOTES

1   PAC Report, p 3/5
2   ibid, p 1/4
3   ibid, p 2/4
4   ibid, p3/4

00 01 03

NHS (England) Summarised Accounts 1998/99

The number of NHS Trusts was reduced by 23 since the previous year, along with 71 health authorities. Fifty-three trusts were "in serious financial difficulties". (Note 1)

As previously reported, the NHS had recognised that fraud existed. A Directorate of Counter Fraud Services was created to identify and neutralise fraud and corruption within the NHS. The directorate had three specific targets: to achieve a 50% reduction in the level of prescription charge evasion by 2002/03; to prevent £9 million in contractor fraud and recover £6 million by 2001/02; to reduce fraud to a minimum within ten years. The directorate had been tasked to develop a facility to measure fraud and incorrectness across main services in the NHS and had been given a target date of March 2000 for completion of a management report about the subject. It did not meet this target and a revised target date of early 2001 was agreed with the NAO. In the meantime, the directorate accepted the measurement exercise previously introduced by the NHS Executive, concentrating on prescription fraud, which identified that the annual loss for the period 1998/99 was £92 million. (Note 2) Fraud in the dental, pharmaceutical, ophthalmic and general medical services areas was not identified in this report, possibly because of the relative insignificance, to the NHS, of the figures involved. The Audit Commission recorded £4.7 million of fraud this year, but the directorate had asked NHS organisations to report suspected frauds to them and received 239 cases, with an estimated value of £14 million. There were 200 fraud suspects, including 36 internal administrators, 25 GPs, 9 hospital doctors and surgeons, 22 nursing staff, 24 dentists, 16 opticians and 27pharmacists.

What did occupy the NAO's interrogating minds was the growing realisation that the clinical negligence obligation was increasing dramatically. They noted that neither the health authorities nor NHS Trusts made any provision for the likely cost of clinical incidents that had not been reported, which might lead to future claims. They had estimated, based on an analysis of delays carried out jointly by the NHS Executive with the Medical Detection Society Ltd and Willis Corroon Ltd, that the amounts incurred for claims before 1995 alone would have amounted to over £1.1 billion. They noted the difficulty of comparing like with like insofar as while the NHS Litigation Authority had applied accounting standard FRS 12 to their 1998/99 accounts, NHS Trusts and health authorities had deferred the application of the standard to 1999/2000.

It would appear that the NHS was not in a position to identify the levels of fraud and suggested that the level of loss was immaterial in a total spend of £60 billion. Indeed, the Comptroller and Auditor General stated, "The overall levels of fraud and incorrectness reported are not significant enough to affect the true and fair view of the accounts and I have therefore given an unqualified opinion on the accounts". (Note 4)

For the purposes of this report a total of £1.206 billion, which includes the pre-1995 analysis of possible claims for clinical negligence, is added to the summary at the end of this section.

SOURCES

NAO Report: *NHS (England) Summarised Accounts 1998/99*, HC356, 5 April 2000

NOTES

1 NAO Report, R5
2 ibid, R44
3 ibid, R48, fig 7
4 ibid, R44

00 01 04

The PFI Contract for the New Dartford and Gravesham Hospital

The contract for the new Dartford and Gravesham Hospital was the first major hospital contract to be awarded under the Private Finance Initiative (PFI) and as such should have been closely monitored, not only by the NHS Executive but also by the Treasury. The contract was agreed in July 1997 and negotiated between shareholders Barclays Private Equity Ltd (previously part of BZW), 32.5%; Tarmac PFI Ltd, 32.5%; Innisfree Ltd, 25%; and United Medical Enterprises with 10%, along with the West Kent Health Authority and the local NHS Trust, whose business plan had been approved by the South East Thames Regional Health Authority, the NHS Executive and the Treasury. To the neutral observer it would seem that the advantages would lie with the shareholders and so it came to pass. The Dartford and Gravesham NHS Trust was one of seven hospitals being bailed out by the Department of Health in a £1.5 billion, 25-year rescue plan, (Note 1) because of their inability to meet their financial obligations. The following paragraphs will hopefully demonstrate why this situation had arisen.

In 1994 the Dartford and Gravesham NHS Trust succeeded the regional health authority as the provider of hospital services to the local population and inherited proposals for a new hospital development at Darenth Park outside Dartford. There were at that time three existing hospital sites, at Joyce Green, West Hill and Gravesend, and it was proposed that the Gravesend and North Kent Hospital be retained by the NHS and that the new hospital built to replace those at Joyce Green and West Hill. The trust examined the possibility of updating the existing resource but concluded that, whilst it was a cheaper option than building a new hospital, it was extremely poor in terms of the quality and efficiency of health services that could be delivered, and accordingly obtained approval in May 1995 from the regional health authority to plan a new hospital, comparing the costs and benefits of a privately financed project against those of a traditionally funded public sector project. The chronology is important, as the decisions about whether to proceed or not were condensed into a fairly tight timescale for such an important project. One would have suspected, as this was the first major hospital contract to be considered for PFI treatment, that all details of the subsequent negotiations would have been scrutinised at a very high level, but this does not appear to be the case. The plan to build a new hospital was advertised, and by February 1996 the trust had received four indicative bids, of which two, the Pentland Consortium and United Healthcare, were, in April 1996, invited to make final bids. United Healthcare had submitted the lowest indicative bid but upon evaluation their bid had been identified by the trust, "as being inferior to the three other bidders in all respects". (Note 2) United Healthcare also indicated as early as January 1996 that they had strong concerns about the final bidding process, primarily because of the short timescale of 2½ months between the invitation to make final bids and the deadline date. The trust thereby created a risk that there might be only one final bid, and that indeed was the outcome as United Healthcare did not submit a final bid.

The Pentland Consortium was therefore in pole position and submitted their bid, which had increased by 33% in real terms compared to their indicative bid. Whilst the NAO make a case that the Pentland Consortium was unlikely to be aware of the United Healthcare withdrawal, commercial reality would dictate otherwise. The trust negotiated with the only bidder and managed to reduce the proposed increase of 33.3% to 17%, making Pentland's final bid £177 million, without appreciating that any good negotiator would present a bid which allows a discount to be negotiated by the potential buyer. Detailed negotiations took place between July 1996 and July 1997, and as a result of those negotiations it was agreed that Barclays Private Equity Ltd and Innisfree Ltd would be repaid some or all of the paid-up value of their investment, in the event of contract termination when the hospital was in operation even where 'termination is due to contract or default', (Note 3) otherwise known as having your cake and eating it. It was also agreed that, once the project was up and running, the trust would pay to Pentland a monthly fee of £879,000 for availability and £441,000 for service provision – both sums subject to increase in line with the Retail Price Index. It was also agreed that the trust would transfer to Pentland three plots of land, which were sold for the benefit of the project for a total of £21.9 million and, whilst they negotiated a claw-back arrangement relating to planning permission for one site, they acknowledged that there may be opportunities for Pentland, and the parties to whom they sold the sites, to generate revenues from the sites, which would not be shared with the trust. Pentland also managed to defer funding of £13 million, which would be replaced by bringing forward the investment of bank finance to improve the cash flow for the project for Pentland, but the trust failed to negotiate a reduction in the contract price as Pentland argued that it would be difficult for them to hold to the contract price agreed in 1996. Pentland also negotiated that their liability for any extra costs arising from changes to health and safety and environmental legislation should be limited, again without any benefit to the trust. In February 1997 both parties agreed that savings of £2.4 million, which had arisen from favourable movements in interest rates between February and July 1997, would benefit the trust through a reduced annual contract price. The trust, in its wisdom, decided to contribute 13% (£300,000) of this windfall to Pentland as a contribution towards Pentland's costs. It was also agreed that any profits which might arise from refinancing the project after the contract was signed would be for the benefit of the investors, even though the trust had provided £29.1 million of the equity represented by land sales.

The trust now needed to convince the regional health authority and the Treasury about the value for money implications of their case, and duly prepared a full business case which was submitted to the regional office in September 1996, and to the Treasury and the NHS Executive in January 1997. Part of this procedure was to convince the relevant bodies that a comparison of the PFI costs with a traditional procurement route would show that the PFI option was the correct decision. The case submitted showed that traditional procurement would cost £193.7 million, whilst the Pentland PFI contract had now settled at £176.5 million, an estimated saving of £17.2 million. However, the NAO report into the matter, (Note 4) identified that £12.1 million had not been included in the figures for the traditional procurement, which reduced the saving to 2.8%. Furthermore, and even more importantly, the trust assumed that the traditional procurement route would be over-budget, and added £44 million to the estimated cost of building and servicing the hospital. Whilst this figure is available in the NAO report as Appendix 7, (Note 5) no comment is made about the assumption. Exclusion of this £44 million would have immediately identified that the PFI option was a non-starter. However, this particular gravy train was a lucrative one for the legal advisers who had offered a preliminary estimate of £308,000 for the necessary work associated with this bid, but who eventually delivered invoices for £2.355 million – an increase of some 700%, as an incandescent PAC subsequently noted. (Note 6)

The new, increased, Pentland bid also identified, to the no doubt well-meaning members of the West Kent NHS Trust in January 1997, that the project would have to be subsidised at the rate of £4.7 million a year, and it was agreed that the trust would make savings of £700,000 a year. West Kent Health Authority would find £2 million a year out of its annual allocation, the NHS Executive would find £1 million a year, to be repaid during years 26 to 60 of the contract, and £1 million would be transferred annually from the West Kent Health Authority allocation for capital maintenance. Also, in January 1997, the full business case was approved by the Treasury and Alan Langlands, Chief Executive, NHS Executive, and no one questioned whether the delicate manoeuvrings carried out to justify the PFI option were highlighted in any presentation. The PFI option did mean that debts incurred for this PFI option are not reflected in the government balance sheet.

The West Kent NHS Trust committed to paying £4 million a year for 25 years to support a flawed PFI proposal, costing the taxpayer a minimum of £100 million. They also paid £300,000 to Pentland, which they were not legally obligated to do, as well as allowing legal advisers to invoice just over £2 million above the estimate they had provided. The issue of land given to Pentland also meant that a £29.1 million loss was recorded for the trust as well as any future development benefits. The total added to the summary at the end of this chapter is £132 million. It must be noted that

West Kent NHS Trust played an important part in convincing government that PFI was the answer to the nation's borrowing problems. Even worse, it convinced commercial organisations such as Barclays, Tarmac, United Healthcare and Innisfree that negotiating with government, whether local or national, was always going to be a win-win situation – for the commercial organisations.

SOURCES

PAC Report: *The PFI Contract for the New Dartford and Gravesham Hospital*, 7 April 2000

NAO Report: *The PFI Contract for the New Dartford and Gravesham Hospital*, HC 423, 19 May 1999

PWC: Dartford and Gravesham NHS Trust. Annual Audit Letter, 30 July 2013

Brown, Jonathan: *The Independent: Struggling NHS Trusts get £1.5 billion Bailout*, 4 February 2012

NOTES

1 Brown, Jonathan, p1
2 NAO Report, p5
3 NAO Report, p38
4 NAO Report, p44, figure 11
5 NAO Report, p71
6 PAC Report, p2/7

00 01 05

The Contributions Agency: The Newcastle Estate Development Project

In November 1993 a team of property consultants, Storey Sons and Parker, who had been commissioned by the Contributions Agency to develop a feasibility study of the options available for one of their sites, recommended phased demolition and rebuilding between 1995 and 2003, at a cost of £83 million, and concluded that there was little potential for private finance on the terms suggested. The agency calculated that the cost of this option over

25 years would be almost the same as that of continuing with the existing buildings, but would offer a much improved working environment for staff, so therefore recommended the option to HM Treasury in May 1994. In June 1994 the Treasury asked that the agency investigate a Private Finance Initiative (PFI) solution whilst not explicitly rejecting the agency's bid. And so began again the saga of what would become "a pioneering Private Finance project in the office sector". (Note 1)

The Contributions Agency, the Benefits Agency, the Child Support Agency and the Information Technology Services Agency occupied most of the Newcastle estate of the Department of Social Security. The Newcastle estate housed over 13,000 staff in 2.5 million square feet, of which 627,000 square feet comprised single-storey buildings at Longbenton on the outskirts of Newcastle. The accommodation had been constructed as temporary accommodation during the 1940s and, as such, needed attention. The Contributions Agency's decisions relating to the project were made by a project board, which included representatives from the aforementioned agencies as well as the Treasury, the Private Finance Panel Executive and the Corporate Director of the Department's Estates. This board was established in November 1994 to provide overall direction and management of the project and reported to the Chief Executive of the Contributions Agency, who in turn reported to the Management Board of the Department of Social Security.

In January 1995 an invitation to potential bidders was published in the *Official Journal*, specifying that the contract type was building and civil engineering work; that the site would be within ten miles of the centre of Newcastle; that it may include an existing building or a green field site at any of the 11 UK Government-owned or leased sites in the area; that the requirement was for a modern office accommodation for approximately 14,000 staff; that the development could also include subsequent management or operation of the new facility; and that the development should be financed by the private sector through the UK Government's Private Finance Initiative (PFI). The deadline for applications was 7 February 1995. By April 1995 the Contributions Agency had assembled projections from the other tenants, which suggested that the requirement by the year 2000 would be to accommodate 13,200 staff. The advertisement generated 58 formal expressions of interest of which 14 submitted themselves for assessment – three of these were chosen for the shortlist to enter detailed negotiations. The three were issued with detailed service requirements in July 1995 and best and final offers were received into February 1996. The bids were evaluated, and in June 1996 the Newcastle Estate Partnership (NEP) was announced as the preferred bidder, with the Tyne Partnership as the reserve supplier. The NEP bid was estimated at £244.6 million whilst the Tyne Partnership bid was estimated at £282.4 million. There were further negotiations for 18 months with NEP but it was accepted that the direct cost to the taxpayer of the PFI deal was £241 million. (Note 2) The PAC was unhappy with the conduct of the negotiations: "In this deal, the Department of Social Security conducted exclusive negotiations with a single preferred bidder for 18 months. We find this incompatible with the Inland Revenue's assertions that the Department of Social Security had relied on stiff competition between rival bidders as a driver of value for money throughout the procurement." (Note 3)

The speed at which the Treasury reacted to a request for funding was unusual but it was also unusual to give the go ahead without a full Public Sector Comparator, (Note 4) which would have estimated the costs of publicly financing a redevelopment of the estate. The Treasury guidance at the time did not require the preparation of a Public Sector Comparator, (Note 5) although this project, for which there was no precedent, would seem an ideal project for such a comparison. The PAC report says, "We fail to see how the Department of Social Security could have gained assurance on value for money in the absence of a systematic option appraisal which, in this case, must have included a public sector comparator. We are therefore disturbed that the Inland Revenue still maintained that the deal is good value for money in the absence of sufficient evidence, we feel that the Inland Revenue has been dazzled by the prospect of getting new buildings". (Note 6) As expected, the department prepared a comparison of the costs and benefits of the deal with those of remaining in the existing estate. This comparison showed that the direct cost to the taxpayer of the PFI deal was £51 million more than if the department remained in the existing premises and converted them to a level compatible with health and safety regulations. One of the arguments of the department was that the £51 million would be recovered through efficiency savings. However, the PAC pointed out, "Such efficiency savings could also have been delivered by a publicly funded construction project". (Note 7) The Inland Revenue attracted more criticism when, in giving oral evidence, they produced revisions to the estimate that the PFI deal would cost £51 million more than the 'Do Minimum' option.

(Note 8) The PAC was surprised that the Inland Revenue had not agreed all of these figures with the NAO and in their conclusion stated, "It is very regrettable that in giving oral evidence to us the Inland Revenue produced figures for efficiency savings expected from the deal which have not been previously shared with the National Audit Office and which, on subsequent examination by the National Audit Office, proved to have been overstated". (Note 9)

There were a few other unique features about this deal. The department transferred the total estate to NEP, who guaranteed proceeds of £9.4 million from the disposal of freehold land and buildings. This sum was not paid in a lump sum but was used to reduce the department's continuing service charge. The agency had also negotiated a claw-back arrangement whereby they would receive 50% of any additional development proceeds above the base value of the £9.4 million, which would be paid as a one-off payment in 2006. When the agency undertook their own valuation of the sites they identified some disparity between valuations obtained by the agency and those offered by AMEC, one of the partners in the NEP consortium, e.g. at Emerson House AMEC paid only £1 million, based on the redevelopment value of the site, whilst the agency's valuation, assuming continued use of the building, was £6.7 million. Another unusual decision was to reject a bid from NEP of around £66 million for the estate and to alternatively negotiate reduced rentals over the contract period.

There seems to have been a degree of flexibility about the potential occupancy of the buildings. When the bid document was circulated it specified that 14,000 staff would occupy the buildings by April 1995, but that requirement was reduced to 13,200 staff. The number was reduced again in December 1995 to 10,700 staff and it was on that basis that NEP was awarded the contract. However, the bid submitted by NEP did not reduce in proportion and NEP were awarded an extension to their contract in 2002 to provide new office accommodation to house the new Department of Work and Pensions (DWP). Indeed, a report indicated that by 2003/04 accommodation may be needed for 13,200 staff. (Note 10)

A further aspect of the deal which irritated the PAC was the increase in procurement costs, which were initially budgeted at £397,000 but which eventually were acknowledged as £4.4 million. The biggest single increase was the cost of legal advice, which was budgeted at £70,000 and cost £2.3

million. The PAC suggests that this type of enormous increase reflects the department's initial failure to understand the complexity of this type of procurement and its own inability to undertake many of the tasks required to negotiate a deal.

The project could have been completed for £83 million, but the Inland Revenue was distracted by the attractions of a new building and the creation of a PFI for office accommodation within the public sector. The overspend of £4 million on procurement should have been avoided. A total of £166 million is added to the summary at the end of this chapter. What has not been taken into account is the loss of valuable freehold property in the Newcastle area.

SOURCES

PAC Report: *The Contributions Agency: The Newcastle Estate Development Project*, HC104, 7 June 2000

NAO Report: *The Contributions Agency: The Newcastle Estate Development Project*, HC16, 25 November 1999

NOTES

1 NAO, p1
2 ibid, p2
3 PAC, p9/12
4 NAO, p5
5 A Public Sector Comparator is now standard requirement for any PFI deal.
6 PAC, p3/12
7 ibid, p3/12
8 The Do Minimum Option involved the refurbishment of existing accommodation.
9 PAC, p5/12
10 ibid, p3/12

00 01 06

Highways Agency: Getting Best Value from the Disposal of Property

"In the case of the A40 Gypsy Corner and Western Circus, in 1995/96 the Agency demolished 200 properties, which had been acquired for £18 million, ahead of planned road building. The scheme was cancelled in July 1997. As a result of demolition, the Agency is likely to realise reduced proceeds when the sites are sold. The Agency had not prepared a business case for this demolition. We were told by the Agency that there had been consultation with the then Secretary of State for Transport but that there had been no written record of approval. The Agency acknowledged that the business case should have been prepared." (Note 1)

The Highways Agency was responsible for the construction and management of England's 6,500 miles of trunk roads and motorways and, as such, had powers to purchase properties along the proposed route of a road or purchase properties in close proximity which would be blighted by the new road or its construction. As a result the agency owned 1,900 properties, of which 300 were non-residential, by February 2000. As in the case of the A40 scheme mentioned above, some of the property acquired was sold because the scheme was cancelled, while in other cases property was sold because it was not needed for the actual construction.

The agency employed commercial agents to manage much of their property portfolio and in many cases delegated responsibility for repair and maintenance to these agents, who had authority to carry out routine repairs whilst consulting the agency in complex and expensive cases. The agency acknowledged that "it was not proud of its record on maintaining properties", (Note 2) and that poor property management by their commercial agents had contributed to the poor condition of some of the agency's properties. The agency also admitted that they "until recently lacked proper records on all aspects of its agents' performance". (Note 3) The result of this lack of attention to their property portfolio resulted in an average loss in value of property, subsequently sold by the agency, of 32% in the period 1994 to 1999, resulting in a total loss in value in the region of £110 million.

An earlier PAC report in 1994 had urged the agency to avoid inflicting blight on properties unnecessarily and as a result the agency had, with the assistance of the former Department of the Environment, examined procedures in other countries for comparison purposes and found that the UK had the most generous arrangements for buying property along the line of a proposed route. In 1997 they published a report outlining a scheme that would replace the existing blight provision but by 2000 this scheme, which would require primary legislation, had not been initiated. The agency continued to buy property which was not required.

A total of £110 million in respect of losses due to poor management of the estate has been added to the summary at the end of this chapter.

SOURCES

PAC Report: *Highways Agency: Getting Best Value from the Disposal of Property*, HC 231, 15 June 2000

NAO Report: *Highways Agency: Getting Best Value from the Disposal of Property*, HC 58, 9 December 1999

NOTES

1   PAC Report, p2/3

2   ibid, p1/3

3   ibid, p1/3

00 01 07

The Passport Delays of Summer 1999

1998 was an important year for the Passport Agency. They had announced in April of that year that children under 16 would require their own passports to travel abroad and that implementation would start in October but also decided that a new IT system, which allowed them to digitalise passports to avoid fraud and improve efficiency, would be trialled at Liverpool. The resulting chaos did not help the agency's reputation.

Forecasts for passport traffic were provided by the Home Office on an annual basis and were tweaked by the agency. In 1997/98, five million passports had been issued, so the suggested target for 1998/99 was 5.1 million. The Home Office believed that because of the cancellation of the

British Visitor's Passport facility in 1995 there was still some slack in the capacity of the agency, although offered no explanation of why that slack should still exist some three years after the cancellation. The Home Office calculations did not seem to have taken into account the requirement that children would need their own passports, and admitted as such to the PAC, who examined the matter. (Note 1) The agency received 800,000 child passport applications in the first six months of 1999. (Note 2)

Digital passports were first considered in 1996 and, after a normal procurement procedure, Siemens were awarded the contract in 1997 with an operational target date of October 1998 for implementation at the three largest offices of the agency – Liverpool, Newport and Peterborough. In doing so they ignored advice from Coopers and Lybrand, who had reported about the implementation of the previous system in the passport offices in Glasgow and Liverpool, who had noted, "As a general principle we would recommend that a system be implemented in one location and all problems resolved, before the system is replicated elsewhere... this was a high-risk decision". (Note 3) Indeed, the Home Office Internal Audit Service noted, "However, the risk is that the pilot may need to have its timescales extended to ensure that robust operational and user procedures and controls are in place". (Note 4) Both the design and development stages overran their schedules by four months and, when the agency tried to conduct further tests on productivity on site at Liverpool in September, they could not do so due to the shortage of time. The system was therefore rolled out in Liverpool, with Newport to follow six weeks later. The Liverpool target was 30,000 passports per week, which was the normal output under the old system, but only 6,200 passports per week were produced, so in November the agency's management board decided to implement the rollout at Newport, "despite serious reservations". (Note 5) The backlog that built up at Liverpool and Newport was reduced by the reinstallation of the old computer system at Peterborough, but by now the effects of the increased application for children's passports was impacting workload.

By the spring of 1999 customer service had deteriorated, with delays of up to 50 days before passports were returned against a specific target for turnaround of ten working days. Questions were asked in parliament and the agency increased their resources by employing 300 extra staff; asking existing staff to work significant overtime hours; introducing a call centre to help ease the pressure on staff; and reached agreement with the Post Office, which allowed 400,000 people to take advantage of a two-year free extension to their passport. These additional measures allowed the agency to meet their ten-day turnaround target by the end of August, but almost 500 passports were not available for people travelling on specific dates who were eventually compensated.

The simultaneous introduction of a new IT system and inadequate forecasting by the Home Office created for the Passport Agency a set of problems which dented their reputation and could have been avoided. The cost for rectifying the problem was around £12.6 million, (Note 6) plus £275,000 compensation due from Siemens which the agency waived. However, the major damage to the agency was to its reputation. A total of £12.9 million will be added to the summary at the end of this chapter.

SOURCES

PAC Report: *The Passport Delays of Summer 1999*, HC208, 28 June 2000

NAO Report: *The Passport Delays of Summer 1999*, HC 812, 27 October 1999

Private Eye: Editions 980, 9 July 1999 and 1023, 22 March 2001

Pollock, Allyson and Price, David: *Public Risk for Private Gain*, Unison, undated

Computer Weekly: Passports Service, September 2008

NOTES

1 PAC Report, p4/9
2 NAO Report, p21
3 NAO Report, Appendix 4: *The Coopers and Lybrand Report 1989*, p59
4 NAO Report, p30
5 NAO Report, p34
6 NAO Report, p48

Two reports about the Child Support Agency were delivered in 2000: a PAC report about 1998/99 in April and a NAO report about 1999/2000 in July.

00 01 08

Child Support Agency: Client Funds Account 1998/99

This PAC report was scathing about the performance of the agency, suggesting on the basis of the statistics quoted that this was an agency out of control and reporting, "The inadequacies of the child support arrangements and the agency's information systems, and the agency's poor performance ever since it was set up in April 1993, are well documented. Yet the fact remains that five years on, 23% of new maintenance assessments made in 1998/99 were wrong, 35% of proceeds from non-resident parents were for the wrong amounts and 79% of maintenance balances were incorrect. All these errors affect hundreds of thousands of people during very stressful periods of their lives, and are totally unacceptable". (Note 1)

The Child Support Agency (CSA) was established as an executive agency of the Department of Social Security (DSS) and was responsible for implementing the 1991 and 1995 Child Support Acts by ensuring that non-resident parents met their maintenance responsibility, whilst also allowing government to recoup the cost of paying benefits to nearly 900,000 single mothers. Prior to the creation of the CSA, child support scheme disputes were handled on a court-based system, whose major flaw was the absence of power to trace non-resident parents. The CSA had two prime functions: to calculate how much child maintenance was due, and to communicate with and collect from the non-resident parent the appropriate amount and transfer it to the person responsible for care.

The agency had the responsibility to vet all new applications for child support maintenance against regulations approved by parliament. This procedure required sensitivity after the birth of the child to a single mother, or after a settlement as a result of a divorce or the breakdown of a relationship. The issues were sometimes complicated, often delicate, regularly emotional, occasionally legal, and were aimed at bringing about financial stability to the children concerned and their parent. The application was assessed and involved the identification of the non-resident parent, as well as confirmation of paternity. The agency would then establish the non-parent's income and/or benefit status, and having finalised the maintenance assessment collect the amount assessed and distribute it accordingly. The agency failed miserably in its duties and at the time of the PAC report the government had agreed a new scheme that was due for implementation in April 2002, which was to be supported by new information technology systems. The PAC noted, "While some will be disappointed that these new arrangements will not be implemented until April 2002, it is essential that they are properly planned and tested". (Note 2)

The PAC noted that, because of the agency's maladministration, consolatory payments had been made to individuals affected by an error. A total of £4.35 million was paid but the PAC noted that the majority of this should have in any case been paid and that £561,663 was the 'true' value of the consolatory payments. The number of individuals involved was 5,466 and this represented an increase of 150% on the 1997/98 figure. The major issue though was the collection of money from the non-resident parent, and by the year end the total debt due to the department was £1.7 billion, of which the department agreed that £1.070 billion was unlikely to be collected and so was written down, whilst a further £690 million was deemed to be either collectable or possibly uncollectable. (Note 3) For the purposes of this exercise it has been assumed that £345 million, i.e. 50% of the money due for collection will not be collected, so the total added to the summary at the end of this section will be £1.416 billion, which includes the consolatory payments and the debt write-downs.

SOURCE

PAC Report: *Child Support Agency: Client Funds Account 1998/99*, HC 184, 20 April 2000.

NOTES

1   PAC Report, p3/4
2   ibid, p2/3
3   ibid, p2/4

00 01 09

Child Report Agency: Client Funds Account 1999/2000

The NAO report into this account was understandably written with some difficulty. The accounts were qualified and it would appear the NAO were reporting on a set of accounts which they felt were totally lacking in content. An executive summary of the Comptroller and Auditor General's report has been used for analysis in the absence of a full report from the archives.

In the previous year the amount written-off that was due from non-resident parents was substantial and this year's report recorded that the amounts "due from non-resident parents at 1 April 1999 and March 31, 2000 are materially misstated. Since these notes do not properly present the maintenance balance due I have qualified my audit opinion". (Note 1) However, the summary indicated that £341 million was written-off from the full and interim maintenance balances. (Note 2) The consolatory payments made because of delays totalled £3.1 million, but had been reduced to £387,000 as a high percentage of the payment was in any case due to the claimant. Monetary errors accounted for £59 million, which includes underpayments, which will have been satisfied from other areas within the benefit system.

Payments of deferred debt can be made when there has been a delay of over 26 weeks between the effective date of an assessment and the actual determination, and these payments cost £2 million; advance payments of maintenance where delays by the agency caused a significant amount of arrears to build up cost £862,000; and refund payments which occur when a non-resident parent has made an overpayment of maintenance that has been passed onto the parent with care but was regarded as not subsequently recoverable by the agency, £4 million.

The total therefore added to the summary at the end of this section is £407 million.

SOURCE

NAO Report: *Child Support Agency Client Fund Account 1999/2000*

NOTES

1 NAO Report, p5
2 ibid, p6

00 01 10

Ministry of Defence: Major Projects Report

The 1998 report by the Public Accounts Committee (PAC) examined in some detail the introduction of the Smart Acquisition Programme which was designed to enable the Ministry of Defence (MoD) to acquire defence equipment faster, cheaper and better. The Smart Acquisition Programme, also examined in some detail in section 00 01 13 of this chapter, introduced a number of checks and balances that would allow the MoD to judge the feasibility of a project and act accordingly. In 1999 the National Audit Office (NAO) commented, "It is too early to tell whether Smart Procurement will fulfil all its aims and in some areas, such as establishing robust whole-life costs for equipments, there is still a long way to go. However, in conducting our analysis of the 1999 Major Projects Report, we have noted some signs that Smart Procurement principles are being put into practice..." (Note 1) There were a number of 'legacy' projects conceived before the implementation of the Smart Acquisition Programme and a number of these are examined in this section.

These Major Projects Reports only examine the 25 largest defence equipment procurement projects, so readers need to understand that losses associated with day-to-day procurement and minor projects avoid analysis.

The collaborative Eurofighter project was due for delivery in June 2002 to replace the Tornado F3 and Jaguar aircraft and was designed as an agile fighter aircraft, primarily offering air superiority but also offering an air-to-ground capability. The 1999 Major Projects Report again confirms that the initial 55 aircraft ordered for the RAF was now over budget by £1.371 billion which was, however, an improvement of £142 million when compared to the previous report.

The delay in the introduction of the Brimstone air-launched anti-armour weapon required the MoD to improve their existing BL 755 equipment and to order modification kits to increase their stocks by some 50% to compensate for those used in the NATO campaign over Yugoslavia. It was later discovered that the additional munitions "were not required for the campaign before it ended although, should they have been, delivery of them was delayed by the late availability of an essential component". (Note 2) The modified but not needed BL 755 bombs were added to stock at a cost of £9 million. An additional £1 million was spent adding a radar proximity sensor which allowed the existing BL 755 bomb to be upgraded to RBL 755 standard. The Brimstone was operating to its revised schedule and the first 12 missiles were due to be delivered in March 2001, but development costs had exceeded budget by £5 million and production costs by £11 million. (Note 3)

The Beyond Visual Range Air-to-Air Missile (BVRAAM) was noted in the 1998 report because it failed to add VAT when calculating the cost of the programme. The programme was now under development and exceeded its budgeted cost by £7 million, "mostly due to a need for additional Defence Evaluation and Research Agency support during the assessment". (Note 4) The NAO report, using the dogma of immateriality, commented that this was only one per cent of the total cost of the project

The Type 45 destroyer was conceived when the Defence Ministers of the United Kingdom, France and Italy agreed not to proceed with development and production of a Common New Generation Frigate, which was intended to replace the existing Type 42 anti-air warfare destroyers. The Type 45 was due to be equipped with a missile system, the Principle Anti-Air Missile System (PAAMS) and was due to enter service in 2007, some five years later than the date originally estimated. The department "estimates that, in net total, it will cost an additional £537 million to operate and support the existing Type 42 destroyers, because of the 57-month delay". (Note 5)

A programme to replace obsolescent sonar equipment and interface the new sonar with the new Submarine Command System (SMCS) was successfully achieved in June 1996, and a final phase to implement acoustic signature measures to reduce counter detection and enhance the submarines' sonar performance was designed to provide the capability to take the Swiftsure and Trafalgar Class nuclear submarines into the third millennium. Development costs had exceeded their budget by £22 million and an increase in production costs added £10 million to that figure. (Note 6)

The Spearfish is an advanced anti-submarine and anti-ship torpedo and was intended to replace Tigerfish in all Royal Navy submarines. Originally ordered in 1982, deliveries were suspended for 62 months because of unreliability. However, a contract was agreed with GEC-Marconi, but the development costs exceeded budget by £190 million, whilst the production costs were below budget by £8 million. (Note 7)

The Sting Ray Lightweight Torpedo entered service in 1983 with a planned service life of around 20 years. The department decided that it should remain in service until around 2020 and the extension programme was approved in May 1995 on a fixed-price basis. However, the development costs exceeded budget by £13 million and the production costs exceeded budget by £9 million. (Note 8)

The Landing Platform Dock (Replacement) was established to cover the replacement of the existing amphibious assault ships, and the contract was awarded to Vickers Shipbuilding and Engineering Ltd (VSEL) in July 1996. The development costs exceeded budget by £5 million and the production costs exceeded budget by £11 million. (Note 9)

The Challenger 2 (CR2) main battle tank was designed to replace the Chieftain tank and supplement the Challenger 1 tank. Two hundred and fifty-nine tanks were ordered from Vickers plc, whilst ammunition already sourced from Royal Ordnance was used. The NAO report says, "This programme is complete and has been fully reported in previous Major Projects Reports. It has spent £235 million against a MoD approval of £211 million", (Note 10) i.e. an excess of £24 million over budget. The report also notes that the project costs overran development and production budgets by £65 million. (Note 11)

A development contract for the Bowman tactical communication system was given by the department to a joint-venture company known as Archer, formed in 1996 and now trading as Archer Communications Systems Ltd. Despite the fact that this was a firm price contract for £132 million the current estimate of costs was £341 million, i.e. an excess of £209 million over budget. (Note 12)

The Tracer reconnaissance vehicle development costs exceeded budget by £6 million. (Note 13)

The Merlin Mk1 helicopter entered service in 1998, replacing the Sea King and was supplied by EH Industries (EHI), a company formed by Agusta of Italy and GKN Westland in the UK. In 1991 the department selected IBM-ASIC as prime contractor to complete Royal Navy Development, integration of the Mission System and production of 44 aircraft. Progress on the project was hampered by accidents, but the first flight was in December 1995 and delivery started to the Royal Navy in 1997. However, the budgeted development and production costs were exceeded by £1.161 billion, in part due to a change in requirement by the department due to deployment patterns as well as early settlement of liabilities with GKN Westland as well as the accidents to the three prototype aircraft.

The total added to the summary at the end of this chapter is £2.144 billion which recognises the reduction in budget for the Eurofighter project.

SOURCE

NAO Report: *Ministry of Defence: Major Projects Report 1999*, HC 613, 6 July 2000

NOTES

1 NAO Report, p51/52
2 ibid, p40/41
3 ibid, p60
4 ibid, p15
5 ibid, p42/43
6 ibid, p163
7 ibid, p151
8 ibid, p155
9 ibid, p120
10 ibid, p87
11 ibid, p88
12 ibid, p82
13 ibid, p168

00 01 11

Criminal Justice: Working Together

The criminal justice system costs the taxpayer about £9 billion to process some 2 million defendants through the criminal courts. Efficient and effective progression of cases depends on the police, the Crown Prosecution Service, the courts and other agencies working closely together, as well as with victims, defendants, witnesses etc. In addition there are defendants, usually represented by lawyers, usually funded from legal aid, and cases may also require work by probation officers, the Forensic Science Services, independent experts, professional witnesses, the Prison Service and the Prisoner Escort and Custody Service. There are also three spheres of influence involved: the Home Office, the Lord Chancellor's Department and the Crown Prosecution Service.

The criminal justice process crosses and re-crosses organisational boundaries, so it is of little surprise that 750,000 magistrates' court hearings had to be adjourned. Twenty-five per cent of ineffective hearings in the magistrates' courts are caused because defendants on bail do not turn up at court. A further 41% (Note 1) of the adjournments in magistrates' courts were caused by error or omission on the part of defendants or their legal representatives. The PAC report into the matter suggested that the cost associated with adjournment was £41 million.

The PAC also identified that Crown Courts also suffered from adjournment caused by error or omission, and estimated the number of adjournments at about 14,000, i.e. 25% of the total number of trials, which suggested that the cost associated with adjournment at Crown Courts was £15 million. They also suggested that one third of Crown Court cases 'cracked' because they were disposed of in some other way. Work by prosecution and defence teams would have been completed, so significant costs had been incurred, and the PAC estimated that some £29 million was wasted in this manner. They noted there a was wide range of variance in the performance of individual courts, e.g. in 1999 only about 12% of trials in the Central Criminal Court in London 'cracked', whilst in Doncaster and Hull the figure was closer to 50%.

The PAC report estimated that costs of the order of £85 million were incurred each year in respect of ineffective hearings and 'cracked' trials and estimated that these unnecessary costs could be substantially reduced by improved cooperation and joint management among the agencies involved. A total of £85 million will be added to the summary at the end of this chapter. This is one of the sections which appears just once in the five years under review.

SOURCES

PAC Report: *Criminal Justice: Working Together*, HC 298, 12 July 2000

NAO Report: Lord Chancellor's Department, Crown Prosecution Service, Home Office: *Criminal Justice: Working Together*, HC 29, 1 December 1999

NOTES

1 PAC Report, p2/3

2 ibid, p2/7

00 01 12

Ministry of Defence: Appropriation Accounts

The contract for a bespoke signal message handling system, known as the Common User Data System, was given to GEC in 1988, who delivered the capability to the Royal Air Force in December 1994 without any caveat regarding functionality. Significant problems with software, operational performance and site processes were identified and in August 1997 the project was terminated with a loss to the taxpayer of £21 million. In February 1998, the MoD implemented a slightly adjusted off-the-shelf solution which cost £1.3 million. It is such stories like this which confirm to taxpayers that their money is not being well spent.

This report concentrates on five issues which can be identified as waste. The five issues to be examined are: an information technology project known as Project Trawlermen; the aforementioned Common User Data System; the Pay Replacement System; evidence of fraud in the Pensions Division of the Army Personnel Centre; and finally the handling of Suspense Accounts within these Appropriation Accounts.

The Trawlermen project related to the development of an information technology system for the Defence Intelligence Staff and was awarded in July 1988 to Data Sciences Ltd, who delivered the system to the MoD in 1995. It was realised on delivery that changes and development in information technology, as well as changes in health and safety legislation, meant that the Trawlermen system could not meet the needs of the Defence Intelligence Staff, particularly as the original specification did not include a requirement for the system to be capable of interfacing with other computer systems. A review followed to see if the system could be modernised, but by November 1996 the MoD decided to abandon the project. In evidence to the PAC they admitted that the project had been overambitious and they had relied too much on what industry told them could be delivered and also agreed with the PAC that they had, in effect, left the management of the project largely to the contractor. The MoD suggested to the PAC that they could not find an alternative and that their requirements were unique. The cancellation of the project cost the taxpayer £40.7 million and the MoD subsequently bought an off-the-shelf package based on Windows NT4 for £6 million.

The Common User Data System was intended to replace teleprinters used for sending and receiving signal messages to about 500 terminals at 13 sites. The system was delivered to the MoD without caveat about functionality so when, in March 1995, the MoD discovered that the system did not fully address the procedure for handling incoming messages, an additional contract was given to GEC at a cost of £250,000. In early January 1996 significant problems with the software were identified and a working group was set up to address and solve the problem. Further operationally unacceptable problems occurred, which the NAO ironically described as follows: "These included the tendency for the system to stop, and failure of side processors." (Note 2) In January 1997 the RAF began to look for an alternative commercial system and cancelled the support contract, valued at £6.5 million, for the system. By August 1997 the project was terminated, and in February 1998 the department began to implement an off-the-shelf solution at a cost of £1.3 million. The value of the contract with GEC was £21 million.

The Pay Replacement System 2 was intended to deliver the Royal Navy's pay and pension system and was initiated in 1993, sponsored by the Second Sea Lord. (Note 3) The contract was awarded in 1994. Within three months it was clear to the MoD that the project was likely to be more complex than originally envisaged. The estimated delivery date slipped by 12 months and the contractor advised that the cost might increase by £4 million. A review team reported in March 1995 that the cost of the project was likely to rise to £41.1 million and added that a delivery delay would stretch to a further three years. On that basis the MoD decided to suspend, run down and then close the project, but not before £8.7 million costs had been incurred. A subsequent report into the fiasco highlighted that the project should have been staffed with experienced personnel from the outset; that requirement should be specified in a testable way; that development risk should be transferred outside the MoD; and that the systems to be used to track the progress of any project should be designed to suit the project's needs. The PAC identified that "the recommendations made by the consultants were little more than managerial common sense", (Note 4) and therefore asked the MoD whether they usually embark on projects with inexperienced personnel and requirements that could not be tested. The MoD agreed "that there had been weaknesses in project management and depressingly familiar problems with underestimating the complexity and scope of the project at the outset". (Note 5)

A civil servant employed at the Army Personnel Centre in Glasgow paid £477,734 into his personal bank account by obtaining the computer passwords of three of the staff, saying that he would process their work whilst they were on leave. This enabled him to reach a key control within the system and he was able to access and authorise payments which were duly credited to his own bank account. It was not a very sophisticated fraud but an effective one and the perpetrator eventually received a four-year prison sentence.

In his report the Comptroller and Auditor General noted that in the examination of 160 suspense accounts, (Note 6) all of which had balances at the year-end of more than £1 million, 20 could not be fully reconciled. For instance, in the suspense account identified as Army Pay Disbursement Suspense, £9.1 million was not reconciled and the MoD explained that whenever the army deployed forces overseas on exercise the soldiers received cash in hand. The amounts were booked as advances and transmitted to the appropriate authority. However, the process for the recovery of this advance of pay was unique, in that whilst the army was satisfied that they had recorded the correct amount they could not match the advances to the recoveries and get precise matches. The NAO took the attitude that this money should be written-off, and accordingly £28.7 million was written off for 1997/98 and 1998/99. The MoD started afresh by replacing the Army Paid Disbursement Suspense account with a Cash Issue Suspense account, but the NAO were disturbed to find by the end of 1998/99 that the balance on this suspense account was already £5.8 million.

A total of £99.6 million has been added to the summary at the end of this chapter.

SOURCES

PAC Report: *Ministry of Defence: Appropriation Accounts 1998/99 (Volume 1, Class I)*, HC11-1, 13 July 2000

NAO Report: *Ministry of Defence: Appropriation Accounts 1998/99 (Volume 1: Class I)*, HC11-1, 19 January 2000

NOTES

1 An appropriation account requires an allocation by parliament to a specific department for a specific financial year.

2 NAO Report, p5

3 The Second Sea Lord in 1993 was Sir Michael Layard who retired in 1996.

4 PAC Report, p5/8

5 ibid

6 Suspense accounts identify receipts and disbursements pending analysis and classification and are regarded as a control risk.

00 01 13

Ministry of Defence: Major Projects Report

The Ministry of Defence (MoD) is responsible for over 35% of all Major Projects initiated by government, and since 1984 has reported to parliament for the performance of these Major Projects on a classified basis. The NAO and PAC reports about Major Projects, which began in 1991, register a mixture of surprise, despair, frustration and disbelief at the MoD's inability to take control of its finances and live within its means.

Major Projects are, per se, usually large-scale and innovative and rely on complex relationships between diverse stakeholders and as such are invariably high risk. They include the introduction of large IT systems and construction of defence equipment such as ships, aircraft and helicopters. By definition they should be well-planned and executed to justify the expenditure of large tranches of taxpayers' money. At the time of writing, 2012, there were 205 projects managed by government of which 72 were managed by the MoD. The whole life value of the 205 projects was some

£376 billion and the annual spend equated to £14 billion. The sheer scale of the programmes and the unhealthy history of many past projects, both financially and operationally, convinced government to create the Major Projects Authority in an effort to improve performance. Created by Prime Minister mandate in 2011, and launched in March of the same year, the authority is a partnership between the Cabinet Office and the Treasury, reporting jointly to the Chief Secretary to the Treasury and the Minister for the Cabinet Office. A National Audit Office (NAO) report into the authority notes that the Treasury had not engaged as strongly at a senior level as the NAO would expect, giving them little confidence for the long-term outlook for the authority. (Note 1)

Encouraged by the NAO, the MoD introduced the Smart Acquisition Programme in July 1998 with the ambition of enabling defence equipment to be delivered faster, cheaper and better. The creation of the programme reflected the sustainment and reinforcement of the initiative across the defence acquisition family, i.e. the Equipment Capability Customer, the Defence Procurement Agency, the Defence Logistics Organisation and the various service users. The Smart Acquisition cycle involved a series of procedures evaluated at two main 'Gates' – an Initial Gate and a Main Gate. At Initial Gate, the business cases were put to the Equipment Approvals Committee to confirm there was a well-constructed plan to take the concept forward to an assessment phase and that such a plan gives reasonable confidence that there are flexible solutions within the time, cost and performance envelope proposed by the presenter.

If a concept is approved it moves to the assessment phase where the Integrated Project Team (IPT) produces a System Requirement Document (SRD) and identifies the most cost-effective technological and procurement solution. By the end of this process the business case will have been assembled for Main Gate approval.

Main Gate is the approval point for the Demonstration and Manufacturer phases. At this stage the assembled business plan, which should recommend a single technical and procurement option, is presented. Also, by this stage, risk should have been reduced to the extent that the Director of Equipment Capability and IPT leader can, with a high degree of confidence, undertake to deliver the project to a narrowly defined time, cost and performance parameter.

The Demonstration and Manufacturer cycles now follow and continue until the equipment enters service. During this phase development risk is aggressively eliminated, the ability to produce integrated capability is demonstrated and the solution to the military requirement is in theory delivered within time and cost limits.

Stage Five of the Smart Acquisition Programme is the in-service phase, when the equipment has been delivered and has proved to be as forecast, with the final and sixth stage, the disposal of the equipment after it has reached obsolescence.

There are two main inhibitions therefore in the process of ordering equipment, i.e. the Initial Gate, which precedes the assessment phase and which the Public Accounts Committee (PAC) says gives "a rational rather than just an enthusiast's opinion of new technology", (Note 2) and the Main Gate, which is the final check before demonstration and manufacturer. Whilst the balances were established by the Smart Acquisition Programme there were a number of legacy programmes which predated the introduction of this concept, and all of the post-Main Gate projects featured in this 1998 Major Project report were conceived prior to the introduction of the Smart Acquisition Programme.

It is also useful to offer information about some of the organisations within the MoD that are responsible for the sourcing and delivery of materials and weapons necessary to conduct the business of war and security. The Defence Procurement Agency (DPA) was established in 1999 with responsibility for the acquisition of materials, equipment and services for the armed forces. Eight years later it merged with the Defence Logistics Organisation to create a new body, the Defence Equipment and Support Agency (DE&S). Also involved in the process is the Equipment Capability Customer Organisation, which was set up to help improve the way the department meets the needs of the armed forces. The responsibility of this latter organisation, in consultation with the armed service, is to decide which capability was needed and how much funding to allocate. It is the responsibility of the DE&S to deliver the agreed capability.

This report (Note 3) into the 20 largest projects initiated by the MoD concluded that "the Department is meeting the technical requirements of customers but not within approved time and cost. There is evidence that since 1997 the Department has been controlling costs better but average project delays are getting longer". (Note 4) This section therefore looks at projects which appear to contribute to the definition of government waste.

The PAC examination of the Major Projects Report 1998 identified that the total cost overrun on the 25 projects was some £2.8 billion.

Eurofighter was a collaborative project with Germany, Italy and Spain and was designed as an agile fighter aircraft, primarily offering air superiority but also with an air-to-ground capability. It was designed to replace the Tornado F3 and Jaguar aircraft and the contract signed in January 1998 covered production for 55 aircraft with a value of some £2.2 billion. The project was managed on behalf of the collaborating nations by a NATO agency, NETMA. The PAC identified that there was a £1.5 billion increase with the cost of Eurofighter and that there was a 42-month delay with delivery.

Brimstone was an air-launched anti-armour weapon and was scheduled to replace the BL 755 but had been delayed by 118 months to coincide with the planned date for the Tornado GR4 package 2 update. The BL 755 had 5% of the capability of Brimstone against modern tanks so it was decided to fit radar proximity sensors to enable the bombs to be delivered from a higher altitude at a cost of £10 million. The PAC recorded: "The delays on Brimstone had occurred because of the Department's decision-making process and not because of work in industry on producing the missile". (Note 5)

The BVRAAM (Beyond Visual Range Air-to-Air Missile) was created for the Eurofighter aircraft. A comment by the PAC needs no embellishment: "The Department continues to make basic errors in estimating programme costs, such as missing £2 million Value Added Tax on the BVRAAM project. The Chief of Defence Procurement is at a loss to explain why such mistakes happen..." (Note 6)

The Tornado aircraft 'enjoyed' a Mid-Life Update that ran over budget by £333 million, which was attributed to the underestimation of the technical complexity of the programme. Under examination by the PAC the department admitted that they had identified that the aircraft did not have enough computing power to integrate all the weapons and other electronic systems, such as friend or foe identification, and handle them all in combination so that they worked together.

The total cost variation is £1.858 billion, which will be added to the summary at the end of this chapter.

SOURCE

PAC Report: *Ministry of Defence: Major Projects Report 1998*, HC247, 16 August 2000.

NOTES

1 NAO Report

2 ibid

3 ibid

4 PAC Report, p1-2/4

5 ibid, p3/4

6 ibid, p2-3/4

00 01 14

State Earnings-Related Pension Scheme: The Failure to Inform the Public about Reduced Pension Rights for Widows and Widowers

A lack of technology, dependence upon manuals, a total lack of interest by middle and senior management and an error by junior members of staff at the Department of Social Security (DSS) will cost the taxpayer at least £2.5 billion and perhaps as much as £13 billion in the period to 2050. This section examines why such a catastrophe was allowed to happen.

The State Earnings-Related Pension Scheme (SERPS) is the earnings-related part of the state retirement pension. It is paid to employees who paid Class I National Insurance contributions on earnings between the lower and upper earnings limit for such contributions in one or more tax years since 6 April 1978, and who reach state pension age after 6 April 1979. SERPS was given effect by the Social Security Pensions Act of 1975, and under the provisions of that act widows and widowers were to receive the full additional pension earned by their spouses (subject to a maximum amount if they were entitled to an additional pension derived from their own contributions). However, Section 19(1) of the Social Security Act (the 1986

Act) replaced that inheritance entitlement, instead providing that widows and widowers would inherit only one half of the amount of additional pension payable to their spouse if death occurred after 5 April 2000. A key objective of the 1986 Act was to reduce the future burden of SERPS as it was felt that "existing provisions were regarded as overgenerous and the proposed changes would bring the arrangements more into line with those in occupational pension schemes", (Note 1) and estimates quoted by the NAO suggest that the cost of SERPS would reduce from £48 billion to £21.9 billion in 2030/31 as a result of the Act. (Note 2)

The Minister of State for Social Security, Norman Fowler, said, "We have every intention of mounting a major publicity campaign to herald the pension changes contained in the present Bill, should it become an Act..." (Note 3) In September 1986 a leaflet was distributed, publicising the 1986 reforms, which mentioned the halving of SERPS for widows and widowers as well as confirming that the new arrangements would become active after 5 April 2000, i.e. some 14 years ahead. In November 1986 the DSS Newcastle-upon-Tyne-based section responsible for promulgating procedures and instructions on long-term benefits contacted other DSS sections about a draft amendment sheet for insertion into DSS leaflet NP32 – a leaflet which was routinely included in claim packs sent to prospective state pensioners. The Newcastle-upon-Tyne section did highlight the need to include, in the proposed revision, the new rules regarding pension calculation. The London section responsible for policy replied, recommending inserting a sentence saying that after April 2000 a widow or widower would be able to receive not more than half of the late spouse's additional pension. The suggestion was not acted upon and an enquiry conducted by the Parliamentary and Health Ombudsman was not able to establish whether any discussion of the London section's suggestion took place, whether other sections offered comment, nor indeed were the interviews conducted with DSS staff able to throw any light on the situation. The leaflet was not amended in any way and the full reprint in April 1987 made no reference to the significant changes to inheritable SERPS due to take place in 2000. To make matters worse, the April 1987 leaflet said: "A widow can inherit the whole of her late husband's pension and add this to her own additional pension... A widower can also make use of this provision if his wife dies when they are both over pension age", (Note 4) thereby contradicting the essence of the 1986 Act. Leaflet NP32 was superseded in April 1989 by leaflet NP46, which was quite detailed but was primarily intended for the use of advisory bodies such as Citizens' Advice Bureaux, whilst this simpler leaflet FB6 was intended for general readership. Again, leaflet NP46 compounded the situation by quoting, "you get all of his Additional Pension..." (Note 5) and this leaflet stayed in circulation until April 1995. The Parliamentary and Health Ombudsman was able to show that, apart from the leaflet produced in September 1986, there was a failure for ten years to refer at all to the future changes in SERPS inheritance provisions and that in a large number of leaflets incorrect information was offered.

DSS staff holding the following instructions and guidance material (the Pensions Instructions and Procedures Code; the Widows Instructions and Procedures Code; and the Pensions Law Code) were told about the changes to the SERPS inheritance rules and advised that appropriate amendments to all three codes would follow in due course. However, only the Pensions Law Code was amended and staff continued to give contradictory advice until January 1999, when a specific bulletin to staff drew attention to the forthcoming halving of the SERPS inheritance entitlement. The NAO report into the matter drew attention to the very limited availability of IT during the period, and the archaic nature of what did exist ensured that much of the work of the DSS on a local office basis was paper-based and that staff did not have much direct access to information in electronic form. The DSS showed a lack of appreciation and a degree of arrogance during this period – they received over 3,500 letters during 1999 alone from customers who were often distressed and concerned and, apart from sending them a standard holding reply, these customers were not advised of subsequent developments. The PAC report into the matter concluded that decisions were taken at a low level by staff who did not appreciate the significance of the issues and who had a rather narrow view of their responsibilities. No senior staff took an interest in the dissemination of information to the customer, including leaflets. (Note 6)

An opportunity arose in 1995 to address the matter when Baroness Gould of Potternewton tabled an amendment in the Lords which would have the effect of introducing a transitional period of ten years, during which the amount of SERPS to be inherited would be reduced in steps of 5% a year from April 2000. In moving her amendment Baroness Gould said it was her understanding that there was little public awareness of the forthcoming change and that the measure would come as a great shock to many people when it happened. The Minister of State for Social Security, Norman Fowler, replying for the then government said, "This reduction... will not come as a surprise... 14 years is a more than adequate lead-in period and more than enough notice to give people who may be affected when the year 2000 comes". (Note 7) The Minister of State had an opportunity to rectify a problem and missed that opportunity.

Age Concern wrote to the minister, then Alistair Darling, in 1998, highlighting that an increasing number of older people had contacted them when they discovered that the amount of SERPS the surviving widow or widower would receive depended on the exact date on which the spouse died. Unhappy with the reply received from the department, Age Concern suggested in July 1999 that the reduction due to be instigated in April 2000 was in breach of Article 1 of the First Protocol to the European Convention on Human Rights, and then in December threatened to commence legal proceedings if the matter was not resolved. Even at this stage the department did not appreciate the implication of the changes in legislation and in February 1999 major newspapers such as the *The Times*, *The Financial Times* and *The Daily Telegraph* were aware of the problem, whilst *The Sun* published an article headed "Biggest Pension Scandal Ever", which was subtitled "The Government Gave Out Bad Advice For 10 Years". (Note 8) By May 1999 the Permanent Secretary to the DSS, Rachel Lomax, had admitted to the Parliamentary and Health Ombudsman that the leaflet produced by the department since 1987 had contained incorrect and incomplete information about the changes to SERPS, and had not been corrected until 1996. She confirmed that the majority of DSS staff were unaware of the changes and had given information to the public based on contemporaneous leaflets, manuals etc. In September 1999, the Parliamentary and Health Ombudsman wrote to the Permanent Secretary and suggested that, in order to make good the effects of their maladministration, the department needed to be capable of providing due redress on a global, rather than individual basis. The amendment, which eventually received Royal Assent on 11 November 1999, provided for the Secretary of State to do one or more of the following: to allow for specified categories of widows or widowers to receive more than 50% of their spouses' additional pensions under SERPS; to postpone the reduction to 50% from April 2000 to a later year; or to set up a scheme to determine who had been misled by incorrect or incomplete information about the reduction of 50% so as to ensure that the reduction was not applied in such cases. The government eventually decided to extend the starting date for changes to SERPS to October 2002.

The NAO estimated that the direct costs in terms of anticipated savings not realised due to the deferral of the legislation until October 2002 would be £2.5 billion between 2000 and 2050. The cost of payments to those eligible for preserved rights will vary depending on the number of successful applicants, and NAO quoted one set of assumptions as £5.7 billion over 50 years. As well as this, the cost of administering a preserved rights scheme over a two-year period assessment was £60 million, making a total cost to the taxpayer of £8.26 billion. The PAC report suggested that the remedy may cost the taxpayer up to £13 billion. As costs are incurred up to 2050, no doubt further actuarial reports will become available with more reliable information. A total of £8.26 billion has been added to the summary at the end of the chapter.

SOURCES

PAC Report: *State Earnings-Related Pension Scheme: The Failure to Inform the Public about Reduced Pension Rights for Widows and Widowers*, 17 August 2000

NAO Report: *State Earnings-Related Pension Scheme: The Failure to Inform the Public about Reduced Pension Rights for Widows and Widowers*, HC 320, 15 March 2000

Parliamentary and Health Ombudsman: *State Earnings-Related Provision (SERPS) Inheritance Provisions*, 15 March 2000

NOTES

1　Parliamentary and Health Ombudsman, p1/5

2　NAO Report, p1

3　Parliamentary and Health Ombudsman, p1/5

4　ibid, p 2/5

5　ibid, p 3/5

6　PAC Report, p4/11

7　Parliamentary and Health Ombudsman, p1/2

8　ibid, p 1/2

00 01 15

Ministry of Defence: Accepting Equipment Off-Contract and Into Service

Giving evidence to the Public Accounts Committee (PAC), Kevin Tebbit, Permanent Under Secretary of State for the Ministry of Defence (MoD), noted that the NAO had looked at £10.7 billion worth of equipment purchased over a five-year period when they examined the MoD's record of accepting equipment off-contract and into service, and said about the MoD's reluctance to pursue damages that "the proportion of £60 million in £10.7 billion does not sound to me a particularly bad record". (Note 1) Immateriality strikes again.

The department had accepted into service some 65 pieces of major equipment, each with a value of above £10 million in a five-year period. The term off-contract is when sufficient testing of the equipment confirms that compliance with the specifications and criteria set out in the contract have been met. The second milestone, acceptance into service, is when the department assesses whether the equipment meets the specific expectations and requirements of the users of the equipment. The NAO examined 43 projects and based their findings on a questionnaire sent to the appropriate project/equipment managers. They regarded 40 of the responses as usable, and supported these questionnaires by visits to five projects and the creation of six case studies, involving equally sea/land/air. In one third of cases the examined contract acceptance criteria did not fully reflect the staff requirement, and in some cases the MoD had to pay for remedial work themselves or sacrifice the equipment performance in question. The NAO also reported that in 50% of the cases where the staff requirement was not fully met, the MoD made concessions that removed from the contract the obligation to make good the shortfall. In all cases, bar one, the NAO reported that "the nature of the shortfalls made it inappropriate for them to be traded off, and the Department agreed the concession because they decided that the shortfall against the requirement would have no effect on overall military capability". (Note 2) Another reason for the MoD agreeing concessions was pressure from users to accept the equipment when the system being replaced was so old as to have a very low level of capability, or because there was an urgent operational requirement for the equipment. It was noted that taking equipment into service before acceptance is complete generally weakened the MoD's negotiating position. The NAO noted that one way of dealing with shortfalls against the staff requirement was to accept the equipment into service with provisos that can bring operational benefit, which can sometimes become concessions.

The worst possible scenario was where the MoD accepted the equipment from the contractor but was forced to remedy shortfalls at their own expense – a circumstance which arose if the staff requirement was not adequately reflected in the contract. In one third of the projects the contract acceptance criteria did not reflect the technical objectives of the staff requirement in all material respects.

The MoD specified to manufacturers that the RB44 Heavy Duty Utility Truck "should be made, rather than the performance it should achieve. As a result, the truck's failure to work properly was not primarily the responsibility of the contractor and the Department ended up paying £3.2 million to rectify the situation". (Note 3) Project Boxer was a high-capacity telecommunications system. The Chief of Defence Procurement told the committee that the department had ignored the advice of the supplier, British Telecom, and had subsequently spent £6.8 million putting the equipment right. The Royal Fleet Auxiliary Fort Programme was accepted off-contract with 13,000 defects, of which half were considered to be significant. It took over 12 months to sort out the defects, by which time the 12-month guarantee had expired, which meant that problems that occurred whilst operating the ship were not covered and had to be rectified at an additional cost of £1.4 million. The Radar Type 996 was purchased for use on Royal Navy ships and was expected to remain in service until 2032. An 'off-the-shelf' purchase was made which did not meet the staff requirement, and the performance required could only be delivered through the procurement of a new track extractor, which was ordered from BAE Defence Systems Ltd at a cost expected to be £45.1 million. The Single Role Minehunter needed rectification at a cost of £1.9 million.

The NAO noted that the department rarely pursued general damages, but if the mind-set of the individuals concerned is that the loss of £58.4 million is immaterial, then some readers might begin to understand why such a catalogue of waste, error and inefficiency exists. The Chairman of the PAC, Mr David Davis, made his feelings known, "I must say, both from what is in this report and from what we have seen in previous reports and indeed anecdotal evidence, the tolerance of underperformance strikes me, frankly, as a culture of low standards, not necessarily one that is just extant today but over a long time in the MoD". (Note 4) A total of £58.4 million has been added to the summary at the end of this chapter.

SOURCES

PAC Report: *Ministry of Defence: Accepting Equipment Off-Contract and Into Service*, HC 319, 30 November 2000

NAO Report: *Ministry of Defence: Accepting Equipment Off-contract and Into Service*, 8 February 2000

NOTES

1 PAC Report, p2/4
2 NAO Report, p16
3 PAC Report, p3/10
4 ibid, p2/4

00 01 16

VARIOUS: This section examines three reports prepared by the Public Accounts Committee in 2000.

Financial Management and Governance at Gwent Tertiary College

Find a Principal who is financially naive, add a complacent Board of Governors, mix in an underperforming external auditor, season with a senior Management Board without any financial discipline, stir with inertia from the Funding Council and the Welsh Office and finally add a Head of Department without a job specification, and you're sure to create a dish which will deliver a financial disaster. That's what happened at Gwent Tertiary College when the board appointed Sue Parker as Principal.

In January 1996 Mrs Parker outlined proposals for a management restructuring for Gwent College, which she estimated would cost between £300,000 and £400,000 and involve an increase in management posts from 56 to 118. The Governing Body approved Mrs Parker's proposals. By 10 July, the Deputy Principal advised the senior management team that the extra costs arising from restructuring was estimated at £1.2 million, but this information was not passed to the Finance and General Purposes Committee.

A meeting attended by the Chairman of the Governing Body and the chairman of each of the committees was told in February 1997 that senior management were now forecasting a deficit of £4.4 million for the financial year 1997/98. The Funding Council had requested that an Executive Board, consisting of a few key governors, be established to monitor what was now a crisis and they were informed that the projected operating deficit for 1997/98 would increase to £6.8 million if no action was taken. The Chairman of the Personnel Committee resigned and Mrs Parker was suspended in June and subsequently resigned, having accepted a 'compromise agreement'. The fiasco that was Mrs Parker eventually cost the college £6.8 million, which is reflected in the adjusted 1997/98 accounts, and a further £1 million in the following year.

Dr Jenny Hughes was seconded to the college from Gwent County Council and was responsible for the Training Shop, which had been established in 1992 to find innovative ways of providing training in the wider community. A subsequent investigation highlighted issues of nepotism and the irregular use of credit cards for foreign cash withdrawals and unsupported expense claims, as well as probable conflict-of-interest issues. In the light of the report by Ernst & Young, the college decided to disband the Training Shop and withdraw from European Union-funded activities, which required them to repay £2.9 million out of the £3.4 million received from the European Social Fund.

The PAC Report said, "We are appalled by the lack of honesty and integrity in the financial reporting by the college", (Note 1) and also commented that "a good part of the responsibility for the College's problems also rests squarely with the Governing Body, the Funding Council and the Welsh Office". (Note 2)

These two individuals not only cost the taxpayer £10.7 million, which will be added to the summary at the end of this section, but also lost for South Wales a European-funded training opportunity.

SOURCES

PAC Report: *Financial Management and Governance at Gwent Tertiary College*, 12 January 2000

NAO Report: *Financial Management and Governance at Gwent Tertiary College*, HC 253, 12 March 1999

Whittaker, Martin: *Back from the Broke*. *TES* Editorial, 29 September 2000, updated 11 May 2008

NOTES

1   PAC Report, p3/5

2   ibid, p3/5

The Arts Council of England: Monitoring Major Projects Funded by the National Lottery

The National Lottery was introduced by John Major's Conservative Government in 1993. Funds were channelled through 12 distributing bodies of which four were for the arts, i.e. the Arts Council of England received 13.88% of the National Lottery Distribution Fund, which in 1998/99 was valued at £240 million. The PAC examined 15 major projects and found 13 were over budget, whilst eight had requested and were given supplementary assistance. The Arts Council normally funded up to 75% of the cost of the project and required the balance to be raised by the grant recipient. Management of the project was the responsibility of the grant recipient, but the Arts Councillors had a duty to safeguard use of the funds and were therefore required to monitor each project.

The PAC report concluded: "It seems to the committee that many of the problems experienced by the 15 projects raise questions about the way the grant applications have been assessed by the Arts Council in the first place." (Note 1) Initially, the Arts Council used the existing Business Assessment and Planning Team, but this was replaced four years after the introduction of the lottery scheme with a Lottery Projects Unit. The PAC "view with some scepticism their assertion that they use the Business Assessment and Planning Team on a 'pilot' basis – the team was in existence before the National Lottery began and was replaced more than four years after the lottery was introduced". (Note 2) The inefficiency of the Business Assessment and Planning Team included ignoring special conditions attached to the granting of an award, an accusation defended by the Arts Council who insisted that "they never waive special conditions, except that they 'relax' and 'defer' them". (Note 3) The PAC report noted "thirteen of the fifteen are over budget, and over half are late. The Arts Council have found it necessary to make grants of £20 million on these projects alone". (Note 4) It is therefore proposed to add £20 million to the summary at the end of this section.

SOURCES

PAC Report: *The Arts Council of England: Monitoring Major Capital Projects Funded by The National Lottery*, HC563-i, 20 January 2000

NAO Report: *The Arts Council of England: Monitoring Major Capital Projects Funded by The National Lottery*, HC404, 14 May 1999

NOTES

1 PAC Report, p3/4
2 ibid, p3/4
3 ibid
4 ibid, p2/4

NHS Executive: Hip Replacements – Getting It Right First Time

A 1996 television documentary drew attention to the failure of the 3M Capital hip prostheses, which led to its withdrawal in 1997. Both the PAC and the NAO subsequently examined the subject of hip replacements: they discovered that there were 30,000 operations carried out per year at a cost to the NHS of £140 million. They also discovered that the cost of the prostheses supplied to the NHS was £53 million, and that only 35 out of 207 NHS Trusts had negotiated satisfactory discounts, and that £7.202 million (Note 1) could have been saved. They also identified that the average length of stay was 11 days, with some patients staying as little as five days whilst others required 30 days. Consultant consultations confirmed that the length of stay could be further reduced and the NAO estimated that the saving could be anywhere between £15.5 million per year for a two-day reduction and £46.5 million (Note 2) for a six-day reduction, releasing beds and other resources for other patients.

On this basis a total of £22.7 million has been added to the summary at the end of this section.

SOURCES

PAC Report: *NHS Executive: Hip Replacements – Getting It Right First Time*, HC513, 20 December 2000

NAO Report: *Hip Replacements: Getting It Right First Time*, HC417

NOTES

1 NAO Report, p59
2 ibid

SUMMARY

A total of £53.4 million, representing a total for the three projects listed above, will be added to the summary at the end of this chapter.

SUMMARY: CHAPTER ONE – 2000

00 01 00	The Home Office: The Immigration and Nationality Directorate's Casework Programme	£1.597 bn
00 01 01	The Sheep Annual Premium Scheme in England	£0.087 bn
00 01 02	NHS (England) Summarised Accounts 1997/98	£3.055 bn
00 01 03	NHS (England) Summarised Accounts 1998/99	£1.206 bn
00 01 04	The PFI Contract for the New Dartford and Gravesham Hospital	£0.132 bn
00 01 05	The Contributions Agency: The Newcastle Estate Development Project	£0.166 bn
00 01 06	Highways Agency: Getting Best Value from the Disposal of Property	£0.110 bn
00 01 07	The Passport Delays of 1999	£0.013 bn
00 01 08	Child Support Agency: Client Funds Account 1998/99	£1.416 bn
00 01 09	Child Support Agency: Client Funds Account 1999/2000	£0.407 bn
00 01 10	Ministry of Defence: Major Projects Report	£2.144 bn
00 01 11	Criminal Justice: Working Together	£0.085 bn
00 01 12	Ministry of Defence: Appropriation Accounts	£0.100 bn
00 01 13	Ministry of Defence: Major Projects Report	£1.858 bn
00 01 14	State Earnings-Related Pension Scheme: The Failure to Inform the Public about Reduced Pension Rights for Widows and Widowers	£8.260 bn
00 01 15	Ministry of Defence: Accepting Equipment Off-Contract and Into Service	£0.058 bn
00 01 16	Various	£0.053 bn
	Total	£20.748 bn
	Total adjusted for inflation to December 2014	£27.284 bn

INDEX: CHAPTER TWO – 2001

01 02 00   Ministry of Defence: Resource Accounts
01 02 01   DVLA: Appropriation Accounts
01 02 02   Inland Revenue: National Insurance Fund Account
01 02 03   Child Support Agency: Client Funds Account
01 02 04   Ministry of Defence: Managing Reductions in the Number of Vacant Family Quarters
01 02 05   Ministry of Defence: Major Projects Report
01 02 06   The Cancellation of the Payment Card Project
01 02 07   Ministry of Defence: Resource Accounts
01 02 08   Sale of Part of the UK Gold Reserves
01 02 09   Various

"The only difference between a taxman and a taxidermist is that the taxidermist leaves the skin."

Mark Twain (1835-1910)

"In Venezuela Chavez has made the co-ops a top political priority, giving them first refusal on government contracts and offering them economic incentives to trade with one another. By 2006, there were roughly 100,000 co-operatives in the country, employing more than 700,000 workers. Many are pieces of state infrastructure – toll booths, highway maintenance, health clinics – handed over to the communities to run. It's a reverse of the logic of government outsourcing – rather than auctioning off pieces of the state to large corporations and losing democratic control, the people who use the resources are given the power to manage them, creating, at least in theory, both jobs and more responsive public services. Chavez's many critics have derided these initiatives as handouts and unfair subsidies, of course. Yet in an era when Halliburton treats the U.S. government as its personal ATM for six years, withdraws upward of £20 billion in Iraq contracts alone, refuses to hire local workers either on the Gulf coast or in Iraq, then expresses its gratitude to U.S. taxpayers by moving its corporate headquarters to Dubai (with all the attendant tax and legal benefits), Chavez's direct subsidies to regular people look significantly less radical."

Naomi Klein, Canadian political and corporate analyst (b.1970)

01 02 00

Ministry of Defence: Resource Accounts

At 31 March 2000 the Ministry of Defence (MoD) had 11 major budget holders with 110 reporting entities. It was in this year that the MoD completed its first set of Resource Accounts. By any measurement the MoD was a major establishment, with assets of over £90 billion, an annual net cash requirement of £22 billion and operating costs of £31 billion.

As a result of the previous government's White Paper, *Better Accounting for the Taxpayers' Money*, published in July 1995, accrual-based accounts – known as Resource Accounts – became the required standard for all government accounts, replacing the traditional Appropriation Accounts. In contrast to the accounting principles applied in the private sector, government departments were not, at that time, required to record expenditure and income on an annual accrual basis, that is to say in the accounting period to which they relate, nor to produce a balance sheet which recorded their assets and liabilities. Resource Accounting was therefore a radical move and regarded by the National Audit Office (NAO) as "the most important reform of central government accounting for over 100 years". (Note 1) Resource Accounts were expected to provide departments with better management information, both on the true cost of their activities and on their asset holdings, and were expected to replace Appropriation Accounts as the principal means by which departments report their financial results to parliament from the 2001/02 financial year. The MoD made a valiant attempt to anticipate some of the problems by initiating a 'dry-run' with their 1998/99 accounts, which were examined by the NAO but was deliberately not accepted as accounts for that year. Despite this exemplary attempt at anticipation, the 1999/2000 accounts still recorded enough uncertainty for the Comptroller and Auditor General to record, "I have particular concerns about the reported values for certain land and buildings, fighting equipment, capital spares, plant and machinery and vehicles and the associated additions and disposals during the year. In addition, inadequate audit trails existed to enable me to gain sufficient assurance regarding the reported balances, particularly those for stock, but also for creditors and accruals". (Note 2) The NAO were sympathetic to the MoD's position and agreed that the department should move forward, even though they recognised many of the balances brought forward at the start of

The Elephant in the Room

the year from 31 March 1999 contained fundamental uncertainties and errors. They suggested that, rather than devote an inordinate effort to remedying the deficiencies in the opening balance sheet for 1999/2000, the department should focus on improving the accuracy and reliability of current and future data. They of course recognised that the errors and uncertainties in the April 1 1999 balance sheet remained largely uncorrected and that therefore there were serious doubts about the material accuracy of the charges recorded in the department's Operating Cost Statement 1999/2000. The implication seemed to be that over the first few years, errors and uncertainties would be identified and corrected.

These Resource Accounts show that some of the properties owned by Annington Homes (Note 3) were mistakenly recorded on the balance sheet at 1 April 1998, so the NAO questioned the validity of the depreciation and the cost of capital charges. They also note that Defence Estates, an agency within the MoD responsible for estate management services, themselves valued properties earmarked for future disposal at £144 million as an open market value. However, the NAO staff noted discrepancies in the treatment of the sales proceeds: "For some sites the surplus represents the difference between the sale proceeds and valuer's estimate likely sales proceeds. For other sites, however, the surplus represents the difference between the sales proceeds and the site's existing (defence) use value" (Note 4) They therefore suggested that in the absence of audit trails for 1999/2000 there was uncertainty regarding the validity of the figure of £144 million recorded by the Defence Estates as the value of unsold surplus defence property at 31 March 2000.

The NAO also noted that most of the army's equipment was managed by the staff of the Defence Logistics Organisation (DLO) and that a managed equipment fixed asset register existed, with the value of some £8 billion recorded. The army had a fundamentally sound and robust management system, known as Merlin, but it was recognised that the underlying records for other forces were less reliable. There is therefore some uncertainty at the start of the 1998/99 financial year as to whether the fixed asset register was indeed accurate, so the department conducted a census exercise which revealed errors in the information held and raised uncertainties about the existence of certain assets and the completeness of asset records. The errors and uncertainties identified by the census initially amounted in value to over £500 million, but a second census reduced that figure to £90 million.

The NAO also recognised that the MoD maintained a large number of logistics management systems, holding details of over 3 million different types of items, which was reflected in the asset base of the balance sheet at some £29 billion at the end of March 2000. They identified difficulties with the reconciliation of the RAF stock collation system and noted that discrepancies at the year-end between the various parts of the RAF Supply System, "pointed to a potential ranging between an overstatement of the reported balances at 31 March 2000 of £297 million, to an understatement of £361 million". (Note 5) They also noted that the Royal Navy stock collation system had rejected some 1.2 million items presented to it for processing and reported, "It is not possible to quantify the financial impact on the Department's Resource Account of these rejections, but the Defence Logistics Organisation believes the amount involved is in the order of £200 million". (Note 6) The NAO identified that the CANVASS stock collation system calculated the annual depreciation charges and recorded accumulated apprecation on certain naval fighting equipment having a value of almost £5 billion. It also identified that the system often calculated incorrect amounts for these charges during 1999/2000 and that it had not been possible to estimate reliably the extent of the possible misstatements. They also noted that "although many of the prices in the army supply systems had been corrected before the end of 1999/2000, my staff estimated value of certain inventory items was overstated by a total of some £145 million at 31 March 2000. Other items were overstated by £22 million, and items with the reported value of £620 million budget, were to be verified". (Note 7) There was uncertainty about whether all the items owned by the department had been included in the accounts.

The adoption of Resource Accounts required the MoD for the first time to correctly identify and quantify their creditor and accrual figures, and the NAO staff involved "expressed concern over the basis on which Equipment Support (Air) had the right creditor and accruals figures". (Note 8) The staff could not verify some 80% of the creditor and accrual figures – a total of £118 million.

The NAO did not comment about the schedule on pages 44 and 45, which showed that the department had entered into off-balance sheet Private Finance Initiative (PFI) commitments totalling £1.198 billion, which stretched to December 2029. It also does not comment about the losses of £49 million, which covered 18,540 cases where details of special payments, gifts and other notes as described in 'Government Accounting' are required to be included within financial statements.

The accounts also mention a loss of £2.2 million following the cancellation of a project to fit a Joint Tactical Information Distribution System to the RAF Tanker aircraft fleet. Similarly, £1.6 million was incurred on the development and production of a software application for an Automatic Routing and Distribution System, which proved not be required.

These first Resource Accounts of the department raise many questions but no doubt the answers will be provided in future years. For the purposes of this exercise a total of £572 million has been added to the summary at the end of this chapter.

SOURCE

Ministry of Defence Consolidated Departmental Resource Accounts 1999/2000, HC 50, 31 January 2001

NOTES

1 MoD Report, p12
2 ibid, p10
3 Annington Homes purchased the majority of MoD family quarters in 1996. See 01 02 04.
4 ibid, p14
5 ibid, p16
6 ibid, p16
7 ibid, p17
8 ibid, p18
9 ibid, p50

01 02 01

DVLA: Appropriation Accounts

The NAO report into the activities of the DVLA examined the introduction of the agency's vehicle computer system sourced from Electronic Data Systems Ltd (EDS) and notes that the introduction of the system was handled in a positive manner. The report also examined tax evasion and outlined some actions taken to resolve the problem.

The £5 million, fixed-price contract to replace the agency's vehicle computer system was originally expected to take two years, with installation planned for October 1998, but eventually was completed in mid-October 2001. However, the direct cost to the agency had remained within the limits set within the Treasury-approved business case, primarily because the agency had prepared detailed user requirements at the outset, concluded a fixed-price contract and kept subsequent changes to a minimum.

The issue of evasion of tax was one which the agency felt it could deal with more efficiently once the information technology issues had been addressed, and in this report the agency estimated that there was a gross evasion loss of £183 million, which was offset by some £86 million recovered through enforcement activities. Twenty-six wheel clamping/Vehicle Excise Duty enforcement campaigns with local police forces were organised and, as a result, some 21,000 vehicles were either clamped or impounded. Over 7,000 of these were released on payment of fees but a total of 10,000 were disposed of, mainly by crushing. At the year-end the remaining 4,000 vehicles were waiting authorisation to crush. (Note 1) A further initiative was a trial of Automatic Number Plate Readers which gathered evidence of unlicensed vehicles on public roads. It would appear that the successful introduction of the DVLA computer system had given the agency the ammunition to reduce tax evasion. A total of £98 million, the difference between the estimated loss and revenue recovered, is added to the summary at the end of this chapter.

SOURCE

Driver and Vehicle Licensing Agency (DVLA) Appropriation Accounts 1999/2000, HC 25-III, 14 February 2001

NOTE

1   NAO Report, R6

01 02 02

Inland Revenue: National Insurance Fund Account

In April 1999, the Inland Revenue assumed responsibility for the management of the National Insurance Fund from the Department of Social Security.

This NAO report identified that the value of errors by officials in assessing Incapacity Benefit amounted to £252 million. Incapacity Benefit was introduced in April 1995 and replaced Invalidity Benefit and Sickness Benefit. It provided support to people under pension age who were unable to work due to their incapacity and who had paid sufficient National Insurance contributions. It was assessed initially through the provision of medical certificates, but subsequently by the application of tests designed to determine whether claimants were capable of carrying out a range of work-related activities. The assessment of Incapacity Benefit was complex because circumstances could affect the level of benefit due in any week and the Benefits Agency were sometimes not told by the claimant when changes in circumstances occurred.

Retirement pension is paid to people who reach state pension age and qualified by meeting the appropriate National Insurance contribution conditions. Widows' Benefit is a generic term covering payment for widows whose husbands were not entitled to a retirement pension when they died, widowed mothers' allowance for widows with at least one qualifying child and widows' pension. The NAO estimated that losses in the calculation of Widows' Benefit amounted to some £32 million, whilst the latest Benefit Review of Retirement Pension estimated that losses could be as high as £40 million.

A Public Service Agreement target had been set to reduce fraud and error by 10% by March 2000 and by 50% by March 2006. These are significant targets bearing in mind that in the year some £50.025 billion was paid out of the fund, of which the largest amount was for Retirement Pension and Widows' Benefit. For the purposes of this exercise £284 million has been added to the summary at the end of this chapter.

01 02 03

Child Support Agency: Client Funds Account

The Child Support Agency Client Fund Account was qualified "because the National Audit Office's examination of a representative sample of cases showed that 35% of receipts from non-resident parents and 80% of maintenance assessment debts were incorrect". (Note 1) Whilst the reports in this book seek to be non-judgemental, it is difficult not to feel sympathy for the staff who had to make such a statement and perhaps explains why the report this year, like the previous year, was terse. Auditing a set of accounts which demonstrated an out of control agency, allied to the knowledge that the rectification of the problem would not happen until new policies and a new information technology system were introduced in 2002, would no doubt determine the NAO's approach to this report. The NAO were well aware of government's history of introducing information technology systems, and possibly foresaw a period in which this agency would continue to absorb and waste taxpayer revenues.

The agency was established in 1993, but after six years was found not to be working efficiently, so legislative change to secure a simpler scheme of child support was incorporated in the Child Support, Pensions and Social Security Act 2000, aimed at the simplification of rules surrounding maintenance assessment. When the new system arrived it was planned to use it initially for new cases, and existing cases would only be transferred when ministers were satisfied that the new arrangements were working well. However, the NAO was aware that high error rates had occurred for a number of years and very conscious that the impact from the conversion of cases from all the old rules to new rules could be traumatic, and that there would be 'losers' as well as winners under the new arrangements. The realisation that the rectification of the problem would not occur for at least two years did not help staff morale and the annual turnover of staff was in the order of 27%.

One of the main targets of the agency was to collect revenue from non-resident parents for onward transmission to either the parent with care or to the Secretary of State, who recovered the money when parents with care were already in receipt of Income Support. It was a thankless and difficult procedure, and in this year the agency assessed that £183 million due by the non-resident parent was probably uncollectable and was therefore written-off. Similarly, a further £99 million was written off from non-resident parents with interim maintenance assessments. (Note 2)

Errors amounted to £375 million for non-resident parents for full maintenance assessments whilst the level for interim maintenance assessments for the same group totalled £31 million. Additionally, overpayments and underpayments by non-resident parents amounted to £17 million.

The total added to the summary at the end of this chapter for error, write-offs and over/under payments is £705 million.

SOURCE

Child Support Agency Client Funds Account 2000/01, 4 July 2001

NOTES

1 NAO Report, p1
2 ibid, p4

01 02 04

Ministry of Defence: Managing Reductions in the Number of Vacant Family Quarters

When the Ministry of Defence (MoD) sold the majority of the Service Family Accommodation (SFA) in England and Wales to Annington Homes Ltd in 1996 they had four objectives: to transfer to the private sector property which the MoD did not need to own themselves; to improve management of the quarters through the greater involvement of the private sector; to secure improvement in the quality of the married quarters by raising sufficient funds to upgrade the bulk of quarters in the United Kingdom to prime condition; and finally to secure value for money through a competitive sale. What they did not seem to appreciate was that some of the proceeds, i.e. the proceeds available when Annington Homes sold surplus property, would revert to the Treasury and not to the MoD. In the period between 1996 and 2006 the total proceeds returned to the Treasury was £140 million. It is unclear how much of the £1.67 billion raised from the sale of the properties was indeed used for the purpose intended, but in view of the negative comments by both the Public Accounts Committee (PAC) and the National Audit Office (NAO) about the state of the housing stock it would appear that not all of the proceeds were used for the purpose intended, or if indeed the MoD received any of the funds.

Every married service person is entitled to family quarters, although they are not compelled to take up their entitlement. The bulk of the estate, some 53,000 homes, is owned by Annington Homes Ltd and was leased back to the department under the terms of the sales agreement, although the MoD remained responsible for the management, maintenance and upgrade of the properties. The size of the family quarters estate had fallen from 75,000 houses in 1991 to around 63,000 in 1999 to reflect a decreasing military establishment, but of much concern to the PAC was the increase in empty properties, which moved from 11,200 houses in 1991 (15% of the total housing stock) to 14,425 in 1999 (23% of the total housing stock). (Note 1) The significance of the vacant family quarters was that Annington Homes still received their rent for these empty properties, which the NAO estimated cost the MoD £39 million in rent and maintenance for 1998/99, (Note 2) and which the PAC estimated cost the MoD £41 million in rent and maintenance for 1999/2000. (Note 3) Whilst the PAC had some sympathy with the MoD about its inability to accurately forecast demand for family quarters because of the uncertainty about force strength and dispositions, it nevertheless was very critical of the fact that, whilst the estate was falling, the number of vacant houses was rising. One of the causes, the PAC suggested, was that local commanders had no financial incentive to release surplus properties, as rent and maintenance costs are met by the Defence Housing Executive (the Executive).

Annington Homes also negotiated within the contract that they receive 'ghost rent' for properties which had been the demolished, but where the MoD retained an interest in the site. The MoD believed that their liability in respect of such empty sites during the first 25-year period of the agreement could amount to as much as £61 million, so the PAC naturally suggested that they should relinquish their interest in such sites as early as possible to reduce the potential liability.

Besides payment for empty homes, 'ghost rent' for demolished sites and payment of 75% of the sale price for properties disposed of, Annington Homes also negotiated a clause which required the MoD to return properties to Annington Homes in 'good tenantable repair'. (Note 4) If this could not be achieved Annington could claim financial compensation for the cost of any repairs needed to restore the property to the required standard. The problem facing the MoD was whether to upgrade the housing stock for disposal or for service personnel.

It is unclear whether the £1.6 billion achieved from the sale of the estate was used to upgrade the properties, as intended. The Executive inherited 53,000 houses, of which only 1,000 rated as ideal standard. The PAC noted that the MoD set the target to upgrade 40% of the estate to the ideal standard by spring 2001, and that the total planned expenditure on the upgrade programme was £600 million – even so, only £48 million was spent in 1999/2000, and a further £68 million was due to be spent in 2000/01. The total planned expenditure figure of £600 million was £1 billion short of the proceeds of the sale to Annington Homes. No wonder then that PAC concluded their report: "After four years of operating the new arrangements, it now appeared that the Department had borne all of the risks with none shared by the owners of the estate. Meanwhile the overall level and cost of vacancies had increased, while the size of the estate had reduced during this period. We therefore asked whether the Department could point to any real management benefit resulting from the sale." (Note 5)

According to *The Daily Telegraph*, Annington Homes had by 2012 achieved sales of £3 billion from the houses and £2.3 billion in rental income. However, what will be included is rents, where known, for empty properties and for ghost rents, both of which could have been avoided by efficient management. A total of £141 million will be added to the summary at the end of this chapter.

SOURCES

PAC Report: *Ministry of Defence: Managing Reductions in the Number of Vacant Family Quarters*, HC 391, 5 July 2001

NAO Report: *Ministry of Defence: Managing Reductions in the Number of Vacant Family Quarters*, HC 435, 22 April 2000

BBC News: news.bbc.co.uk/1/hi/uk/115903.sim, 28 November 2007

Ebrahimi, Helia. *The Daily Telegraph: Guy Hands set for £3.5 billion Army Housing Deal*, 16 November 2012

NOTES

1   NAO Report, p1
2   ibid, p2
3   PAC Report, p1/9
4   NAO Report, p7
5   PAC Report, p4/6

01 02 05

Ministry of Defence: Major Projects Report

Vice Admiral Blackham, Deputy Chief of Defence Staff (Equipment Capability) stated in evidence to the Public Accounts Committee (PAC) that "he had never been prepared to send any ship to sea without sonar, and agrees that the sonar is a vital part of a ship, without which ship should not be accepted at all". (Note 1) He went on to admit that "the words in the Comptroller and Auditor General's report concerning the fitting of sonar to the Type 45 destroyer had hit home inside the Department and had caused the Department to have a rethink". (Note 2) The National Audit Office (NAO) report concerned had identified that "the lack of sonar could impose operational and ship scheduling constraints on the initial ships until it is fitted. For example, without sonar it is unlikely that the Type 45 destroyers could be deployed alone to theatres where significant submarine threat is perceived". (Note 3) It does seem odd that the auditors in Buckingham Palace Road were able to spot a glaring omission missed by the professionals in the Ministry of Defence (MoD).

The 2000 report by the NAO identified that this would be the first report produced in the new format, reflecting the changes in project accounting and approvals brought about by the introduction of the Smart Acquisition Programme and the introduction of Resource Accounting and Budgeting.

The Smart Acquisition Programme was dealt with in Sections 00 01 10 and 00 01 13. The NAO noted, "All of the post-Main Gate projects featuring in the 2000 Major Projects Report were conceived prior to the introduction of the Smart Procurement initiative", (Note 4) and accordingly the PAC recognised that the MoD "does not expect there to be big improvements in the timescale performance reported in the Major Projects Report until 2002, some four years after Smart Acquisition was first introduced. Whilst the timescale performance reported in the Major Projects Report will continue to reflect pre-Smart Acquisition projects for some years, we will expect to see signs of improvement as new 'smart' projects come through". (Note 5)

Resource Accounting was introduced in April 1999, in line with government-wide change, and required departments to include all resource elements such as interest on capital, government-furnished equipment and investment in capital assets in all future reports. They also required the department to forecast outturn prices and reflect the amount that is forecast to be spent in each year, including the forecast impact of inflation. Essentially, government moved from a cash accounting philosophy to an accrual philosophy.

The collaborative Eurofighter project received a deal of attention from the PAC, as the MoD had reduced the cost of the project by deciding that a gun was no longer required for each aircraft. The PAC suggested that "it would be wise for the Department to cross check why our Eurofighter partner nations are still fitting the gun and why other countries fit guns to their aircraft". (Note 6) The project variance cost increased to £1.468 billion – an increase of £97 million over the previous year.

The PAC judged the MoD's strategy for meeting its anti-armour weapon requirements "to have evolved incoherently". (Note 7) The MoD had paid a premium to buy additional BL 755 cluster bombs for the Kosovo campaign which were not used, reduced the number of Brimstone missiles being procured, with no prospect of a proportional saving in price, and purchased Maverick missiles at extra cost. The delays to Brimstone were now noted as costing the MoD £48 million – £26 million of which is recognised in the 1999 report, so £22 million has been added to the summary

The opening paragraph of this report notes the pressure felt by the MoD about budgets established for the Type 45 destroyer. Besides the embarrassment of the sonar issue the PAC also established that "our ships would not be able to defend themselves if the United Kingdom were involved in an operational scenario similar to the Falklands conflict", (Note 8) as the Sea Dart, the anti-air missile system deployed on the Type 42 destroyer, was not designed as an anti-missile missile. The cost of running on the Type 42 destroyers was now £565 million – an increase of £28 million on the previous year. Assessment costs had overrun the budget by £21 million, so a total of £49 million has been added to the summary.

The programme cost to replace obsolescent sonar equipment for the Swiftsure and Trafalgar Class submarines increased by an additional £18 million. The variation between budget and forecast cost decreased for the Spearfish torpedo programme, so a total of £80 million will be deducted from the summary. However, the variation between budget and forecast cost increased for the Sting Ray project, primarily due to a slippage in delivery

The Elephant in the Room

time, adding £15 million to the final cost. The Challenger 2 (CR2) main battle tank procurement costs were £122 million, of which £65 million were noted in the 1999 report. The Tracer reconnaissance vehicle development costs had now been contained and were running at the variation of £1 million over approved costs, allowing a £5 million positive adjustment to be recorded in the summary.

The Bowman tactical communication system was conceived to replace the Clansman combat radio, which had been in service since the mid-1970s. The assessment phase was approved in 1988 and a contract placed with two competing consortia. In 1996 the two members of the consortia joined forces to create Archer Communications Systems Ltd (Archer) who were tasked to define systems integration requirements and demonstrate technical progress prior to major production, but by 2000 the MoD had decided to withdraw from the programme after Archer was taken over by BAE Systems, and suggested to the PAC that withdrawal from the programme would cost between £35 million and £102 million. However, the MoD calculated that £183 million had been invested in this programme. For the purposes of this analysis £100 million will be added to the summary.

The Microwave Landing System (MLS) was being assessed to establish the practicality of building a Precision Approach Landing System for both MoD aircraft and airfields, allowing safe runway approaches at night and in adverse weather conditions. The forecast cost of the assessment phase was £80 million against an approved cost of £40 million. (Note 9)

The cancellation of the medium-range Trigat anti-tank guided weapon system motivated the PAC to look closely at the project. They noted it was initiated in 1979 and also noted that the requirement was not expected to be met until at least 2005 and commented that "this is equivalent to the commissioning of a weapon at the end of World War I and not receiving it until the end of World War II". (Note 10) The MoD cancelled because of continuing and open-ended delays by their collaborative partners. The PAC noted that the department spent £115 million on development costs.

The Merlin Mk1 helicopter was mentioned in the 1999 report (see Section 00 01 10). The variance between forecast cost and approved cost had reduced by £201 million. The High Velocity Missile (HVM) was an army requirement to attack armoured helicopters and low-flying aircraft. The procurement costs exceeded the approved cost by £16 million. The Astute class of submarine was the planned replacement for the Swiftsure class and an initial contract for the design, build and support for three units was placed with GEC-Marconi in 1997, with delivery scheduled in 2005. The variation between forecast cost and approved cost was £42 million.

A total of £569 million will therefore be added to the summary at the end of this chapter.

SOURCES

PAC Report: *Ministry of Defence: Major Projects Report 2000*, HC 368, 28 November 2001

PAC Report: *Ministry of Defence: Major Projects Report 2000 – The Role of the Equipment Capability Customer*, HC 369, 28 November 2001

NAO Report: *Ministry of Defence: Major Projects Report*, HC 970, 20 November 2000

NOTES

1 PAC Report, p5/12
2 ibid, p5/12
3 NAO Report, p19
4 ibid, p3
5 PAC Report, p9/11
6 PAC Report, p8/12
7 ibid, p8/12
8 ibid, p5/11
9 NAO Report, Appendix 3, p163
10 PAC Report, p3/11

01 02 06

The Cancellation of the Payment Card Project

When British company ICL plc created Pathway to handle this PFI contract, and were awarded the contract to create a benefit payment card, they were third on a list of three based on the ten factors used to evaluate the best company to handle the project. However, they did come first in two categories which met with the assessors' approval, i.e. price and PFI compliancy.

The evaluation team who assessed the bids reported that they "had a low belief in Pathway's appreciation of, and empathy with, either of the purchasers' business requirements or ability to deliver a service which would meet the required service levels". (Note 1) If that were not damning enough they also reported that "Pathway had weak authentication procedures, the weakest security proposals and that Pathway had manifest lack of understanding of the management of fraud risk". (Note 2) Just in case the message had not been received they also reported that "Pathway's performance in managing the demonstration phase of the procurement has been substantially below those of the two other providers", (Note 3) and "Pathway had not shown itself to be adept at foreseeing and preventing problems". (Note 4) It is with these less than positive endorsements that ICL set out to provide the Benefits Payment Card.

The Department of Social Security (DSS) had responsibility for the payment of benefits to those who were entitled to them, and fulfilled this requirement by issuing order books and/or Giro cheques, which could be cashed at convenient post offices. £51 billion was processed by order books, £6 billion by Giro cheques and the remainder was processed by bank transfer during the year. The cost of handling the transactions was astronomical and the system was also open to fraud. The DSS investigated alternatives and, with the Post Office Development group, agreed that automation would be the answer. The banks and building societies provided an instant solution but the department's desire to use the latter had been blocked repeatedly by ministers in 1983, 1992 and 1994, on the basis that the compulsory imposition of a system using the banks would have limited the beneficiaries' choice but also put at risk the national network of post offices. The DSS had a further objective in seeking improvement in the handling of benefit payments. Their accounts had been qualified partially because of the fraudulent encashment of order books and Giro cheques, but also because they were unable to reconcile payments and receipts.

Post offices regarded the footfall gained from beneficiaries as important to their existence and were therefore delighted when the Secretary of State,

Peter Lilley, announced to the National Federation of Sub-Postmasters an intention to create a new automated system for payment. However, one of the problems not identified was that the involvement of two Departments of State (Post Office Counters Ltd was a public corporation and controlled by the Department of Trade and Industry (DTI)) who each had different objectives, i.e. the DSS sought to reduce their costs, solve the fraud problems and get their audit achieved without qualification, whilst the DTI sought to protect the post offices against the reduction in footfall and to retain the turnover generated by the DSS, would not lead to an easy relationship.

It is against this background that in 1994 an invitation notice to potential bidders was published and subsequently three bidders, including Pathway – at that time a vehicle created by ICL, De La Rue and Girobank, an operation within the Post Office. The tenders were accepted in April 1996 and all three bidders were asked to resubmit their tenders on 16 April with the revised acceptance date of 22 April, which no doubt allowed the bidders to adjust their tenders to suit the market. Despite having only 13 days to re-evaluate the bids and despite the unease expressed by the evaluation team who assessed the bids, the status of preferred supplier was awarded to the ICL consortium. The NAO noted without irony that at this stage, "The project had a high probability of failure as soon as the contract was signed". (Note 5) The target date for operational trials was June 1997 with a complete rollout planned by 1999, and in 1996 a limited early version of the hardware and software was rolled out to ten post offices in Stroud, Gloucestershire. This version was limited to the payment of only child benefit and had limited volume flexibility. ICL now realised that the rollout of the full system throughout the UK would have to be moved to 2001 and the DSS, the Post Office and Pathway became increasingly aware of the difficulty they faced. In February 1997 a 'no-fault' re-plan agreed to postpone the delivery dates and for all parties to bear their own costs in doing so. The DSS and the Post Office alleged that Pathway was in breach of contract, but Pathway denied such liability and wrote to the DSS, suggesting that either the existing contract be maintained but with prices increased by 30%, or that the contract be extended by five years and the prices be increased by 5%, or finally that the contract be terminated. The DSS was, according to *Private Eye*, entitled to charge Pathway for damages, but neglected to do so as it might result in the scheme collapsing – which it did anyway. They quote a NAO report which revealed that "the purchasers

(DSS and the Post Office) did not in the end demand damages from Pathway when the project began to slip. They felt this would not encourage Pathway to succeed and could deflect the firm's attention away from delivery to a legal battle". (Note 6)

An interdepartmental working group made up of officials from the Treasury, Cabinet Office, DSS and DTI considered the matter and, in April 1999, reached agreement with ICL plc that the Benefits Payment Card System would be cancelled, that ICL plc would be given a fixed payment contract to roll out by 2001 a basic post office automation infrastructure which would support the national use of barcoding to reduce encashment fraud for benefit order books, that the Post Office would develop a network banking strategy in good time for the withdrawal of paper-based benefit payment methods in 2003, and that the DSS would take no active steps in marketing bank transfers as their normal method of payment until 2003, to allow the Post Office an adequate period to manage the transition.

As a result of this fiasco the DSS wasted some £127 million associated with the creation of a link to the Benefits Payment Card, whilst the Post Office recorded in their accounts an exceptional charge of £571 million "for acquiring assets which has not at this stage yielded sufficient income to justify the cost". (Note 7) ICL claim they lost £180 million, which was written off in their 1998/99 accounts, but a UNISON report said, "Meanwhile, the private contractor avoided losses on the deal by brokering new, advantageously priced contracts with the Post Office worth between £600 million and £1 billion. According to the Public Accounts Committee, these deals were a covert form of bailout for the private sector: the impression remains of an essential political deal to ensure that ICL has a substantial contract with the PO at a price which seems to have been largely determined in advance of contractual negotiations, as a means, however inadequate, of making up some of the £180 million written off by ICL in its 1998/99 accounts". (Note 8)

For the purpose of this exercise a total of £698 million has been added to the summary at the end of this chapter.

SOURCES

PAC Report: *The Cancellation of the Benefits Payment Card Project*, HC 358, December 2000

PAC Report: *Improving the Delivery of Government IT Projects*, HC 65, 5 January 2000

NAO Report: *The Cancellation of the Benefits Payment Card Project*, HC 857, 18 August 2000

Pollock, Allsyon and Price, David: *Public Risk for Private Gain? The Cancellation of the Benefits Payment Card Project*, UNISON

Private Eye: Edition 1010, 8 September 2000

NOTES

1 NAO Report, p65

2 ibid

3 ibid

4 ibid

5 NAO Report, p49

6 *Private Eye*, p27

7 NAO Report, p36

8 UNISON, Case Study 5

01 02 07

Ministry of Defence: Resource Accounts

This was the second year in which the Ministry of Defence (MoD) prepared Resource Accounts. The move from appropriation to resource accounting has already been mentioned in Section 01 02 00. The accounts were again qualified by the NAO who, however, recognised not just the difficulties faced by the department, but also the sheer magnitude of the task. It was acknowledged that before the introduction of the resource accounting initiative, the department had little information on the value or extent of its asset base, and it struggled to compile acceptable accounts. It was also acknowledged that the department had made significant efforts to improve the standard of its financial accounting and that these efforts had led to progress and improvements to the quality of its accounting records. However, it also mentioned that the department had many old information systems, which were no longer suited to the production of accurate and timely accrual-based information and, accordingly, the NAO were still not able to confirm the value for fixed assets and for consumption and depreciation charges.

The matter of married quarters and their acquisition by Annington Homes was outlined in Section 01 02 04 of this chapter. There were still problems about the sale of property and the NAO reported that "some of these problems continue to have an impact on the 2000/01 accounts. For example, the Defence Estates Agency disposed of 203 sites during 1999/2000 but in three cases the sites remained in the accounts of the top-level budget holder concerned. The total value of these properties at an existing use value, namely £44 million, has been written off in 2000/01, overstating the department's net expenditure for the year". (Note 1)

The report noted that the Defence Logistics Organisation had been able to improve the accuracy of the opening balances for this year and the army noted that, whilst the prices of certain capital spares had been validated and revised downwards, the accounting systems could not be updated with these values in time for the accounts, so estimated that the net book value of capital spares was overstated in the balance sheet by £58 million.

The MoD's price validation work confirmed that many of the items held on the Supply Systems were in excess of requirements or obsolete, because the equipment they supported was no longer in use and, accordingly, a consistent policy for the army, navy and air force was agreed about how the value of consumable stock should be written down. "The Department had not been able to calculate the write down of stock accurately as not all the information required is at present held in a readily accessible form, and it has yet to resolve the feasibility of gathering this data." (Note 2) However, the Defence Logistics Organisation estimated that the stock balance could be overstated by as much as £145 million. This report notes that "deficiencies in its records could have resulted in the Balance Sheet of 31 March 2001 being over or understated by as much as £150 million". (Note 3)

The move from appropriation accounting to resource accounting required the department to provide financial, as well as stock data, and this led to problems with all three services. The supply system used by the Royal Air Force was unable to differentiate whether an item received from the contractor was a new or a repaired item, suggesting that a number of repaired items had been double accounted on the balance sheet, so a misclassification of £639 million during the depreciation of fixed assets and the surplus/deficit on assets and disposals had arisen. The army could not explain why there was a £77 million deficiency between the Supplied Systems data and its accounting systems and had to write-off the amount. The navy also experienced difficulties with its stock control system and discovered that the movements of stock in the accounting records had been erroneously rejected, forcing the department to make manual adjustments of some £500 million at 31 March 2001.

The NAO also identified that some of the systems used did not account for depreciation in line with specified requirements and noted that, whilst the department operated a single fixed-asset register to account for the majority of the army's equipment and vehicles when an asset life was changed, the register calculated what the depreciation charge should have been over the whole life of the asset and compared this to the depreciation charges already made. This methodology had resulted in depreciation of some £180 million being understated in the Operating Cost Statement during the year.

It has already been noted that the opening balances for tangible and intangible assets for the department were regarded with caution by the NAO and this report confirms that the department could not support, with an appropriate accounting trail, some £89 million.

The NAO report offers just four examples of losses for the cancellation of procurement or development projects because of changing needs. This report noted the cancellation of the ALR Radar Warning equipment, which the RAF "concluded that the project would never work at a satisfactory level", (Note 4) so the project was cancelled at a cost of £12 million. The department also wrote-off £30.7 million in trying to create an integrated stores and engineering information system, code-named 'Upkeep', of which they accepted that there was no clear indication of how long it would take before the project could be made operationally effective, nor indeed an indication of the possible cost. The department also reported a loss of £205 million arising from a decision not to procure variants they wanted of the Long Range Tricat – an anti-tank guided weapon system which had been superseded by the purchase of Apache helicopters, which came complete with weapon systems. The fourth example, cancellation of the Medium Range Tricat has been dealt with elsewhere.

"The Department has provided for £3.755 billion for stock write down in its balance sheet", (Note 5) so that amount, the Annington Homes amount of £44 million, plus £248 million for cancelled projects has been added to the summary at the end of the chapter.

SOURCES

NAO Report of the Comptroller and General Ministry of Defence: Departmental Resource Accounts 2000/2001, 18 December 2001

Likiermanm, Andrew: *Resource Accounting and Budgeting: Rationale and Background*, 1995

NOTES

1 NAO Report, p17

2 ibid, p8

3 ibid, p14

4 ibid, p19

5 ibid, p7

01 02 08

Sale of Part of the UK Gold Reserves

The Bank of England's handbook on Foreign Exchange Reserves Management (Note 1) details the traditional reasons for holding gold. The war-chest argument – gold is seen as the ultimate asset to hold in an emergency and in the past has often appreciated in value in times of financial instability. Gold has traditionally kept its value against inflation and has always been accepted as a medium of exchange between countries. Gold is 'nobody's liability' and so can't be frozen, repudiated or defaulted upon. Gold's historical role in the international monetary system is the ultimate backing for domestic paper.

Gold has never had a value of less than zero and, since the times of King Tutankhamen, people have understood the value and scarcity of gold and used it as a symbol of wealth and power. Between 1816 and 1931 the pound was linked to the value of gold and, after World War II, the Bretton Woods Agreement established a standard that pegged the dollar to gold at a rate of

$35 per ounce – a standard which was ended by President Nixon in 1971. It is estimated that the world gold reserves totalled 160,000 tonnes and is growing at a rate of approximately 2,500 tonnes per annum.

The UK Government sold 395 tonnes of gold using 17 auctions between July 1999 and March 2002 at an average price of US$275 per ounce. Both the NAO and PAC issued reports in 2001, but their remit was restricted to analysing whether the process of using the auction option was the correct procedure and both reports reach conclusions within the parameters established. Readers might think a more meaningful investigation would identify why the UK Government chose to sell just under 50% of its gold reserves.

The subsequent Treasury report (Note 2) was self-congratulatory and did not address whether the sale of these assets represented value to the taxpayer. The rationale for selling gold (Note 3) were threefold: the government felt that holding 50% of taxpayer reserves in gold was risky and it made sense to reduce that risk; the investment return for gold was half of 1% whilst other assets may return 6%; and gold was bulky and difficult to store. Government papers made available under the Freedom of Information Act indicate that the Chancellor's, then Gordon Brown, approval was solicited in spring of 1998 and discussed with the Governor of the Bank of England in early January 1999. Both the Chancellor and the Governor agreed with the recommendations.

Choosing July 6, 1999 as the date of the first auction was not the government's finest choice. They chose to value gold based on a 20-year period, during which it had soared from $130 an ounce in 1976 to $500 at the end of 1979 as a result of climbing oil prices and rising inflation, and then had rocketed to $850 an ounce in the first three weeks of 1980. The rise in the price of gold can be swift, but so can the downturn, and any analysis needs to consider a term much in excess of 20 years. The government's position was not helped by the prior announcement on 7 April 1999 that it would be disposing of its gold reserves, triggering a collapse of 10% in gold prices. (Note 4) Prices continued to slide just before the second auction option on 21 September 1999, but started to recover when the European Central Bank (ECF) and 14 Central Banks made a joint statement about a limitation on sales for a period of five years from September 1999. Gold immediately rose to an average of $325 an ounce, and when the PAC investigated why the September option had not been postponed to a date after the ECF meeting it was told, "It would not have been right for the UK to be opportunistic and rely on insider information." (Note 5)

The Treasury raised £2.1 billion and spread their risk by purchasing Euros, US Dollars and Japanese Yen. However, in doing so, they forfeited the opportunity of selling the gold at the height of the market when gold was valued at over $1,900 per ounce. At the time of writing (Note 7) the value of gold has decreased to $1,205 per troy ounce, so a sale at today's rate would net the Treasury £9.46 billion, indicating that by their actions the Treasury realised £7.36 billion less than they could have achieved. A total of £7.36 billion has therefore been added to the summary at the end of this chapter.

SOURCES

PAC Report: *The Sale of Part of the UK Gold Reserves*, HC396, 19 December 2001

NAO Report: *The Sale of Part of the UK Gold Reserves*, HC98, 9 January 2001

HM Treasury Review of the Sale of Part of the UK Gold Reserves, October 2002

Hope, Christopher: *The Daily Telegraph: Gordon Brown's decision to sell half of the UK's gold reserves cost UK £5 billion*, 7 January 2009

Henry, Robin: *The Sunday Times: Gold Losing its Lustre*, 25 September 2011

NOTES

1 Rugee, J: *Handbooks in Central Banking Foreign Exchange Reserves Management*, p15-19

2 *Review of the Sale of Part of the UK Gold Reserves.*

3 HM Treasury, note 20

4 PAC Report, p3

5 ibid, p3

6 Gold prices are quoted in dollars on the world market and differentials quoted between the sale benefit in 2000 and the sale in 2014 can be also be attributed to differentials in dollar/sterling rates in that period.

7 4 December, 2014

01 02 09

This Various section deals with four projects ranging from a housing association to a prison.

Housing Corporation: Overseeing Focus Housing Association

Between 1991 and 1995 Keith Hinson and John Hartshorn accepted at least £21,750 from Darshan Ram to facilitate the sale of houses to the Focus Housing Association (Focus) for £1.1 million more than market value.

Focus was based in Birmingham and received during the period grants of £104 million from the Housing Corporation, which was used for property investment, e.g. new-build schemes, conversions or rehabilitations. Hartshorn was the Deputy Director for Focus with responsibility for rehabilitation, and Hinson was a development manager in the same department and, as such, both were involved in the purchase of 142 properties between 1991 and 1995 for which the association, according to the District Valuer, paid £741,200 more than necessary. A subsidiary association, Focus Two, similarly overpaid £344,850 for 81 further properties. Ninety-six of the properties were certified by an architect employed by Focus as 'satisfactory dwellings' but were in such poor condition that an average of £5,000 needed to be spent on each (£467,000 in total) before they could be let.

Concerns about Hartshorn, Hinson and Ram were raised on at least six occasions, but investigations were either not completed or, if investigated, were regarded as inconclusive, until the relatively new Chief Executive received anonymous allegations of serious fraud and passed the matter on to West Midlands police in December 1995. The three were brought to trial on 17 April 2000 and pleaded guilty to charges of corruption and sentenced to 12, nine, and 18 months imprisonment respectively and also ordered to pay costs of £10,000, £3,000 and £7,500 respectively.

The PAC report noted the lack of co-operation between the Housing Corporation and the NAO, who had requested information about similar property transactions but were advised that this information was not available "on the grounds of taxpayer confidentiality", (Note 1) which delayed the NAO report by six months.

The management organisation chart for Focus showed that Hartshorn and his deputy answered to a development director who answered to an operations director who answered to a chief Executive who answered to a committee of management. (Note 2) It would seem that the conclusion of HACAS, who reported on the matter in April 1996, that there was "a general disregard for policies, procedures, controls and the ways of working that they imply", (Note 3) was indeed an accurate description of an organisation without strong, if any, management control. A total of £1.567million has been added to the summary at the end of this section.

SOURCES

PAC Report: *The Housing Corporation: Overseeing Focus Housing Association*, HC 365, 2 May 2001

NAO Report: *The Housing Corporation: Overseeing Focus Housing Association*, HC 741, 24 July 2000

Serious Fraud Office Press Release: *Three jailed in housing association fraud*, 17 April 2000

NOTES

1 PAC Report, p2/4

2 NAO Report, p7

3 ibid, p15

The Refinancing of the Fazackerley PFI Prison Contract

Fazackerley Prison Services Ltd (FPSL) made £9.7 million from the refinancing of their joint contract with the Prison Service and managed to increase the rate of return to shareholders from 16% to 39%. The Prison Service received £1 million for consenting to the refinancing and waived £500,000 of charge payments withheld from FPSL for performance shortfalls. This PFI contract was one of the first of its sort. "When this contract was in 1995, the Prison Service estimated that they would only deliver marginal savings of £1 million compared with conventional procurement", (Note 1) but what it did offer to the Treasury was the Holy Grail of capital expenditure off the government balance sheet. FPSL "initially sought only a 12.8% shareholder return from the Fazackerley prison project which was considerably less than the return it would expect on hospital projects". (Note 2)

They quickly identified that an additional return could be generated by refinancing. The Prison Service did not have any contractual rights to share the benefits of refinancing, but their consent was required and their "position strengthened when FPSL's lenders decided it would be prudent to seek consent". (Note 3) They had never before "been faced with refinancing", (Note 4) so asked Rothschilds for advice. "The Service made this arrangement because the refinancing had been proposed by FPSL and it was FPSL who would receive most of the resulting benefits." (Note 5)

FPSL offered the service £100,000 for their consent, then £300,000, and agreed to £1 million when it came under pressure from lenders. Part of the negotiation required the service "to waive £500,000 which they had retained because of FPLS's underperformance in delivering the required service". (Note 6) The PAC noted that "Carillion agreed with us that as the prison opened in December 1997 this meant that the FSPL's shareholders had achieved the payback of their investment in two years". (Note 7) It also noted that "splitting benefits 50:50 between the public and private sectors was a more reasonable outcome, in terms of taxpayers' interests, then the Prison Service had achieved in respect of the Fazackerley prison refinancing". (Note 8) A total of £5.3 million, representing the waiver of the £500,000 and the value lost by not negotiating a 50% share of the net gain, has been added to the summary at the end of this section.

SOURCES

PAC Report: *The Refinancing of the Fazackerley PFI Prison Contract*, HC372, 4 July 2001

NAO Report: *The Prison Service – The Refinancing of the Fazackerley PFI Prison Contract*, HC584, 29 June 2000

Pollock, Allyson and Price, David: *Public Risk for Private Gain? Case Study 6: Refinancing of Fazackerley Prison*, UNISON

Fazackerley Prison Services Ltd: *Annual Report and Financial Statements for the Year Ended 31 March 2005*

NOTES

1   PAC Report, p4/8

2   ibid, p4/7

3   NAO Report, p3

4   ibid, p44

5   ibid

6   PAC Report, p3/7

7   ibid, p3/7

8   ibid, p5/7

NHS (England) Summarised Accounts 1999/2000

Fifty-nine health authorities, an increase of 11 over the previous year, and 150 of the 377 trusts, an increase of 52 over the previous year, had declared a deficit in this financial year. At the end of March 2001, NHS organisations were investigating 484 cases of suspected fraud with an estimated value of some £18 million, and work was ongoing to measure accurately the level of fraud and 'incorrectness' across all areas in the NHS. No further details were offered about fraud or inefficiency, so £18 million has been added to the summary at the end of this section.

SOURCE

NAO Report: *NHS (England) Summarised Accounts 1999/2000*, 12 July 2001

The Renegotiation of the PFI-type Deal for the Royal Armouries Museum in Leeds

This was one of the first PFI deals signed for this type of project. Just one bidder competed after the Madame Tussaud organisation decided not to tender. This project had the misfortune to suffer the same fate, i.e. over-optimism about visitor numbers, as the Millennium Dome and the Channel Tunnel.

The Royal Armouries wanted additional display space and decided on a site close to the Leeds/Liverpool Canal. Approximately 65% of the funding for this £42.6 million development was provided by the Royal Armouries, Leeds Development Corporation and Leeds City Council, with the remainder provided by Royal Armouries (International) plc (RAI), a specially created company. Completed in March 1996 it became apparent by 1998, when revenues were £1.4 million against a target of £3.4 million, that the operation was financially challenged and that change was necessary. The Royal Armouries sought detailed financial information from RAI without success, and by October 1998 RAI expressed to the Armouries "its willingness to work on joint proposals with a view to ensuring the museum's long-term viability". (Note 1) By this time the RAI debt had mushroomed to £10 million. RAI suggested downsizing its operation and retaining the profitable corporate entertainment and car parking activities, as well as catering. As well as retaining ownership of the collection and providing curatorship, the Royal Armouries assumed the other loss-making parts of the operation.

The Department for Culture, Media and Sport assumed the annual cost of £900,000 for servicing the RAI debt, and also agreed to increase the grant-in-aid to £1 million per year from 1999 until 2015. The PAC noted that "while RAI have retained responsibility for the debts of £21 million they ran up when building and operating the museum, they have also the profitable elements of the museum's business, such as corporate hospitality and car parking, worth in total over £10 million". (Note 2) A total of £32.3 million, representing the grant-in-aid and the debt servicing costs, has been added to the summary at the end of this section.

SOURCES

PAC Report: *The Renegotiation of the PFI-type Deal for the Royal Armouries Museum in Leeds*, HC359, 19 December 2001

NAO Report: *The Renegotiation of the PFI-type Deal for the Royal Armouries Museum in Leeds*, HC103, 15 January 2001

Royal Armouries (International) plc: *Report and Financial Statements 31 December 2012*

NOTES

1 NAO Report, p20

2 PAC Report, p2/3 para 56

The total added to the summary at the end of this chapter is £57.2 million.

SUMMARY: CHAPTER TWO – 2001

01 02 00	Ministry of Defence: Resource Accounts	£0.572 bn
01 02 01	DVLA: Appropriation Accounts	£0.098 bn
01 02 02	Inland Revenue: National Insurance Fund Account	£0.284 bn
01 02 03	Child Support Agency: Client Funds Account	£0.705 bn
01 02 04	Ministry of Defence: Managing Reductions in the Number of Vacant Family Quarters	£0.141 bn
01 02 05	Ministry of Defence: Major Projects Report	£0.569 bn
01 02 06	The Cancellation of the Payment Card Project	£0.698 bn
01 02 07	Ministry of Defence: Resource Accounts	£4.047 bn
01 02 08	Sale of Part of the UK Gold Reserves	£7.360 bn
01 02 09	Various	£0.057 bn
	Total	£14.531 bn
	Total adjusted for inflation to December 2014	£18.992 bn

INDEX: CHAPTER THREE – 2002

02 03 00   Tobacco Smuggling

02 03 01   The Millenium Dome

02 03 02   DVLA: Appropriation Accounts

02 03 03   Ministry of Defence: The Risk of Fraud in Property Management

02 03 04   The Channel Tunnel Rail Link

02 03 05   Ministry of Defence: Redevelopment of MoD Main Building

02 03 06   Construction of Portcullis House

02 03 07   NHS (England) Summarised Accounts

02 03 08   CRAMS

02 03 09   The BBC

02 03 10   NHS: Handling Clinical Negligence Claims in England

02 03 11   NHS Direct in England

02 03 12   Ministry of Defence: Major Projects Report 2001

02 03 13   The Misuse and Smuggling of Hydrocarbon Oils

02 03 14   Collection of Fines and Other Financial Penalties in the Criminal Justice System

02 03 15   Ministry of Defence: Resource Accounts: Departmental Resource Accounts 2001/02

02 03 16   Ministry of Defence: Major Projects Report 2002

02 03 17   Various

"The art of taxation consists in so plucking the goose as to obtain the largest possible amount of feathers with the smallest possible amount of hissing."

Jean Baptiste Colbert (1619-1683), Minister of Finances for Louis XIV of France

"The way to crush the bourgeoisie is to grind them between the millstones of taxation and inflation."

Vladimir Lenin, Russian Revolutionary (1870-1924)

02 03 00

Tobacco Smuggling

"The majority of cigarettes smuggled into the country have been manufactured here." (Note 1) With this surprising comment the Public Accounts Committee (PAC) addressed not just the problem of lost revenue for the Exchequer but also the more fundamental problem about who runs the UK: big business or our representatives in Westminster? Examination of the issue of lost revenue through tobacco smuggling might provide some clues.

The EU single market began in 1993, and routine frontier controls between EU states were removed in order to facilitate the free movement of trade. Restrictions on the amount of excise goods that could be imported by individuals from other EU states were also removed, and since that time a large market in smuggled cigarettes has developed in the United Kingdom. By 1999/2000, Customs estimated that 21% of all cigarettes smoked in the UK had been smuggled and that the cost to the UK taxpayer was £3.5 billion. Of this total £2.4 billion related to cigarettes; £0.7 billion related to hand rolled tobacco (HRT); and £0.4 billion to other tobacco products. Customs also estimated that up to 80% of smuggled cigarettes were being transported into the country principally in deep-sea ship containers on 'roll on roll off' ferries. Most of the remainder was smuggled in light vehicles through the Channel ports and the Channel Tunnel: the so-called 'white van' trade.

Some four million containers pass through UK ports each year and, as just 2,400 freight containers of cigarettes could supply the entire illicit market in the UK, the task of identifying appropriate containers was not without its challenges. Customs accepted this challenge, authorising X-ray scanners at 43 approved points of entry, excluding airports and railheads. The first was introduced in November 2000, and by January 2002 Customs had 12 in place. Whilst the NAO report into the matter noted "at one freight container port the number seized during the last quarter of 2000/01, the period when the scanner was deployed, fell to 20 million cigarettes from 100 million cigarettes only six months earlier. At first this may indicate that scanners may have acted as a deterrent, and that smugglers are having to use more complex, costly methods of smuggling (or have discontinued altogether) or they have revised their routes and smuggling modes into the UK". (Note 2) A more common sense conclusion might be that smugglers decided to use ports without scanners. Customs had a range of sanctions to tackle the problem and, whilst prosecution was an option, it was one which was not favoured during 2000/01, so prosecutions decreased by 19% from the previous year. The alternative policy which was adopted was one of seizure of private vehicles, such as transit vans, used to smuggle, and 10,219 vehicles were seized. Similarly, Heavy Goods Vehicles were seized, although the NAO report does not record a total figure. Asset seizures were also a sanction used, but in 2000/01 Customs only achieved about 60% of their £15 million target. The requirement introduced in June 2001 that all UK-bought cigarettes and HRT should be marked 'UK DUTY PAID' forced the sale of smuggled products away from legitimate outlets and also offered enforcement agencies, such as Trading Standards, highly visible indications of which products were tax paid.

Customs' attempts to stem smuggling were not helped by the realisation that as much as 65% of just two brands of cigarettes exported by Imperial Tobacco were smuggled back into the UK. Customs hoped that UK tobacco manufacturers would pursue export policies that did not encourage the reimport of previously exported cigarettes. However, Imperial Tobacco's profits from the UK market were decreasing, as usage in the domestic marketplace decreased, and they sought to compensate for this by exporting to various international markets and thereby increase their international profits. Amongst the many overseas markets approached by Imperial Tobacco were Afghanistan, Latvia, Kaliningrad, Moldova and Andorra. The two brands chosen by the company for export to these markets were Regal and Superkings, and 65% of all production was exported to these five markets. The PAC report dryly noted that "these locations did not seem to be among the most promising of UK export markets". (Note 3) PAC member Richard Bacon, the MP for South Norfolk, asked the unfortunate Imperial Tobacco employee representing the company why Imperial Tobacco had exported 1.7 billion cigarettes to Latvia, "enough for every man, woman and child to consume 722 cigarettes a year". (Note 4) The unfortunate representative also had to face questioning from George Osborne, Chancellor of the Exchequer from 2010, who asked, "One comes to the conclusion that you are either crooks or you are stupid and you do not look very stupid. How can you possibly have sold cigarettes to Latvia, Kaliningrad, Afghanistan and Moldova, in the expectation that those were just going to be used by the indigenous population or exported legitimately to neighbouring countries and not in the expectation that they would be smuggled? You must know – you only have to read a newspaper every day, a member of the public could tell you, these are places which are linked to organised crime, that the drug trade passes through all of these countries, that prostitution passes through all of these countries. Did you not know that?" (Note 5)

Customs had introduced a system of red and yellow cards to identify to companies the concerns they had about the reimport of previously exported tobacco. Red cards were issued in cases of more serious concern and Customs would expect a tobacco manufacturer to take action against any of its customers who re-exported to the UK, whilst yellow-carded customers would expect to be the subject of enquiries. "Customs had not found it necessary to issue any cards to British American Tobacco, only two to Gallaher, but 17 to Imperial." (Note 6) Imperial's attitude to tobacco smuggling was defined when, in May 2002, they bought the German tobacco company, Reemtsma, who manufactured the West brand of cigarette, which according to the World Customs Organisation was the most frequently smuggled cigarette brand in Europe. Incredibly, the Imperial Tobacco witness before the PAC said he was "unaware of the situation, or of the criminal prosecution being brought against Reemtsma by the German Customs authority". (Note 7) Profits at Imperial Tobacco continued to improve and, as planned, international profits increased more rapidly than domestic profits, and by 2001 international sales contributed 48% of total profits. To add insult to injury, Imperial Tobacco took seven years to settle a dispute with UK Revenue about Corporation Tax and in 2013 decided to close their UK manufacturing base in Nottingham and move it overseas.

The PAC report examined suggests that the total tax revenue lost through tobacco smuggling for this year was £3.5 billion. However, examination of various reports for the five-year period under consideration indicates that in 1999/2000 a total of £3.45 billion worth of tobacco products were smuggled; in 2000/2001 the figure was £3.7 billion; for 2001/2002 it was £3.5 billion; for 2002/2003 it was £3.18 billion; and for 2003/4 it was £2.7 billion. The total which has been added to the summary at the end of this chapter is £16.53 billion.

SOURCES

PAC Report: *Tobacco Smuggling*, HC143, 10 January 2002

NAO Report: *Appropriation Accounts 1998/99, Volume 16: Class XVI Departments of the Chancellor of the Exchequer*, HC11, 18 February 2000

NAO Report: *Appropriation Accounts 1999/2000, Volume 16: Class XVI Departments of the Chancellor of the Exchequer*, HM Customs and Excise HC25-XVI, 19 February 2001

NAO Audit of HM Customs and Excise under Section 2 of the Exchequer and Audit Departments Act 1921, 31 January 2002

NAO Report: *HM Customs and Excise Appropriation Accounts 2000/01*, 13 February 2002

NAO Report: *HM Customs and Excise: Standard Report 2002/03*, 18 December 2003

NAO Report: *Comptroller and Auditor General's Standard Report on the Accounts of HM Customs and Excise 2004/05*, 7 October 2005

Joossens, Luk: *Smuggling, The Tobacco Industry and Plain Packs*, undated

Tobacco Tactics: Imperial and Gallaher Involvement in Tobacco Smuggling, undated

NOTES

1 PAC Report, p8

2 NAO Report 2004/05, R24

3 PAC Report, p10

4 Tobacco Tactics, p3/4.

5 Joossens, p2/3

6 PAC Report, p12

7 ibid, p12

02 03 01

The Millennium Dome

Alton Towers is the largest visitor attraction in the UK and averages some three million paying visitors per year. The prospectus circulated to potential private sector operators interested in working with government to develop a visitor attraction to acknowledge the beginning of the new millennium suggested, "As a minimum it is envisaged that the exhibition will attract 15 million people" and also stated that "a figure in excess of 30 million is unlikely to be achievable". (Note 1) The Accounting Officer (Note 2) sought a direction (Note 3) when instructed to arrange the funds to allow English Partnerships, the government's urban regeneration agency, to purchase land on the peninsula at Greenwich. There has been a history of over-optimism by government when assessing usage figures for major projects and the Millennium Dome was no exception.

In 1993, John Major's government created the Millennium Commission with a brief to help communities acknowledge the end of the second millennium and the start of the third. The funds would originate with the National Lottery and within 12 months the concept of a national exhibition, loosely based on the Great Exhibition of 1851 and the Festival of Britain in 1951, was mooted to the Commission. One of the keenest supporters of the concept was the then deputy Prime Minister, Michael Heseltine, who quickly identified not only the morale-boosting benefits of such an exhibition, but also identified the possibilities of cleaning a toxic area, encouraging subsequent development. In 1996, Greenwich, with the obvious advantage of its association with Mean Time, was chosen as the appropriate site, and in 1997 the site was purchased by English Partnerships. Government decided that the project should be delivered in the public sector by a limited company whose sole shareholder would be a government minister, and thereby created the New Millennium Experience Company Ltd (NMEC). Jennifer Page CBE was appointed as chief executive in February 1997 and brought with her the experience of being Accounting Officer at the Millennium Commission. She believed that she and her employers had the tacit support of politicians, but in a lecture to the Royal Society of Arts she suggested that "there was a belief that an incoming Labour Government would reshape or reject this exhibition: this meant hold-ups". (Note 4) The Commission saw some challenges ahead, one of which was the parallel problems of actually building the structure, whilst at the same time creating an organisation which would deliver the concept of the exhibition. Advice was sourced from BDO Stoy Hayward Public Sector Consulting Services, who suggested in June that a technical director who had experience in running a large complex visitor attraction should be recruited as early as 1999. This advice was ignored.

Naturally, the company needed to establish budgets and quickly realised that the revenue from paying visitors and from sponsorship would not allow them to balance the budget, and therefore applied for a grant of £449 million to the Millennium Commission. This budget assumed that £50 million would be repaid to the Commission at some future stage. However, the budget also assumed that 12 million paying customers would visit the site, so the Commission employed Deloitte and Touche Consulting Group to review the visitor numbers. They downgraded the possible visitor numbers to 8 million as a worst-case scenario and suggested that the NMEC estimate of 12 million visitors would be at the high end of achievement. The PAC report into the matter noted that "it meant that the Dome would have to attract in just one year, and from a standing start, more than four times as many visitors as the next most popular UK 'pay to visit' attraction (Alton Towers) achieved in 1999. In approving the target of 12 million visitors the commissioners went against the advice of their own staff, who recommended planning on the basis of 8 million". (Note 5)

The General Election in May 1997 saw New Labour assume power with a large majority. One of the urgent pending files was the decision about whether the exhibition would go ahead, and because of tight schedules a decision was made within six weeks of the new government gaining office. Andrew Rawnsley's book, *Servants of the People*, outlines an interesting account of the decision-making process, which resulted in Prime Minister Tony Blair announcing on 19 June 1997 in Greenwich that the project would go ahead with the words, "These plans require a leap of faith". (Note 6) Within 15 months NMEC realised that their budgeting had been less than satisfactory and suggested to the Millennium Commission that its grant requirement had risen by £42 million. Their request was kicked into the long grass, so by June 1999 the company sought permission to meet day-to-day operational expenses from their contingency fund and permission was granted in the autumn of that year. However, by November the company had spent all but £7 million of its grant and all but £5.7 million of its contingency fund, and the identification that they had only sold £3.9 million worth of tickets against expectations of £18.9 million, and raised only £82.7 million in sponsorship (Note 7) against expectations of £125.5 million, indicated that significant cash flow issues would shortly arise. The chief executive met with the Commission's Accounting Officer, Mike O'Connor in early December and, accordingly, a detailed study was requested to report in late 2000 when NMEC would have hard evidence of operational experience.

The Dome managed to increase its problems by organising a New Year launch celebration for 10,500 of the great and mighty of the London

Establishment. The evening started badly, as severe delays were experienced by those instructed to arrive by Tube – in some cases the delays were up to two hours. The guests included senior personnel from the world of press and television, and whether one regards subsequent reportage as fair or not is immaterial. The verdict about the evening, and by implication about the Dome, was highly critical, and comments from Mayoral candidate Trevor Phillips were not unique. Speaking to the *Sunday Telegraph* editor, Dominic Lawson, he raged, "The New Millennium Experience Company has been given £1 billion for this! After £1 billion there can be no excuses for this! That should be your front-page headline this Sunday! After a billion pounds, no excuses". (Note 8)

In late January 2000, the Commission accepted the inevitable and approved a further grant of £60 million, which was paid in February. Chief Executive Jennifer Page was sacked and replaced by Frenchman Pierre-Yves Gerbeau, whose previous experience included Disney World in Paris, who assumed operational but not financial control. A further additional grant of £29 million was paid in May 2000 and the situation became so fraught that the Board of NMEC sought indemnification should the company fail, and were given such indemnification save where a person acted dishonestly, in bad faith or recklessly. Another grant of £43 million was made in August 2000 and David James CBE, whose reputation as an expert in company rescue was well recognised, was recruited as executive vice chairman. PriceWaterhouseCooper (PWC) was employed to prepare a report and to assess whether there would be any benefit from early closure. David James wrote to the Millennium Commission confirming that the company was insolvent and that in his opinion it had been since February 2000. He confirmed that early closure would not deliver appropriate savings and requested further funding, which was allocated in September in the sum of £47 million. NMEC struggled through to the end of December 2000 having absorbed £628 million worth of National Lottery/Millennium Commission funding.

The failure of NMEC can be attributed to the creation of a budget that suggested that 12 million paying customers would visit the Dome, and the failure of the commissioners to accept the advice of their staff and consultants. The actual throughput was a creditable 5.5 million paying customers which was no mean feat. The sponsorship target of £175 million was not reached and a shortfall of £92.3 million was recorded. The company/Millennium Commission also ignored the advice of their consultants about employing someone with operational experience of such a visitor attraction until the situation was irrecoverable. The fiasco of the New Year's launch party ensured that the Dome received negative press coverage for almost the first half of 2000. The structure created to operate this project was complex both politically and operationally. At one stage there were three accounting officers involved from the company. Similarly, there were 15 commissioners involved and, unusually for the NAO, their report stated that "all of the Commissioners, during their time in office, were responsible for the decisions made by the Commission during the course of the project". (Note 9) Jennifer Page, in a lecture to the Royal Society of Arts, said that "the scale and novelty of the Dome meant that no one person could be asked to take on the final responsibility". (Note 9) This lack of clear management structure cost the taxpayer £628 million, which will be added to the summary at the end of this chapter.

In April 2002 the NAO reported on the winding up of NMEC Ltd and suggested that £25 million of the Lottery grant might not be required, although this was not guaranteed. An adjustment has not been made in respect of this sum.

SOURCES

PAC Report: *The Millennium Dome*, HC 516, 1 February 2002

NAO Report: *The Millennium Dome*, HC 936, 9 November 2000

NAO Report: *Winding-up the New Millennium Experience Company Limited*, HC749, 17 April 2002

Annual Report and Financial Statements: The New Millennium Experience Company Ltd, 4 July 2001

Rawnsley, Andrew: *Servants of the People*, Hamish Hamilton Ltd, London, 2000

Page, Jennifer CBE: *My Crown of Thorns – The Guardian*, p8, 4 May 2000

NOTES

1 PAC Report, p3
2 Accounting Officer – the equivalent of a financial controller/director in the private sector.

3 An accounting officer is required to seek a written direction if instructed by the minister to pursue a course of action that he would not feel able to defend to the Committee of Public Accounts as representing value for money.

4 Page, p8

5 PAC Report, p4/10, para 26

6 Rawnsley, p56

7 A further £34.5 million sponsorship was received 'in kind'.

8 Rawnsley, p325

9 Page, p8

02 03 02

DVLA: Appropriation Accounts

"I am pleased that the DVLA has been able to implement the substantial changes to the vehicle excise duty regime with minimum disruption to the motoring public. I commend the agency's staff for their efforts in processing well over one million applications for rebates of duty from hauliers and private motorists in just a few months, without jeopardising the achievement of the agency's other key strategic targets." (Note 1) Praise indeed from Sir John Bourn, Comptroller and Auditor General of the NAO.

The DVLA had in the previous year introduced a new computer system within budget, primarily because it identified user requirements before concluding a fixed-price contract – hence such praise. The agency had also satisfactorily implemented the Graduated Vehicle Excise Duty reform announced by the Chancellor in the 1999 and 2000 budgets and handled the complex reform of the Heavy Goods Vehicle (HGV) excise duty scheme, which resulted in the processing of refunds of duty for some 240,000 HGVs.

Now that the DVLA had access to up-to-date information they were able to tackle the problem of excise duty evasion through a variety of enforcement activities. They continued with their wheel-clamping initiative, giving owners the option of either producing a valid disc or having their cars crushed. Since the scheme started in 1997, some 36,000 cars had been disposed of. In July 2001, having obtained Home Office approval, an Automatic Number Plate Reader (ANPR) system was introduced, collecting images from moving vehicles from roadside video cameras. The initial capacity for this scheme was 11 vehicles for the UK and Northern Ireland and at the time of writing, whilst the pilot scheme was successful, the actual results have not been detailed. The introduction of the Statutory Off Road Notification (SORN) regulation closed a loophole which allowed evaders to skip licensing their vehicles for a month or more, while still using it.

The DVLA even made progress with the thorny challenges of excise duty evasion, which was estimated at £150 million (a decrease of £33 million on the previous year) whilst the recovery figure was £95 million (an increase of £9 million on the previous year). The net result was that the amount of fraud was £55 million, compared to £97 million in the previous year. Northern Ireland had high evasion levels and the estimated fraud here was £11.2 million.

Excise duty evasion totalling £65.2 million has therefore been added to the summary at the end of this chapter.

SOURCE

NAO Report: *Driver and Vehicle Licensing Agency Appropriation Accounts 2000/01*, 20 February 2002

NOTE

1   NAO Report, PR Release, p1

02 03 03

Ministry of Defence: The Risk of Fraud in Property Management

Giving evidence to the PAC about overcharging by contractors and assuring them that the practice was no longer widespread, Kevin Tebbit CMG, then Under Secretary at the Ministry of Defence (MoD) said, "One change is that we used to have a rather strange method of setting a limit, of saying 'we want to bid within this limit', which seemed to me to be a rather strange way of doing it because everyone would bid up to the limit". (Note 1)

Add to the 'limit' philosophy, the fact that establishment works consultants (Note 2) only provided estimates in 35% of high-value transactions, and that in 88% of all cases where they did provide estimates there was no evidence that they had based the estimates on site inspections. In addition, 40% of the estimates provided for high-value transactions were over 50% different from the price actually paid. It is not surprising that the PAC report into the possibilities of fraud in property management within the MoD concluded that, whilst the department recognised that inspection of property was key to the prevention and detection of fraud, yet fewer inspections had been carried out; that there was evidence of poor standards of control over cost estimating; that the department had taken steps to ensure that the risk of fraud occurring in three establishments visited by the NAO was low and ignored the other 200 establishments incurring property management expenditure; and the department had not been successful in monitoring the prices charged. It was not surprising that fraud did occur, and that the only area of disagreement between the NAO and the PAC was one about quantum.

The MoD estate was and is diverse and included more than 45,000 properties on over 2,500 sites. To manage this estate 200 property managers, supported by a number of establishment works consultants, provided technical support and advice, and a further number of works services managers were responsible for engaging and monitoring contractors to carry out the necessary work. The annual budget for such work was £900 million. The department recognised that property management was an area susceptible to fraud but found it difficult to ensure that controls were consistently applied across the sites where expenditure was incurred.

The department did not have an up-to-date fraud risk assessment model when the NAO were considering this matter, so the NAO created their own model which showed that £135 million worth of expenditure on property management was potentially at risk from fraud. Alan Williams, Labour MP for Swansea West, suggested to Mr Tebbit that he was taking a rather sanguine approach to the matter of fraud and emphasised, "You realise that over the five years of this report that means that £675 million worth of property contract money is being at risk of fraud, £675 million". (Note 3)

The MoD gave the impression of being the originators of their own misfortune. They created a fraud committee in 1998 which only met three times in three years, and by 2002 had not agreed formal terms of reference about which the PAC recorded, "It seems to us, I think you will understand, rather naive to suggest that there is not much degree of urgency on the part of either you, nor on the part of your colleagues in your department". (Note 4) The department had not communicated its fraud policy to contractors employed and the PAC found that "the department's stated policy of 'zero tolerance' is hard to reconcile with its long record of having taken no disciplinary action, and few prosecutions". (Note 5) Since 1994 the department prosecuted only three cases of fraud and there had been no cases of disciplinary action against staff for control or management failings.

The department operated its own anti-fraud activity at an annual cost of £4.2 million and this budget resourced a Police Fraud Squad of about 30 officers; some forensic investigations by consultants; and activity by the Defence Agency. Recovery in 2000/01 had been £2.4 million. The department also operated a fraud hotline but this had only been activated 22 times since February 1999. The implications from both the NAO and PAC reports were that the department did not consider the likelihood possibilities of fraud existing in property management.

The NAO estimate of fraud was 15%. However, the figure taken to the summary at the end of this chapter is £675 million, i.e. the figure suggested by Alan Williams.

SOURCES

PAC Report: *Ministry of Defence: The Risk of Fraud in Property Management*, HC647, 20 March 2002

NAO Report: *The Risk of Fraud in Property Management*, HC469, 18 May 2000

NOTES

1 PAC Report, p2/4
2 Establishment works consultants provided technical support and advice to the 200 property managers in the department. They were generally employed by a firm specialising in building and property consulting and were contracted to support the property manager by planning works and maintenance programmes, inspecting buildings and works to ensure that they comply with legislation, and monitoring the work of the work services manager, who was also an independent contractor, for value for money and probity.
3 PAC Report, p3/4, q1
4 ibid, p1/3, q23
5 ibid, p2/9, note 4

02 03 04

The Channel Tunnel Rail Link

"If the market is unwilling to subscribe sufficient equity capital it is a clear signal regarding the riskiness of the project, the implications of which need to be thought through by the department concerned." (Note 1) This NAO report records that, "The government saw the project as one of national prestige", and suggested that "the Link is one of a number of high priority projects for the development of high-speed rail routes across Europe. This has given the Link priority status in the government's overall transport policy". (Note 2) The Link was a 103km high-speed extension from the Channel Tunnel to a terminus in London.

To facilitate the PFI agreement, significant public assets (including St Pancras and Manchester International stations and the North Pole depot, as well as EPS (Note 3) and Union Railways (Note 4)) were handed to London Continental Railways (LCR), whose original shareholders were Bechtel, Warburg, Virgin, National Express, SNCF, London Electricity, Arup, Halcrow and Systra, all of whom could gain from the construction of the Link. The department agreed to provide LCR with grants totalling £1.730 billion for the construction of the Link (now known as HS1) and its use by domestic train services. The LCR shareholders contributed just £60 million worth of equity finance to the scheme. They had intended to raise private finance from a stock market flotation and the issue of debt, and expected to service that debt from revenue generated by Eurostar. However, Eurostar did not perform to expectations and carried just over five million passengers in 1997, against a target figure of 9.5 million.

The shortfall in revenue motivated LCR to request from the department a further £1.2 billion in grants, a request which was rejected by the then Deputy Prime Minister, John Prescott. Instead, the project was restructured with HS1 divided into two sections, one from the Channel Tunnel to near Ebbsfleet on the outskirts of London and the second section from Ebbsfleet to St Pancras. The construction of this section was given to Railtrack, (Note 5) who were also given the option to purchase the section once completed. The shareholders of LCR were allowed to convert 95% of their equity into preference shares, accruing interest at 7% a year, thereby protecting their investment. The department's rationale for this generosity was the risk that the shareholders would not have agreed to the restructuring and that the project would have to be restarted. In restructuring the PAC suggested "the department put in place complex arrangements that will expose the taxpayer to substantial risk for many years to come. For instance, some £4 billion of bonds were issued by London and Continental, subject to government guarantees, and in addition, it is likely that further substantial sums of taxpayers' money will have to be lent directly to the company to keep it afloat". (Note 6) Rather than obtain government funding, the department decided to use Government Guaranteed Bonds, which attracted extra funding costs of £80 million. Eventually, some £6.630 billion worth of bonds were issued by LCR and guaranteed by government.

The restructuring has all the appearance of a smoke and mirror operation. Apart from the bond issue, LCR also sold and leased back 11 of its train sets, with the government guaranteeing LCR's obligation to a limit of £230 million; Railtrack were obliged to buy Section 1 from LCR but the cost was not specified in either the PAC or the NAO reports; Railtrack guaranteed up to £700 million of commercial bank borrowing by LCR for the specific purpose of financing the construction of Section 1; the department guaranteed payments from Eurostar UK to Railtrack and provided a loan facility for LCR to draw on, depending on Eurostar's performance. It would seem that the department made every effort to facilitate the continuation of the LCR contracts which, bearing in mind the corporate quality of the shareholders, should have been facilitated commercially. The winners in this set of negotiations seems to have been LCR shareholders who had awarded themselves contracts worth over £90 million by the time the project got into trouble, and also managed to retain their initial investment whilst receiving government guarantees against future borrowing. Without quantifying a figure, the NAO also noted that the significant public sector assets, which had been transferred a year before the planned completion of the external financing of the project, had been returned to the department with the added encumbrance of the private sector debts which had been raised by LCR. (Note 7) The NAO were also critical about the timing of the transfer of the assets as it increased the risk to the department.

HS1 was not completed at the time these reports were written and, whilst the PAC suggested that the taxpayer would be exposed to a high level of risk, the only quantifiable loss is the £80 million, which was the increased cost of LCR raising finance using bonds rather than using gilts. £80 million has therefore been added to the summary at the end of this chapter.

SOURCES

PAC Report: *The Channel Tunnel Rail Link*, HC630, 21 March 2002

NAO Report: *The Channel Tunnel Rail Link*, HC302, 26 March 2001

Hope, Richard: *Railway Gazette*, 1 March 1998

NOTES

1 NAO Report, p8
2 ibid, p7
3 EPS was the British arm of the joint Eurostar operation.
4 Union Railways became the construction company for HS1.
5 Railtrack was the infrastructure holding company.
6 PAC Report, p2/6
7 NAO Report, p9

02 03 05

Ministry of Defence: Redevelopment of MoD Main Building

The PFI deal to centralise MoD staff into two buildings in London was agreed at a cost of £746 million over a 30-year period. A parliamentary question from Labour MP John Mann identified that actual payments over 30 years, taking into account inflation, were estimated at £2.35 billion. (Note 1)

The contract, agreed in May 2000, involved reducing staff numbers in London from just over 6,000 to 4,300, of which 3,300 were to be housed at Main Building and the remaining 1,000 at the old War Office. A month before the contract was due to be signed, the MoD, following an extensive review of staff numbers employed in London, identified that up to another 1,000 non-Head Office staff needed to remain in London, and accordingly leased Georges Court for 20 years and refurbished it to accommodate these staff. Staff numbers were therefore back up to 5,300, which was close to the 6,000 staff employed before the redevelopment of the Main Building. The realisation that they had miscalculated the accommodation requirements, and the timing of this realisation, would suggest that the original case for the redevelopment of the Main Building was flawed.

All PFI arrangements are subject to a Public Sector Comparator (PSC) which estimates the cost of an equivalent conventionally procured project. The MoD had created a PSC in 1995 when they first planned this redevelopment and this analysis was updated to take account of changes in specification, time lapses and extra requirements. The final PSC had a base cost of £643.3 million, but to that was added £102.9 million, representing risk, giving a new total of £746.2 million. Risk is subjective and the NAO acknowledged that extensive comparative data was lacking and that "this lack of comparative data on redevelopments added therefore to the degree of uncertainty in the PSC". (Note 2) What was noticeable is that the contract eventually signed was for £746.1 million, i.e. a figure just £100,000 below that which the PSC prepared, which included the £102.9 million contingency allowance.

Two consortia reached the final bidding stage and one of them, Modus, had a bid of £647 million accepted as the preferred bidder. Their bid was to increase by £99 million between the period when they were appointed preferred bidder in January 1999 and before the deal was closed in May 2000. The £99 million was justified on the basis of additional work; by an increase in the level of debt and reserves required to reflect capital costs; and an increase in finance costs. It was incredibly prescient of Modus to pitch their new bid just £100,000 less than the PSC. No doubt a close look at Modus' accounts would identify whether the £102.9 million contingency allowance was needed or became extra profit for shareholders.

The increased costs of £99 million, which the MoD allowed between appointing Modus as preferred bidder and signing the contract, should not have been sanctioned and this is therefore taken to the summary at the end of this chapter. No cost is available for the miscalculation of staff numbers, leading to an increased requirement for accommodation, nor for the increased costs identified by John Mann.

SOURCES

NAO Report: *Ministry of Defence: The Redevelopment of MoD Main Building*, HC748, 18 April 2002

Drury, Ian: *Mail Online*, 29 July 2013

NOTES

1 *Mail Online*, p1
2 NAO Report, p24, para 2.50

02 03 06

Construction of Portcullis House

In 1993 the House of Commons Commission approved plans for office accommodation for 210 Members of Parliament and their staff, together with meeting rooms, catering and other facilities. The plans specified a high quality of material, architectural design and workmanship consistent with the building's status and the perceived status of the occupants.

House officials chose a technique known as 'construction management' and monthly reports on the progress of the project were made to the Accommodation and Works Committee, while a steering group of House officials oversaw the project, but met infrequently between 1992 and 1998. Portcullis House was built on top of Westminster Underground station and work could not commence until the reconstruction of the station was largely complete. London Underground did not receive ministerial approval for the Jubilee Line extension until 1993, and at this stage both the budget was agreed by the House of Commons Commission and a timetable agreed with London Underground. On this timetable, construction of Portcullis House was scheduled to take 30 months, from 2 February 1997 to 2 August 1999.

When the project was approved, the building was forecast to cost £151 million, but a delay in the completion of the Underground meant that the construction of Portcullis House did not begin until 5 January 1998, almost a year late. The delay allowed the project team to resolve some difficulties that may have otherwise delayed the construction, as well as allowing them to increase the amount of off-site prefabrication of building components. In the period between 1993 and 1998, the House of Commons Commission approved increases in the forecast cost of the building to £187 million but the project team managed to deliver the project just £28 million over the 1993 budget.

However, the House also incurred legal and other costs totalling some £10 million after it was successfully sued by an unsuccessful tenderer for unfair treatment and contravention of procurement regulations, as well as having to pay £3.3 million on some associated works and removals, and releasing additional accommodation for the project team.

Once again, an established budget, (Note 1) upon which decisions were discussed and confirmed, morphed into a figure which bore no relation to the original figure. In this case, the budget was exceeded by £28 million and this figure, together with the extra legal fees of £10 million and the £3.3 million for other associated works, i.e. a total of £41.3 million will be added to the summary at the end of this chapter.

SOURCE

NAO Report: *Construction of Portcullis House, The New Parliamentary Building*

NOTE

1   Budget: the amount of money needed or available for a specific item.

02 03 07

NHS (England) Summarised Accounts

This report identified that clinical negligence was now a major source of expenditure for the NHS, rising by £500 million this year. The total provision made by the NHS for this liability reached £4.4 billion, recorded in Section 02 03 10.

The NHS Counter Fraud Service had been established as a result of a fraud strategy initiated by the Department of Health. It had overall responsibility to prevent, detect and measure fraud and corruption, and had an annual budget of £5.4 million and employed some 115 staff. The Counter Fraud Service was given three published targets: to achieve a 50% reduction in the level of prescription charge evasion by the end of 2002/03; to prevent £9 million in contractor fraud and recover £6 million by the end of 2001/02; to reduce fraud to an absolute minimum within ten years. The NHS Counter Fraud Service recognised the need to establish a baseline figure for fraud, and accordingly developed a Risk Measurement Project. They encountered problems with the availability of suitable NHS data and had to develop a methodology as they progressed.

By the time of this report they were able to establish that fraud by patients in the pharmaceutical area totalled £186 million for the period 1998 to 2000; that dental patient fraud totalled £17.3 million in the period 1999 to 2001, with a further £59.7 million at risk from dental contractor fraud; that fraud by patients in the optical area had reached £13.25 million in 1999/2000, and that £20.9 million was at risk from fraud initiated by contractors. (Note 1) An additional £17 million had been reported to the Counter Fraud Service during the year. (Note 2) It is clear from the report that the fraud measurement exercises were still a work in progress, e.g. the report about fraud in health authorities and NHS Trusts had just commenced.

The total added to the summary at the end of this chapter is £314 million.

SOURCE

NAO Report: *NHS (England) Summarised Accounts 2000/01*, HC766, 24 April 2002

NOTES

1 NAO Report, p18, fig 8
2 ibid, p19, para 5.14

02 03 08

CRAMS

A report commissioned by the Home Office in early 2000 from PA Consulting found that the programme team assigned to handle this project were under-resourced, with misaligned skills, and that the Home Office failed to recognise at an early stage the need for appropriate resources to manage the programme. The report also identified that at times there had been as few as five or six people working on the contract.

The NAO report into the matter also identified that "over the course of the project, from 1993 to the end of 2000 there had been seven programme directors in charge of the National Probation Service Information Systems Strategy programme (NPSISS), of whom only two had significant experience of managing major IT projects. The programme management team also suffered frequent changes of staff. Technical experts and specialists within the team tend to be consultants working on short-term assignments". (Note 1)

It therefore came as no surprise when the Home Office Minister, Paul Boateng, announced the cancellation of the project.

The NPSISS was approved in November 1993 with the aim of creating common standards, using the same technology for the 54 autonomous and locally-managed probation services. The strategy was the development of a Case Recording And Management System, CRAMS, which would be based on an existing system developed and used by Northumbria probation service. The Home Office gave the contract to Bull Information Systems Ltd (Bull) who suggested that they should pursue the design and development of a bespoke option. Bull was given a seven-year contract and an Information Systems Strategy Board (ISSB) was created to identify the strategy requirements of the 54 units. In practice, local probation services were expected to make their own decisions about how CRAMS should be implemented in their own local area, including the establishment of local implementation teams and directly liaising with Bull and its subcontractors. In practice, the 54 probation services had different management structures, priorities, methods of working and experience of managing IT.

By November 1995, CRAMS was been trialled in two areas, Surrey and West Midlands, but problems with the software resulted in the withdrawal of the product in early 1996. The Home Office commissioned a report from the Central Computer and Telecommunications Agency (CCTA) who found that the management structure and communication lines had not always proved adequate in addressing problems. The CCTA "report also noted that there was much pressure from the Home Office and the probation service to implement CRAMS as soon as possible". (Note 2)

"The NPSISS Programme Management Board agreed in June 1996 that a telecommunications strategy was needed to get the right information at the right level to the right people. However, no further action was taken to introduce a communication strategy." (Note 3) The report and its findings was the catalyst for a dissatisfaction letter written by the Home Office to Bull in November 1996, and by May of the following year the Home Office issued a formal warning to Bull about the lack of progress with the CRAMS programme.

The new version of CRAMS was introduced to the service in October 1997 and whilst it was accepted that this was an improvement on previous versions, there was still unease about user interface. A report in February 1999 from University College, London noted that "the CRAMS user interface contained 'defects' that 'compromise the ability of users to perform their work'". (Note 4) The company testing the system for year 2000 compliance identified 306 issues and faults in the software, of which 191 had been present in earlier versions and 25 could be classified as major. In March 1998 the Home Office ordered specialist software, GOL, but this order was subsequently suspended "because there was a lack of clarity about who the business owner for the project was; the business needs it was trying to meet; and who wanted it". (Note 5) The Home Office announced in September 1999 that work on the development of the CRAMS system would stop.

The original budget was just over £62 million for a seven-year period but the actual cost was £118 million; an additional £7 million was spent by individual probation services for supplementary equipment and software; £28.5 million was spent by probation services implementing and managing the standard NPSISS infrastructure and CRAMS; £4 million was spent by probation services for personal computers and remote access capability; and £2.2 million was spent to supplement NPSISS software to the end of March 2001. A total of £160 million has been added to the summary at the end of this chapter.

SOURCES

PAC Report: *The Implementation of the National Probation Service Information Systems Strategy*, HC357, 3 May 2002

NAO Report: *The Implementation of the National Probation Service Information Systems Strategy*, HC401, 26 April 2001

Inspectorate of Probation Report: *Using Information and Technology to Improve Probation Service Performance*, October 2000

NOTES

1 NAO Report, p7
2 ibid, p20
3 ibid, p21
4 ibid, p17
5 ibid, p23

02 03 09

The BBC

The BBC does not need an introduction. This report concentrates on the evasion of TV licence fees.

For the period under examination the BBC were responsible for the collection of licence fees and collected some £2.3 billion pounds from some 23 million licensees. The money collected was passed to the Department for Culture, Media and Sport (DCMS) who passed it on to the Exchequer. The money was returned to the BBC as a grant, equivalent to the amount of licence fee income collected, less the department's costs. The BBC contracted out the bulk of the collection and enforcement activity to third parties, and in the three years between 1999 and 2002 had changed these arrangements three times, eventually appointing Capita Business Services Ltd to take over responsibility as TV Licensing Agent.

The cost of collecting the television licence fees was £132 million, which was about 5.6% of the fees generated but the evasion rate, the proportion of potential licence fee revenue that remained uncollected, was £141 million. The rate of evasion was calculated using a statistical model developed and maintained by the DCMS, but the calculation was not regarded as a precise science. Indeed, revision of the model analysed in March 2001 suggested that the evasion figure might be 50% more than expected. (Note 1)

This is one of the subjects only examined once in the five-year period under review but this report does acknowledge that evasion was relevant since 1991/92. (Note 2) A total of £705 million, i.e. a multiple of five of the £141 million identified this year will be added to the summary at the end of this chapter.

SOURCE

NAO Report: *The BBC: Collecting the Television Licence Fee*, HC821, 15 May 2002

NOTES

1 NAO Report, p3, para 8
2 ibid, p2, para 6

02 03 10

NHS: Handling Clinical Negligence Claims in England

Major reports were completed by both the PAC and the NAO about this subject. The NHS is legally liable for the clinical negligence of its employees, including hospital doctors and surgeons, but excluding GPs. The NHS takes responsibility for dealing with any claims, including funding the defence of the claim, and for the legal costs or damages that may become payable. By 31 March 2001 provisions within the NHS budgets had risen to £4.4 billion to meet existing outstanding claims, as well as providing for claims expected to arise from incidents that had occurred but not been reported. Cerebral palsy and brain damage accounted for 80% of outstanding claims by value but 26% of claims by number. Over 10,000 new claims were received in 1999/2000 alone, and for significant claims, i.e. those over £10,000, the average time from claim to payment of damages was 5½ years. In 65% of the settlements in this year, below £50,000, the legal and other costs of settling claims exceeded the damages awarded.

There were three public organisations directly involved in clinical negligence claims: the NHS Healthcare Providers, the NHS Litigation Authority and the Legal Services Commission.

Until 1989, individual practitioners were responsible for claims for clinical negligence against them, but in 1990 the NHS took over responsibility for outstanding and future clinical negligence claims for its staff, but not for GPs or dentists. The NHS initially investigated and assessed medical incidents, and either referred claims to the Litigation Authority or managed the case themselves and paid the first £10,000 of any settlement.

The NHS Litigation Authority was set up in 1995 to operate the Clinical Negligence Scheme for trusts and had, as members, all but one trust and all primary care trusts. At the time of the report the Litigation Authority oversaw the management of 42% of claims and exerted, as the body who appoint and manage a panel of specialist solicitors, a powerful influence over solicitors and claims. The remainder of the claims, usually lower value, were handled by the trusts. The decade before these reports had seen a decade of much change: the rate of new claims per thousand finished consultant episodes had risen by 72% between 1990 and 1998. In 1999/2000 the NHS received some 10,000 new claims and cleared 9,600, but this still left a backlog of 23,000 claims outstanding. The NHS Litigation Authority took responsibility for this important area which reduced the responsibility of the health care trusts.

The Legal Services Commission (LSC) funds any claimant able to satisfy its means and cost benefit tests as set out in its funding code. In practice, the majority of people meeting these criteria were either in receipt of state benefits or were children. To qualify, claims must have at least a 50% chance of success and the commission awards a quality mark to those solicitors' offices that meet their criteria for competence and management. The LSC was created under the Access to Justice Act 1999 to replace the old civil and criminal legal aid schemes. The LSC assessed schemes and provided funds as appropriate.

The NHS Litigation Authority and the LSC sought to deal with cases in a cost-effective and timely manner and regarded an early settlement as preferable, so it made sense for them to cooperate. Early settlement was wanted by patients, whilst delayed settlement increased costs. Until February 2001 the two bodies had not shared information about the thousand or so cases over five-years old that appeared to be supported by legal aid, and after a recommendation by the NAO they had started to assess possible areas of cooperation.

The movement of claim management from the trusts to the Litigation Authority allowed increased transparency for both the public and the NAO, who noted their frustration at the lack of information: "We establish there was little information on the total number of claims. And there was very little aggregate information about the time it takes to settle claims and the costs that have been incurred." (Note 1)

The PAC was told by the Department of Health that the rising number of claims could be a reflection of a more litigious culture, i.e. 'ambulance chasing'. However, the Lord Chancellor's Department had taken steps to make conditional fee (no win no fee) agreements more attractive by enabling claimants' solicitors, from April 2000, to charge a success fee recoverable from the losing side if the case is won. These conditional fee arrangements would be available to those not eligible for legal aid for financial reasons. Inadvertently, the Lord Chancellor's Department created a scenario which helped establish the medical claims industry.

The NAO did not examine measures taken to prevent negligent incidents from happening. Although fundamental to the issue of clinical negligence, they offered no explanation. The PAC recognised the need to reduce negligence as a primary issue and noted that the Department of Health had launched an array of initiatives to improve clinical governance in the NHS, which included the creation of the Commission for Health Improvement, the

National Institute for Clinical Excellence, the National Clinical Assessment Authority and the National Patients' Safety Agency. Whilst no doubt set up with the best of intentions, the PAC noted that "by March 2000, almost a quarter of all NHS Trusts had not achieved even the basic risk management standards set by the Clinical Negligence Scheme for Trusts, and a further two thirds had not achieved more than basic standards. Despite the wide range of actions to improve clinical governance, the Clinical Negligence Scheme for Trusts remains voluntary and the department merely 'hope' that the majority of scheme members will achieve strong standards by 2003/04". The PAC report suggested, "The Department should make membership of the scheme mandatory, and set each trust a clear target of raising its risk management standards to the minimum level and then to the highest level". (Note 2)

It would seem that the NHS was still establishing a knowledge base about the quantum of clinical negligence and about which action would be taken to reduce the obligation. £4.4 billion will be added to the summary at the end of this section representing claims already made and claims acknowledged.

SOURCES

PAC Report: *Handling Clinical Negligence Claims in England*, HC280, 13 June 2002

NAO Report: *Handling Clinical Negligence Claims in England*, HC403, 3 May 2002

NOTES

1　NAO Report, p11
2　PAC Report, p7

02 03 11

NHS Direct In England

1.358 million voters, representing almost 3% of the electoral register, work for the NHS, so it is little wonder that the political parties treat the organisation sensitively and seriously. If the number of suppliers who depend on the NHS is added to this figure then the 'clout' of NHS voters is indeed formidable. The NHS is almost a state within a state and has been virtually impregnable to political interference for the last 40 years. As individuals, we have direct experience of GP's surgeries or of hospital stays and for most people the experience has been largely positive.

Up to the arrival of the recession, generous NHS budget and remuneration packages were available to senior employees, i.e. influencers within the organisation. The recession dictated that the largesse of previous years was no longer available, and under a Conservative government the NHS had to fund their requirements through 'efficiency' savings. The efficiency savings identified in the four years from 2010 were in the order of £20 billion, which begs the question about what money was wasted through inefficiency, fraud or error in the years prior to 2010.

The NHS is protective of its situation and very adverse to criticism. Whistle blowers have generally been compensated by payments involving confidentiality clauses, and whilst there has been some movement towards openness, the organisation is still wary and unwilling to share with its taxpayer funders and customers the negative side of the organisation. The outbreak of antibiotic resistant infections such as MRSA and Clostridium Difficile, as well as the medical scandals such as Alder Hey, Bristol and Mid Staffs, have suggested to the public that maybe everything within the NHS is not perhaps as perfect as the NHS would like us to believe. The NHS attitude to sharing information with outsiders can be illustrated by the 2005 report of the Counter Fraud and Security Management Service (CFSMS). Hope that the CFSMS would eliminate the culture of fraud was quickly dashed when it was established that within the report of 12,000 words, just 54 were devoted to the elimination of fraud and error in the NHS.

NHS Direct was announced in December 1997 and its target was to create a telephone helpline, providing information and advice on health care in England and Wales. Calls would initially be taken by a call handler who would assess whether immediate emergency assistance was necessary and, if appropriate, pass calls through to a nurse adviser. If not, available arrangements would be made to call customers back as soon as an adviser was free. The service did not have a comprehensive framework of detailed objectives, but by the year 2000 offered coverage countrywide and was taking 60,000 calls a week. It had invested in a national computerised decision support system at a cost of £70 million that included technical support over a seven-year period, which was in place at all sites by October 2001. NHS Direct was an initiative which effectively offered access to NHS services and, accordingly, stakeholders' views, ranging from GPs to voluntary organisations, were initially sought.

The successful introduction of NHS Direct was acknowledged by the PAC who complimented the NHS about the introduction of the £70 million call centre computer and who noted the annual running costs of £80 million. However, the NAO noted that the introduction of this service typically added £44 million per year to NHS costs saying, "The additional cost to the NHS of carrying out a consultation with these callers through NHS Direct, as opposed to their theoretical actions in the absence of NHS Direct therefore amounts to between £43 and £45 million". (Notes 1 and 2) It is therefore proposed to add to the summary at the end of this chapter £88 million as the unbudgeted cost of routing enquiries through NHS Direct in 2000-02.

SOURCES

PAC Report: *NHS Direct in England*, HC610, 17 June 2002

NAO Report: *NHS Direct in England*, HC505, 25 January 2002

NHS Report: *The Counter Fraud and Security Management Service Annual Accounts 2004/05*, HC135

NOTES

1 NAO Report, p29
2 All costs calculated by the University of Sheffield's Medical Care Research Unit 2001.

02 03 12

Ministry of Defence: Major Projects Report 2001

Major Projects Reports have been prepared by the NAO yearly since 1991. This report dealt with the NAO's evaluation of the progress of the Smart Acquisition Programme (see 00 01 13). It reached the conclusion that there was evidence of continued improvement in cost control; that delays were being brought under control; and that the MoD was expecting to meet the majority of the technical requirements of its customer.

This report dealt with 20 post-Main Gate projects and ten pre-Main Gate projects, allowing analysis in depth of those projects which exceeded approved costs. Where appropriate, each project is dealt with in the order detailed in the NAO report.

The Eurofighter project was designed to replace the Jaguar and Tornado F3 aircraft used by the RAF. The report (Note 1) showed that the variation on budget had increased to £1.5 billion, an addition of £37 million from the previous year. The report identified the cost of each unit as £57.9 million and noted that late delivery, 46 months at the date of the report, had added £37 million to the support cost of the existing Jaguar and Tornado equipment.

The Extended Range Ordnance/Modular Charge System (ERO/MCS) was a programme to upgrade the AS90 self-propelled Howitzer. (Note 2) Initially, the ERO was developed with the Unimodular Propelling Charge System (UPCS). Following technical difficulties with the latter, an alternative MCS programme was approved. Assessment work had not been carried out prior to Main Gate approval for the development and production of the ERO and UPCS programmes, leading to a budget overrun of £22 million and a further £22 million cost for necessary modification to the ERO. The change from UPCS to MCS saved £8 million, but unforeseen currency conversion costs added £1 million to the budget. Altogether, an overspend of £48 million was incurred because of the decision to proceed with UPCS without carrying out the appropriate assessment work.

The High Velocity Missile (HVM) (Note 3) was designed for use by the army to attack armoured helicopters and low-flying aircraft. The contract for first development and production was placed in 1986 and deliveries were first achieved in September 1997 – a delay of 81 months. The approved cost of £927 million was exceeded by £6 million, due mainly to technical factors.

Two Landing Platform Dock Replacement (LPDR) vessels were ordered to replace current capacity. The two new vessels were contracted with BAE Systems Marine Ltd in July 1996 and delivery was anticipated for December 2003. However, delivery was delayed for at least 31 months, in part due to computer design and industrial loading difficulties and partly due to a lack of competition in the tendering process, as BAE revisited their bid to reflect a NAPNOC situation. (Note 4) The estimated cost of running on with current equipment was £57 million, but support cost not incurred was estimated at £26 million. Extra costs incurred were therefore £31 million, although the MoD was hoping for a £6 million repayment as damages as a result of the delay. Giving the MoD credit for the £6 million repair payment meant that a total of £26 million has been recognised as overspend for the LPDR programme.

The Nimrod MRA4 aircraft was the replacement for the Nimrod MR2 – the RAF's maritime patrol aircraft. A four-way competition resulted in BAE receiving approval in July 1996, but the contract encountered difficulties and the contract was renegotiated in May 1999, suggesting delivery would start in December 2004. The report (Note 5) noted that the additional cost of continuing with the existing Nimrod fleet would be £61 million.

It was decided that the Stingray Lightweight Torpedo should have an extended life to 2025, so a programme was approved in May 1995 and a contract awarded to GEC-Marconi on 10 July 1996 on a non-competitive fixed-price basis. The in-service date for these torpedoes had been extended by 41 months due to delays and contract negotiation, reassessment of programme timescale and the need to match the department's programme with its cash flow. The delay meant that the existing equipment will need extra support at a net cost of £5 million, while the forecast cost exceeded the approved cost by £42 million. £37 million has already been accounted for in Section 00 01 02, so £5 million will be added to the schedule at the end of this section

The resolution of the sonar obsolescence programme, as well as the integration of a new submarine command system for the Swiftsure and some Trafalgar class submarines, was completed in June 1996. The aim was to deliver enhanced military capability to the new version Trafalgar class, principally through a new integrated sonar suite (SMCS) and through improved noise reduction measures. The sonar contractor, Thomson Marconi Sonar, experienced major difficulties with software engineering and associated signal and data processing, which led to a slippage of 24 months and a projected budget variation of £68 million. £50 million has already been accounted for in Section 00 01 10, so £18 million will be added to the schedule at the end of this section.

The medium-range Trigate has been mentioned in Chapter 1, Section 00 01 11. However, the deficiency had reduced and, accordingly, a credit of £6 million will be noted in the schedule at the end of this section.

The Bowman project has also been dealt with in Section 00 01 10 but costs had increased by a further £69 million.

The total added to the summary at the end of this chapter is £257 million.

SOURCES

NAO Report: *MoD Major Projects Report 2001*, HC 330, Appendix 2, pp 27-180

PAC Report: *MoD Major Projects Report 2001*, HC 448, 4 July 2002

NOTES

1 NAO Report, pp65-71
2 ibid, pp72-78
3 ibid, pp85-89
4 NAPNOC: No acceptable price, no contract.
5 NAO Report, pp117-122

02 03 13

The Misuse and Smuggling of Hydrocarbon Oils

At the time of this report there were 700 filling stations in Northern Ireland, of which 450 sold illicit fuel to some extent and 250 sold only illegal fuel. It is little wonder, therefore, that the PAC and the NAO paid attention to this loss of revenue. Customs were conscious that they were also losing revenue on the mainland but recognised that the reasons were different.

HM Customs and Excise collected £22.6 billion in taxes and duties from hydrocarbon oil duties in 2000/01, so it represented a significant percentage of total government receipts. Refined hydrocarbon oils fall into two categories: light oils, such as petrol; and heavy oils, such as kerosene and diesel. Most of the revenue collected was from unleaded petrol and diesel, and the duty was generally collected when the oil left the refinery storage depot of one of the nine large refiners, who account for approximately 80% of the total amount of duty collected by Customs. The nine large refiners own or franchise most of the service stations on mainland UK, whilst the service stations in Northern Ireland were independent.

The smuggling of fuel was a significant problem in Northern Ireland and the price difference in fuel between oils purchased in the Republic of Ireland and Northern Ireland acted as a powerful incentive for smugglers. Customs' efforts to deter smugglers were hampered by their inability to impose sanctions extreme enough to deter. Customs could not close filling stations selling illicit fuel as they were not the licensing authority, whilst they also found it difficult in many cases to even identify the ownership of the filling stations. They were further hampered by having to deal with a border over 300 miles long with almost 300 crossing points, allowing smugglers flexibility to rapidly change routes. Laundering plants, created to remove the dye and chemical marker used in rebated fuels to identify the lower duty paid on these fuels, had the capacity to produce up to 200,000 litres of fuel a week and represented another source of difficulty for Customs. During the year they closed down 17 such laundering plants, but again were unable to identify the owners. Customs were also hampered by the political considerations relating to Northern Ireland.

On the mainland, the main risk was from the illegal use of rebated fuel in road vehicles. It was an attractive proposition for those dishonest enough to find an illegal supplier. The duty rate on normal diesel at the time was 45.82p per litre, whilst the corresponding duty on chemically-marked rebated gas oil, commonly referred to as red diesel, was 3.13p per litre. The marking process had been introduced to allow Customs to detect whether rebated fuels were being used illegally and the process was usually actioned at the refineries. The strategy of tackling evasion by undertaking roadside checks was supported by the initiative of tracking the distribution of kerosene and red diesel and identifying unusual and suspicious transactions. Customs had also disrupted a substantial number of laundering plants, and sought to improve the effectiveness of the markers used to identify rebated fuel by adding a European Union marker called Solvent Yellow. They also sought, from the Chancellor, legislation to provide for an approval scheme for all distributors of rebated fuels to allow improved intelligence data. They found little evidence of smuggling, although there was some evidence about the smuggling of 130,000 litres of rebated fuel from the Republic of Ireland in container lorries, and the decanting of fuel, i.e. where lorries had tanks which held larger than usual amounts of fuel that was bought overseas and returned to the UK for use by other vehicles.

In Northern Ireland, Customs estimated that revenue losses were a further £380 million, a figure that included legitimate cross-border shopping, i.e. an individual purchasing fuel in the Republic of Ireland rather than Northern Ireland. (Note 1) The estimate for revenue lost on the mainland was £600 million in 2000, (Note 2) an increase of over 100% on the previous year. An NAO report for 2003/04 identified that losses for 1999 were £700 million, for 2000 were understated by £20 million, for 2001 were £950 million, for 2002 were £750 million and for 2003 were £850 million. (Note 3) The total added to the summary at the end of this chapter will be £4.25 billion.

SOURCES

PAC Report: *The Misuse and Smuggling of Hydrocarbon Oils*, HC649, 18 July 2002

NAO Report: *The Misuse and Smuggling of Hydrocarbon Oils*, HC614, 15 February 2002

NAO Report: *National Audit Office Standard Report 2003/04*

NOTES

1 PAC Report, p6/11
2 NAO Report 2002, p8
3 NAO Report 2003/4, p110

02 03 14

Collection of Fines and Other Financial Penalties in the Criminal Justice System

On April 1 2001, responsibility for executing warrants for the arrest of defaulters who had ignored fines and other financial penalties imposed by magistrates' courts became the responsibility of the court rather than the police. The Lord Chancellor's Department estimated there was a backlog of 106,000 unexecuted warrants in England and Wales, which in some cases went back three or four years. Statutory responsibility for the efficiency and effectiveness of magistrates' courts, including the collection of fines, rested with the 42 magistrates' court committees throughout England and Wales. However, the monitoring of fine collection was hampered by the lack of reliable, consistently-produced management information, and in some cases committees could not distinguish between financial penalties collected as part of the criminal justice system and civil impositions, such as maintenance payments. The committees used three different computer systems which did not share information electronically, even between courts using the same system, so if a financial penalty was passed to another court the collection needed to be done manually. According to the NAO, "The collection of financial penalties is hampered by poor record-keeping and a paucity of reliable information on overall enforcement performance". (Note 1)

Collection was also affected by the generally limited financial means of the defaulters, many of whom had other financial penalties outstanding and were multiple debtors. Typically, 80% of male defaulters were unemployed and 90% of female defaulters were in restricted financial circumstances, usually without any employment and with dependent children. Fines collected act as a form of punishment; sometimes ensuring that victims were recompensed; and sometimes ensuring that prosecutors' costs were offset. However, whilst magistrates' and crown court judges were required to take account of offenders' means when imposing financial penalties, most did not have systematic arrangements in place to verify the original information, and indeed at some courts magistrates were not provided with information about outstanding fines. Some defaulters became adept at frustrating the courts by giving false addresses or not telling the court about a change of address. One of the first actions by the Lord Chancellor was to designate that information about defaulters could be traced through the Department for Work and Pensions (DWP). It was proposed that committees would also be able to trace defaulters when similar arrangements had been concluded with the Employment Service and Inland Revenue.

It is of little surprise, then, to note that for 2000/01, £74 million was written-off largely because the offenders could not be traced, and a further £77 million was cancelled by the court. Cancellations occur for a variety of reasons, including a successful appeal against the imposition; because the penalty has been satisfied by a term of imprisonment; or because the offender's circumstances changed so much that there is no prospect of the fine being paid. The PAC report suggested that "there is also a risk that areas cancel impositions rather than write them off to mask weaknesses in their enforcement processes", (Note 2) but neither report qualifies any sum in respect of this theory. Cancellations are, however, a judicial decision, and for that reason an attempt is not made to identify how much of the £77 million, and indeed the following year's £90 million, was cancelled because of weak enforcement processes. The PAC report identified the 2001/02 written-off figure as £58 million and the cancellation figure as £90 million.

It is therefore proposed to add to the summary at the end of this chapter a total of £299 million.

SOURCES

PAC Report: *Collection of Fines and Other Financial Penalties in the Criminal Justice System*, HC999, 6 November 2002

NAO Report: *Collection of Fines and Other Financial Penalties in the Criminal Justice System*, HC 672, 15 March 2002

NOTES

1 NAO Report, p4
2 PAC Report, p9

02 03 15

Ministry of Defence: Departmental Resource Accounts 2001/02

This was the third year in which the Ministry of Defence (MoD) prepared resource accounts. The NAO report about the subject noted that progress was being made, and that they were no longer unhappy about the accountancy treatment regarding the stock of departmental housing property; about the treatment of the costs for major refits and overhauls of ships, submarines and aircraft; about the identification and quantification of creditor and accrual figures; and about the calculation of stock provisions. However, the accounts were still qualified primarily because of the issues outlined below.

The Defence Logistics Organisation (DLO) has been mentioned previously in Section 01 02 07. It still maintained 13 principal logistics management systems, collectively known as supply systems. Within these systems were details of over 3 million different types of items, which included consumable stock, fixed asset items, certain items of plant machinery and capital spares. "The department had identified that many of the items held on the supplied systems are in excess of requirements, or obsolete because the equipment they support is no longer in use." (Note 1) The scrapping of obsolete equipment should be reflected in resource accounts, and accordingly in these accounts the DLO had provided for £3.513 billion of stock write-down. (Note 2)

Some assets belonging to the department were held offsite by contractors who were either carrying out repairs or were incorporating into new-build items which were supplied by the department. The gross value was adjusted to £1.057 billion and provisions of £466 million for obsolescence and depreciation in the current year reduced the asset figure to £591 million. (Note 3)

"At the introduction of the resource accounting and budgeting initiative the department had little information on the value or extent of its asset base, and it struggled, initially, to complete acceptable accounts." (Note 4) In the previous year's accounts the department had noted a net balance of £1.178 billion, representing tangible and intangible fixed assets. They also noted that they could not accurately support some £89 million of such assets, but this year's report showed that the level of tangible and intangible fixed assets had dropped to £118 million and that the NAO were satisfied with the explanations about why the amount had reduced so dramatically.

The department suffered further losses through changes in policy regarding the operation of the Harrier aircraft. It was decided that the Sea Harrier, flown by Royal Navy personnel, and the Harrier GR7, flown by the RAF, would be replaced by a common aircraft type, which initiated the disposal of 15 Sea Harriers at a cost of £262 million. This review also led to the decision to scrap three Tornado aircraft and 14 Lynx and Gazelle helicopters, which generated further write-offs of £76 million. At the same time the department identified a reduction to the carrying values for a class of submarine, amounting to £59 million, and a series of smaller changes to the carrying values of a range of fighting equipment and capital spares resulted in further charges of £175 million. (Note 5)

The department also decided that the Skynet satellite communications programme had not functioned as planned since its launch. A review of the operational capability of the satellite concluded that there was an impairment and that it was appropriate to adjust the value to reflect this, so some £106 million has been written-off to reflect this situation.

A total of £5.842 billion will be added to the summary at the end of this chapter.

SOURCE

NAO Report: *Ministry of Defence: Departmental Resource Accounts 2001/02*, 21 November 2002

NOTES

1 NAO Report, p3
2 ibid, p4
3 ibid, p8
4 ibid, p1
5 ibid, p13

02 03 16

Ministry of Defence: Major Projects Report 2002

This report listed 20 Main Gate and ten pre-Main Gate projects. The major theme of the report was an examination of the assessment phase of the Smart Acquisition Programme, i.e. the phase between Initial Gate and Main Gate, as well as assessing some innovative initiatives created by some Integrated Project Teams. For background information about the Major Projects concept and the Smart Acquisition Programme, see Sections 00 01 10 and 00 01 13.

The report was generally favourable about the assessment phase but it noted that projects were taking longer in the assessment phase than planned. As the objective of the assessment phase was to spend the right amount of time and money to reduce risk to an acceptable level for Main Gate approval it would seem that any time spent in assessment was time well spent.

The innovative initiatives highlighted by the report involved aircraft leasing to buy time, whilst a long-term solution to a capacity problem was solved, as well as unique procurement strategy for the Type 45 destroyers and a PFI initiative for the Skynet 5 satellite system.

The A400M aircraft was a collaborative programme involving eight European nations, and within the UK was intended to serve all three services by offering an airlift capability to move large single items, such as attack helicopters, to and from well-established airfields or semi-prepared rough landing areas in extreme climates and in all weathers. The UK commitment to the programme was for 25 aircraft with a delivery forecast for 2009. To meet short-term requirements before the aircraft were delivered the existing fleet of C130K and C17 aircraft would incur unbudgeted support costs of £34 million, whilst the extra cost of leasing C17 aircraft, some £86 million, would be offset by savings from the delay in the introduction of the A400M. The unbudgeted differential added to the summary at the end of this section is therefore £34 million.

Astor was designed as a new capability, providing long-range all-weather theatre surveillance and target acquisition system, comprising five aircraft and eight mobile and transportable ground stations which would meet both army and navy requirements. The first aircraft and ground stations were due for delivery in 2004 with final delivery anticipated in 2008. A favourable exchange rate led to variations of £86 million (Note 1); £9 million due to change requirements; and £11 million due to changes in the contracting process were offset by the deletion of the £12 million air fuelling facility; a delay in contract awards saved £17 million; and £2 million was saved by accounting adjustments and redefinitions. A total of £75 million therefore has been added to the summary at the end of this section.

The replacement for the Lynx Mk7 helicopter was the WAH64 Apache attack helicopter, produced by Boeing using Westland Helicopters Ltd as a prime contractor and fitted with Rolls-Royce engines. The requirement was first identified in 1991 and definitive bids were invited in 1995, with the contract finally placed in 1996, assuming delivery of the 67 helicopters between 2000 and 2004. Delivery slipped by 13 months. However, an increased variation in the total cost of £75 million was caused by 21 changes alone in budgetary priorities; inflation added another £5 million; the contracting process added £14 million to the cost; and some accounting adjustments added a further £29 million. On the credit side, ten of the change requirements saved £41 million and exchange rate gains saved £10 million. The programme "was based on an off-the-shelf buy of the complete weapon system through a prime contractor". (Note2) Having bought on that basis, and presuming that the base aircraft delivered from Boeing were standard, it would seem naive to initiate 31 changes – the programme was no longer an off-the-shelf item and had been converted to bespoke. A total of £72 million, i.e. over £1 million per aircraft is therefore added to the summary at the end of this section.

The Eurofighter project had already been addressed in previous reports and it is noted that the variation to budget had decreased to £1.269 billion in 2002, i.e. an overall reduction of £236 million. There were a number of movements to support this reduction and one is of particular significance – one of the reductions was £165 million, which is described as an "introduction of benefits to be assumed from planned implementation of Smart procurement process". (Note 3) A forecast assumption would not seem to be justification for including a major saving in any budgetary calculation. The recognition that there would be significant costs associated with the need to run on with the Tornado and Jaguar fleet had not been altered. There was also an increase of £42 million associated with technical factors and procurement strategy variations relating to the in-service date. A deduction of £236 million has been added to the schedule at the end of this section.

The army's High Velocity Missile (HVM) programme, designed to create a weapon to attack armoured helicopters and low-flying aircraft, was reported to be running 81 months late. There was a variation of £3 million against approved costs that will be added to the total at the end of this section.

TRACER, the Tactical Reconnaissance Armoured Combat Equipment Requirement, was due to replace the ageing Combat Vehicle Reconnaissance facility, and an initial feasibility study reported in 1994 was followed by a more detailed report in 1996. The latter report identified that the UK requirement was in line with the US requirement for a Future Scout and Calvary System (FSCS), so the UK and US entered a collaborative project definition phase for TRACER. Two UK/US industrial consortia were awarded independent work aimed at winning a competition for a single demonstrate and manufacture contract, scheduled to start in 2003. However, in 2001, the MoD decided not to proceed with any future phases of the programme, but even so the completion of the contract remained a high priority with an assessment phase expected to complete on schedule in

2002. The decision to terminate was a joint UK/US decision and the US had decided to meet their requirement internally for the FSCS. The report (Note 4) into the matter did not identify any specific reason why the decision was reversed but did note that the likely cost of termination was £131 million – a figure which has been added to the total at the end of this section.

A total of £77 million, which acknowledges the credit of £236 million for the Eurofighter project, has been added to the schedule at the end of this chapter.

SOURCE

NAO Report: *Ministry of Defence Major Projects Report*, HC 91, 4 December 2002

NOTES

1 NAO Report, p49
2 ibid, p67
3 ibid, p85
4 ibid, p177

02 03 17

VARIOUS. This section records a number of smaller value reports.

The English Sports Council Accounts

Richard Caborn, MP and Minister for Sport in the Blair government did not want Derek Casey to remain as Chief Executive of Sport England. In a meeting with Mr Casey, attended by Trevor Brooking, Mr Caborn approved a severance package which cost Sport England £494,000. Mr Caborn was advised by his department that "Mr Casey's continued employment was a matter for Sport England; that it was for Sport England to decide whether he should move on; that the terms of any severance were for Sport England, subject to putting a case to the department and, depending on the scale, to the Treasury". (Note 1) The department reviewed the package and discussed it with the Treasury. Both had concerns about the regularity of the process and at the scale of the departure package. However, they both reluctantly approved the package as proposed, "since the legal advice indicated that

Sport England would be unlikely to resist successfully any legal claim that the binding contract was made on June 14". (Note 2) A total of £494,000 has therefore been added to the summary at the end of this section.

SOURCE

NAO Report: *The English Sports Council Accounts 2000/2001: Costs of Departure of Derek Casey, former Chief Exec of Sport England*, 22 February 2002

NOTES

1 NAO Report, R1
2 ibid, R2

Human Fertilisation and Embryology Authority Accounts

The NAO criticised the authority for not invoicing clinics for services provided over the period of the previous nine years and estimated the amount as in the region of £600,000 to £1.25 million. A total of £925,000 has therefore been added to the summary at the end of this section.

SOURCE

NAO Report: *Human Fertilisation and Embryology Authority Account 2001/02*, 18 July 2002

Office for National Statistics

The Office for National Statistics misjudged the rate of return for forms distributed by post for the 2001 Census. They estimated 70% of recipients would return the form, but 88% of recipients did so, leading to an overspend of £5.8 million for field staff. They also failed to recover £244,000 of advance payments made to field staff and paid compensation of £294,000 to field staff whose payments were delayed because of administrative problems. The total added to the summary at the end of this section is £6.388 million.

SOURCE

NAO Report: *Outsourcing the 2001 Census*, HC1211, 18 October 2002

Community Legal Service

New arrangements were introduced in 2000 for the funding of civil legal aid. This report noted that the Legal Services Commission (LSC) disallowed a significant proportion of the costs claimed for help and advice work by solicitors. Audits conducted by the LSC suggested that 35% of suppliers were over-claiming in excess of 20% of actual costs.

The Legal Service Fund totalled £734 million, of which £258 million was 'controlled work', which consisted of legal help and legal representation before certain tribunals. The decision about whether to provide a service lay with the supplier, i.e. the solicitor or advice centre, under a pre-agreed contract that limited the number of cases per supplier. The total spent on 'licensed work' was £476 million, and this work was generally managed under an individual contract with the LSC. It is impossible from this report to identify the monetary values in respect of claims, but what is identifiable is the £20 million written off by the LSC as irrecoverable costs and contributions from funded clients. (Note 1)

A total of £20 million will be added to the summary at the end of this section.

SOURCE

NAO Report: *Community Legal Servers: The Introduction of Contracting*, 22 November 2002

NOTE

1   NAO Report, pp18/19, fig 8

SUMMARY

The total added to the summary at the end of this chapter for these four sections is £27.8 million

SUMMARY: CHAPTER THREE – 2002

02 03 00	Tobacco Smuggling	£16.530 bn
02 03 01	The Millenium Dome	£0.628 bn
02 03 02	DVLA: Appropriation Accounts	£0.065 bn
02 03 03	Ministry of Defence: The Risk of Fraud in Property Management	£0.675 bn
02 03 04	The Channel Tunnel Rail Link	£0.080 bn
02 03 05	Ministry of Defence: Redevelopment of MoD Main Building	£0.099 bn
02 03 06	Construction of Portcullis House	£0.041 bn
02 03 07	NHS (England) Summarised Accounts	£0.314 bn
02 03 08	CRAMS	£0.160 bn
02 03 09	The BBC	£0.705 bn
02 03 10	NHS: Handling Clinical Negligence Claims in England	£4.400 bn
02 03 11	NHS Direct in England	£0.088 bn
02 03 12	Ministry of Defence: Major Projects Report 2001	£0.257 bn
02 03 13	The Misuse and Smuggling of Hydrocarbon Oils	£4.250 bn
02 03 14	Collection of Fines and Other Financial Penalties in the Criminal Justice System	£0.299 bn
02 03 15	Ministry of Defence: Resource Accounts: Departmental Resource Accounts 2001/02	£5.842 bn
02 03 16	Ministry of Defence: Major Projects Report 2002	£0.077 bn
02 03 17	Various	£0.028 bn
	Total	£34.538 bn
	Total adjusted for inflation to December 2014	£44.724 bn

INDEX: CHAPTER FOUR – 2003

03 04 00 The 2001 Outbreak of Foot and Mouth Disease

03 04 01 Individual Learning Accounts

03 04 02 NHS (England) Summarised Accounts

03 04 03 Ministry of Defence: Reducing Stocks

03 04 04 Tackling Benefit Fraud

03 04 05 Tackling Benefit Fraud: DSS Appropriation Accounts

03 04 06 Tackling Benefit Fraud: DSS Appropriation Accounts

03 04 07 Tackling Benefit Fraud: DSS Resource Accounts

03 04 08 Tackling Benefit Fraud

03 04 09 Ministry of Defence: Devonport Submarine Facilities

03 04 10 Ministry of Defence: Resource Accounts

03 04 11 The Libra Project

03 04 12 Ministry of Defence: The Apache Helicopter

03 04 13 NATS

"Nothing is so well calculated to produce a death-like torpor in the country as an extended system of taxation and a great national debt"

                William Cobbett, farmer and pamphleteer (1763-1835)

"As we peer into society's future, we – you and I, and our government – must avoid the impulse to live only for today, plundering for our own ease and convenience the precious resources of tomorrow. We cannot mortgage the material assets of our grandchildren without risking the loss also of their political and spiritual heritage. We want democracy to survive for all generations to come, not to become the insolvent phantom of tomorrow."

                Dwight D Eisenhower, 34th President of the United States (1890-1969)

03 04 00

The 2001 Outbreak of Foot and Mouth Disease

The television coverage of the 2001 foot and mouth disease outbreak was horrific, with images of either the vast funeral pyres of burning animals or the humongous burial sites shown on our screens nightly. Six million animals were killed, of which four million were killed for disease control purposes and a further two million for welfare reasons – a rather unfortunate description as far as the animals were concerned.

The outbreak was discovered at an abattoir in Essex on 19 February and was confirmed the next day. Investigations confirmed that a farmer called Waugh from Heddon-on-the-Wall had fed undertreated pig swill (a process now banned) to his pigs and failed to notify the authorities when his animals subsequently showed tell-tale signs of having contracted the disease, before delivering them to the abattoir for slaughter. Foot and mouth spreads quickly and easily, and by the time the outbreak was identified there were outbreaks in at least 57 premises.

The contingency plans drawn up by the Department for Environment, Food and Rural Affairs (DEFRA) assumed an outbreak in a maximum of ten premises, so the situation in which they found themselves on 19 February 2001 was beyond their calculation.

In July 1998 the department had initiated a report by Richard Drummond, (Note 1) which was delivered in February 1999 to the State Veterinary Service and made a number of prescient recommendations, including one which expressed concern that the rapid spread of foot and mouth disease could quickly overwhelm resources available to the Veterinary Service. Some of the measures recommended by Drummond were acted upon, but in July 2000 the Chief Veterinary Officer, Jim Scudamore, expressed concern that key issues had not been resolved. Indeed, the NAO report into the matter stated that "many of the problems encountered by the State Veterinary Service in 2001 had been anticipated by an internal study in 1999, the Drummond Report". (Note 2)

In evidence to the PAC on July 3 2002, Mr Brian Bender CB, Permanent Secretary to DEFRA, admitted, "There were other major priorities for the State Veterinary Service at the time, more importantly the public health issues surrounding BSE". (Note 3) In the previous year, during the outbreak of classical swine fever, which affected only 16 farms, 80% of the State Veterinary Services' 200 staff, as well as 25% of its administration staff, were devoted to disease control tasks. The recommendations of the Drummond Report had, in modern-day parlance, been 'kicked into the long grass', whilst the majority of resources were allocated to the BSE problem.

After this crisis, government initiated not one, but three separate reports. One, chaired by Dr Ian Andersen, reported on the political handling of the crisis; a second, by Mr D Curry, examined the future of British farming as a result of the crisis; and a third was provided by the Royal Society on the future handling of infectious animal diseases. What was missing, according to *Private Eye*, (Note 4) was what Margaret Beckett called "the all singing, all dancing public enquiry". (Note 5)

So what were the financial implications of the DEFRA handling of the crisis? DEFRA made compensation payments of £1.369 billion to farmers for animals slaughtered. This was a legal requirement under the Animal Health Act 1981, which required compensation to be made based on the value of the animal immediately before it became infected or was slaughtered. Values were determined by professional valuers and the valuations increased threefold during the crisis, on the basis that increased prices would result when the market reopened. Farmers were allowed to select valuers of their own choice and, as fees paid to valuers were based on a percentage of their stock valuation, there was no incentive for valuers to reduce costs. It is of note that when standard rates were introduced by the department in March 2001, because the valuation process was thought to be delaying the slaughter of animals, only 4% of farmers used these standard rates. When DEFRA applied to the EC for £960 million support they were initially offered £230 million on the basis that many of the valuations were spurious – the EC quoted one claim for £240,715 for animals which had not been slaughtered and another for 317 at £2,035 each, described as "mostly pedigree breed from top sires", (Note 6) but all without appropriate certificates. Six rams bought in October 2000 for £60 each were valued at £635 each in a claim to DEFRA.

What seems unreal is that DEFRA should have accepted and compensated such claims without examination, and even more unreal is that DEFRA should have tried to pass the bill on to the EC. There was precedent for the valuation issue and the Northumberland Report, (Note 7) which considered the 1967/68 foot and mouth outbreak, had identified the same problem, which they referred to as a scam by the valuers, and accordingly recommended that senior government valuers be appointed to monitor independent standards of valuation. The department's standing instructions envisaged acceptance of this recommendation, and eventually the appointments were made in July 2001 – some 33 years later.

A further £1.279 billion was paid for haulage, disposal of carcasses, building work, staff costs, administration, payments to other government departments and various miscellaneous costs. Amongst the costs listed by the NAO was a cost of £304 million paid to farmers for the fencing and disinfection of their farms. There were over 10,000 farms, so the average cost per farm was £30,400. The department considered this to be cost-effective, as no case of reinfection occurred. However, in the Netherlands where the cost of disinfection was the responsibility of the farmer/owner, the average cost was between £70 and £550, depending on the size of the farm. The NAO report into the matter dryly notes that "no cases of re-emergence occurred in the Netherlands or any of the other countries affected in 2001". (Note 8)

This was an unnecessary outbreak, and implementation of the Northumberland Report would have ensured the department avoided the valuation scam, whilst common sense could have avoided the cleansing and disinfecting overpayments. The impression is given of a department with limited resources dealing in quick succession with the classical swine fever and BSE outbreaks and ignoring the appropriate Drummond recommendations. The cost of government resources allocated to the outbreak was estimated at £412 million. The total cost of this outbreak, i.e. £3.030 billion, is added to the summary at the end of this chapter.

SOURCES

PAC Report: *The 2001 Outbreak of Foot and Mouth Disease*, HC487, 5 March 2003

PAC Report: *Foot and Mouth Disease: Applying the Lessons*, HC563, 1 November 2005

NAO Report: *The 2001 Outbreak of Foot and Mouth Disease*, HC939, 21 June 2002

NAO Report: *Foot and Mouth Disease: Applying the Lessons*, HC184, 2 February 2005

Private Eye, Edition 1035, 24 August- 6 September, 2001

NOTES

1   Richard Drummond, head of the Northern Region of the State Veterinary Service, reviewed the department's ability to deal with animal disease outbreaks and reported his findings in 1999.

2   NAO Report 2005, p26

3   BSE: Bovine Spongiform Encephalopathy

4   Edition 1035, p26

5   Mrs Beckett was at that time Secretary for State for DEFRA.

6   NAO Report 2005, p42

7   The Northumberland Report made a series of recommendations about tightening import controls and animal hygiene regulations following the 1967/68 foot and mouth epidemic. There was not another major epidemic of foot and mouth until February 2001.

8   NAO Report 2005, p32

03 04 01

Individual Learning Accounts

Naseem Iqbal, Waheed Iqbal, Zafar Iqbal and others chose to register as providers of courses for Individual Learning Accounts (ILA), and between July and November 2001 were paid a total of £723,678 in respect of 3,717 students. The Crown prosecuted them for conspiring to commit fraud through the dishonest abuse and manipulation of the ILA programme, and contended that many of the so-called students were not in fact students but members of the public who had never enrolled as students and who had not received any coursework apart from a CD which itself had been pirated. The three defendants were convicted and each sentenced to 3½ years in prison.

What was an ILA and how did the scheme go so horribly awry? Whilst the Iqbals managed to claim such a large sum, the NAO report into the matter suggested that the total sum lost to fraudulent and other irregular payments could be estimated as high as £97 million.

The ILA philosophy was introduced in the 1997 New Labour manifesto as a "pledge to encourage people to invest in and take more responsibility for learning throughout their working lives". (Note 1) The scheme's ambition was to offer learners, including the self-employed, a scheme where the learner would be able to pick courses of their choice and timing. Initially, the Department for Education and Skills (DfES) sought the involvement of banks and other institutions in setting up accounts for individuals, but after two years of research and a less than enthusiastic reaction from the private sector, the department concluded that the scheme, as suggested, was not popular with the potential user, the providers of the product or other financial institutions approached. The search for private finance echoes the Millennium Dome (see 02 03 01) and the Channel Tunnel (see 02 03 04) experiences, which found that if a project is feasible and likely to be profitable the private sector would find the finance.

Failure to source private finance meant that a system of subsidy was introduced, which was funded from the budgets of the soon-to-be defunct Training and Enterprise Council (TEC), together with additional funding from the DfES, giving the scheme a two-year budget of £199 million. The department still sought a public/private partnership for the design and implementation of the scheme, and by January 2000 had one bidder – Capita. Capita had 300 contracts with government and would provide a call centre for enquiries about learning accounts; an administration centre for the registration of both learners and providers; process new accounts; maintain records of when learning started for those accounts; and provide the DfES with financial details.

Providers were free to market and promote the scheme to prospective participants, and learners could find details about the scheme from providers, libraries and UK online centres. The learner had to apply to Capita for registration, then pass their unique account number to the learning provider, and could book their chosen learning episode up to six months in advance. Providers would advise Capita which course had been chosen and claim payment from the learner's learning account once the course started. Capita were mandated to provide weekly and monthly payment schedules to the DfES, and these would be paid directly to the providers by the department. The subsidy/incentive available to the first million applicants from September 2000 was a contribution of £150 towards the cost of learning, whilst the applicant was expected to pay a contribution of at least £25 per course. Initially, the department required the provider to be registered with an ILA centre approved by Capita and to produce evidence of public liability insurance, but apart from those weak requirements there was no investigation into the quality of courses on offer, nor indeed was there an assessment of quality of delivery.

It is little wonder then that the number of providers mushroomed from 2,241 when the scheme was launched to 8,910 by the time it closed in November 2001, and that a large number of the providers had never before been involved with public-funded educational training. One of the attractions to this new breed of training entrepreneurs may have been the knowledge that confirming to Capita that individuals had commenced training would trigger payment to the provider. Unscrupulous or fraudulent operators like the Iqbals could, and did, assemble names, addresses and signatures for a payment of £5, confirm to Capita that training had begun and immediately trigger a payment of £150. To add to the providers' ability to defraud, the department allowed providers to complete bulk application forms on behalf of learners. The Iqbals were not the only entrepreneurs to face trial over the matter and the NAO recorded 20 providers, who received over £1.5 million for courses provided. The fact that payment was made when the course started rather than when the course was completed increased the motivation for fraudulent behaviour.

The scheme was introduced in a hurry by the department, under pressure from their political masters to have this scheme in situ during the run-up to the 2001 General Election. David Normington CB, Permanent Secretary to the DfES, suggested in evidence that the decision to instigate the scheme was influenced by the manifesto commitment to deliver one million accounts within the lifetime of the parliament. (Note 2) Edward Leigh, Chairman of the Committee, asked Mr Normington, "And you were up against a timetable?" Mr Normington replied, "We were up against the manifesto commitment". Mr Leigh then asked, "Which was influencing your decision?" and Mr Normington further replied, "There was a manifesto commitment to deliver a million accounts by 2002". The department did consult with KPMG and Oakleigh Consulting but chose to ignore certain pertinent recommendations suggested by both companies. (Note 3) They also ignored appropriate advice from Capita, who had drawn up a business plan which included the possibility of attracting larger numbers. Capita, who on one hand were regarded as a PPP partner in this relationship, was, however, treated as a contractor, and despite many requests were not allowed involvement with the Project Board.

The department were initially delighted by the result of the launch, with some 781,000 learners joining the scheme by the end of April 2001 and one million by the end of May 2001. Neither Capita nor the department were monitoring the courses on offer – it is not therefore surprising that courses on offer included Learning about Season Tickets; Summer Glastonbury; Chronic Cats; North Star Crystals and a National Powerboat Certificate. It quickly dawned, however, that exceeding their target of learners so quickly would also mean that they would exceed their fixed budget. Capita were providing the department with financial information and management data, but this was largely ignored. The PAC was particularly incensed because the department had recently been censored for irregularities in funding for Further Education Colleges (FECs). They wrote about FECs: "The newly announced package of improvements to governance and audit arrangements should go some way towards preventing further cases and re-establishing the credibility of the sector." (Note 4) The department replied, "The Department and the Funding Council remain committed to tackling the problems highlighted by the committee. The Funding Council will monitor the new measures closely to gauge their effectiveness and arrangements will be in place by January 2000". (Note 5) The recommendations were ignored and the department rushed to implement a scheme where they not only invited fraudsters to participate, but also reduced the barriers which might have deterred them.

Whilst the NAO confirms that the fraudulent and irregular payments were likely to total £97 million, no one will ever know the full extent about how many genuine learners participated in useful courses. An argument could be made to allocate the total spend of £273 million to the summary at the end of this chapter but the evidence quotes £97 million and, accordingly, that figure will be added.

SOURCES

PAC Report: *Individual Learning Accounts*, HC 544, 17 March 2003

NAO Report: *Individual Learning Accounts*, HC1235, 25 October 2002

NOTES

1   NAO Report, p3

2   PAC Report, ev 3

3   The department maintained the excellent record of Whitehall departments employing consultants, and then ignoring them.

4   PAC Report, ev13. The exchange between Mr Gerry Steinberg, MP for the City of Durham, and Mr Normington, is worth a read in its entirety.

5   PAC Report, p41

03 04 02

NHS (England) Summarised Accounts

The issue of clinical negligence continued to be a major issue for the NHS. A further £850 million was provided for in these summarised accounts, increasing the total provision to £5.25 billion. There were two main reasons for the increase: one was because of the revised assumptions applied by the actuaries in calculating estimates, after the transfer of the Existing Liabilities Scheme and the Clinical Negligence Scheme for trusts' claims to the authority; and there was a decrease in new claims from 4,115 to 2,068. The authority expected that all payments in respect of these claims would be settled within five years.

What did seem to unsettle the NAO was the lack of progress in establishing estimates for fraud in most areas of NHS expenditure. They noted in this report that estimates had been calculated for most areas within Family Health Services, but this only represented £11.99 billion of the total NHS spend. The report (Note 1) suggested that the NHS was losing £118 million through fraud on this expenditure, and also noted that "there is not sufficient data to extrapolate the measured fraud over the remaining expenditure, so there is a need to extend the measurement programme to cover remaining areas of Departmental expenditure". (Note 2) The NHS Counter Fraud Service, established in 1999 to identify and solve the problem of fraud, found that records kept by pharmacists and general practitioners did not allow them to meaningfully estimate fraud in those areas of expenditure. In effect, a budget of £41.2 billion was not examined, and the NHS had no estimate of the level of fraud or error.

Despite the lack of examination, the NAO found that the loss through fraud and error did not distort the truth and fairness of the accounts and therefore gave them an unqualified audit opinion. For the purposes of the summary a total of £968 million, i.e. the clinical negligence figure and the identified fraud figure, will be added to the summary at the end of this chapter.

The Elephant in the Room

SOURCE

NAO Report, *NHS (England) Summarised Accounts 2001/02*, HC, 21 March 2003

NOTES

1   NAO Report, p24, para 5.8
2   ibid, para 5.9

03 04 03

Ministry of Defence: Reducing Stocks

A Strategic Defence Review of 1998 concluded that there was scope for significant reductions in stock held by the Defence Logistics Organisation (DLO), due in no small part to the post-Cold War environment; Britain's changing role in the world; and experimentation in the methodology of waging wars. The Ministry of Defence (MoD) estimated that it held stocks valued at £19 billion, of which £11 billion was non-munitions and £8 billion munitions. (Note 1) Of these figures, some £2.7 billion was represented by consumable items, i.e. items readily available from multiple suppliers in industry. The Strategic Defence Review set a reduction target of 20% for the period to April 2001, and this NAO report examined whether the DLO had met that target.

The NAO had some significant obstacles to overcome in their assessment work. They quickly established that the baseline figures of £11 billion for new non-munitions stock had not been established robustly, and closer examination of the department's 1998 balance sheet showed that stock figures could have been over or understated by 20%. The examination could not establish whether items owned by the department, but held by contractors for repair, had been included in the accounts. They also identified that records had not been updated when stock was consumed, suggesting that the balance sheet for such items was overstated. Accurate prices were not available for many stock items, and in 75% of cases there was no documentation to support the prices recorded on the inventory.

There was inconsistency by the three services in the way stock was evaluated in calculating target achievement, i.e. the air force and navy

The Elephant in the Room

environments ring-fenced equipment values at April 1998, and correctly measured changes in stock value for those items, whilst the army included new stock purchased in the period April 1998 to April 2001. There were also different treatments of items identified for disposal. The navy excluded items awaiting disposal estimated at £300 million from its baseline valuation, even though they still owned the items, whilst the army and air force regarded items as part of their estate until disposals were complete. There was uncertainty regarding valuation policy. The department had identified that many stock items were overpriced at April 1998 and should be reduced, so the air force reported a reduction of £755 million, some £402 million of which is accounted for by a write-down in stock prices, i.e. there is no reduction in volume. There was no consistency in the valuations of stock – the army used professional valuations but also used contractors' prices; the air force used average prices; and the navy "used a variety of methods". (Note 2) Some items had little value, and the DLO had to undertake a great deal of work to establish appropriate prices, which resulted in an uplift of £100 million. The department's policy had been to apply inflation factors to book values, which further inflated values.

Individual eccentricities found during the audit included recognition that the air force had 1,775 long-distance fuelling tanks with a stock value of £41 million, of which four units were used a year, i.e. the air force held a stock sufficient to last 440 years. The navy held an inventory of items valued at £192 million, which were eventually identified as 159 special personal computers, each valued at £12,000. The army had a stock of 4,000 Radiac meters valued at £10 million – these were radiation detection items sourced during the Cold War. The air force had a stock of 170 obsolete hydraulic trolleys valued at £28 million. The navy had 53 obsolescent voice encoding machines valued at £1 million. The air force had 59 Tornado anti-missile containers with a value of £22 million, which could not be used because they had exceeded their specified flying hours. The hunt was on for the service which had a value in the stock system of £83 million, which when researched turned out to be 1,175 brass nuts.

The department held some 1.5 million items, most of which were classified as slow-moving stock, e.g. two thirds of the stock had a stock turnover of ten years. (Note 3) Close examination of the army stock showed that £58 million worth of stock was obsolete, and a further £79.5 million had no forecast demand. The air force figure was more dramatic, with a no-forecast demand figure at £5.4 billion, of which £1 billion was considered inactive and a further £1 billion where the stock turnover was 60 years. Comparison can be extended to the navy, as the latter did not hold demand data for 8% of its stock, but the NAO estimated that over £2 billion of its stock had a stock turnover of more than ten years.

The NAO qualified the department's claim that for the period April 1998 to April 2001 they had achieved reductions in stock of £2.8 billion, thus exceeding the target established by some £600 million. The department had considered that it would be sensible to monitor progress against gross book values rather than the net book value, (Note 4) so another analysis was prepared which showed that in net book values the department had reduced stock by £3.485 billion. The NAO felt however, that "because of weaknesses in the measurement regime we are not fully able to validate performance". (Note 5) The NAO suggested that 83% of the cost of holding stock related to the cost of capital tied up in the stocks, while the remaining 17% referred to buildings, staff, overheads, packaging and transport costs. (Note 6)

The final two paragraphs of the Committee of Public Accounts (PAC) report recorded that "it is not clear what volume of stock was disposed of during the exercise. The Department was not able to give a precise figure for the percentage of stock disposed of by volume, but estimated it to be around 50%. The impact on depot rationalisation was also unclear, although the Department estimated that it had reduced its required storage capacity by 18% as a result of the stock reduction exercise. Despite the evidence provided by the Department that it had indeed disposed of a large amount of stock, the NAO was unable to validate whether or not the stock reduction target had been achieved. Three main factors stood in the way of the validation. The original baseline was not reliable, as it could have been over or understated by 20% – the same as a stock reduction target itself. The basis of measurement was not consistent between the services, particularly in terms of including new stock and counting disposals. And the reporting of achievement was not accurate, due to the difficulty of comparing like with like over the three-year period". (Note 7)

It is difficult to identify what figure should be used to highlight the waste associated with the disposal of stock by the Ministry of Defence because of the variables, but the NAO identified £3.755 billion of stock write-down in the MoD Resource Accounts 2000/01 (see Section 01 02 07). Recognition of the £2.8 billion target achievement claimed by the MoD could be duplication.

SOURCES

PAC Report: *Ministry of Defence: Progress on Reducing Stocks*, HC 566, 20 June 2003

NAO Report: *Ministry of Defence: Progress in Reducing Stocks*, HC898, 20 June 2002

NOTES

1. The figures are taken from the department's Defence Review, CM 3999, July, and 1998, paragraph 185, and are based on the department's balance sheets at April 1998.
2. NAO Report, p10
3. Stock turn measures the time it will take for current stocks to be issued to users.
4. Gross Book Value translates to Net Book Value with the deduction of depreciation, stock provision, storage and other costs.
5. NAO Report, p8
6. ibid, p17
7. PAC Report, p12

03 04 04

Tackling Benefit Fraud

Of all the examples of waste exposed in this book, none causes more angst than that of waste in the benefit system. This is the first set of accounts from the Department of Social Security (DSS) to be examined, and sadly it confirms the reader's worst fears. The report examined four areas of fraud and error: Income Support; Jobseekers Allowance; Child Benefit Fraud; and Instrument of Payment fraud.

This Public Accounts Committee (PAC) reported on the matter in January 2000. Peter Mathison, Chief Executive of the Benefits Agency, gave oral evidence to the PAC about the performance of the agency. Despite commercial experience with Coca-Cola and Jacobs, Mr Mathison seemed to have assimilated the ethos of the Civil Service about materiality, by stating that he regarded the year in which the agency wasted over £3.1 billion through fraud, inefficiency and error, as a satisfactory performance for his department. Because of this level of fraud and error the accounts were again qualified, as indeed they had been for the previous ten years.

Income Support was available to people between 16 and 64 whose income and capital was below a certain level, and in general was only available to people not required to be available to work, i.e. single parents, disabled people and those who were sick. It was a means-tested benefit which depended on the honesty of the applicant, who needed to be working fewer than 16 hours a week and not have in excess of £8,000 in combined savings or capital. During this year the gross level of error was £555 million, and the department had achieved a level of accuracy in 81.7% of cases. The agency felt that inadequate computer systems were a key constraint in detecting fraud and also suggested that the complexity of the regulations was a barrier to achieving 100% accuracy. The department "saw little further scope for simplification given the necessity of targeting those in need. They pointed out that Income Support was designed for people who needed financial support, and was complex by nature because it was means tested and effectively tailored to the financial needs and circumstances of the individual". (Note 1) It would appear the agency's view was that it was more important to support those who needed financial support with some support rather than ensure that they receive the correct support.

Jobseeker's Allowance was introduced in October 1996 as a replacement for Unemployment Benefit and that part of Income Support applicable to employed people. It was intended as a means of support whilst an unemployed person looked for work, and Jobseeker's Allowance (contribution-based) was paid to those who had a sufficient National Insurance contributions history, whilst Jobseeker's Allowance (income-based) was paid to those without such a history. In the 1996/97 accounts there were estimated errors of £137 million, and the agency did admit that part of the problem was that they had recruited new people to deliver Jobseeker's Allowance even though the allowance itself was new. In addition, the agency had to deal with the impact of problems with the NIRS2 computer system.

The level of fraud, as opposed to error, with Income Support and Jobseeker's Allowance was £1.53 billion, and the PAC suggested that a key cause was the complexity of the regulations and stated that "this is poor administration, which creates confusion and uncertainty for those most in need, extra costs, and high levels of debt much of which is not collectable". (Note 2) The Department Public Service Agreement introduced a target to reduce benefit losses from fraud and error by 10% by March 2002, and by 30% by March 2007.

The agency admitted that over £184 million per year was lost through Child Benefit fraud and that the most common method of fraud involved claimants saying that their children over 16 were still in full-time education. The PAC pointed out their surprise that the agency depended on the statement of the claimant alone and were concerned that the agency "had not extended their checks to getting confirmation from schools and colleges that the individuals are indeed in full-time education. From such a simple procedure, the agency could save up to £53 million a year". (Note 3) The agency admitted that their only check was to ask the parent(s) whether the child was in full-time education, and they tried to justify this action as "they had to target their resources, and there were larger sums of fraud in other areas of the benefit system that took priority". (Note 4)

The agency agreed that the fraudulent encashment of order books and giro cheques cost the taxpayer £119 million – up from £102 million the previous year. Again the agency advised that "the majority of the Agency's fraud resource had been targeted at benefit fraud where the financial savings were greater". (Note 5) They also suggested that the anticipated roll-out of the benefit payment card had distracted their attention from this area of fraud and the PAC noted that "the Agency allowed their attention to be diverted from this problem while plans for introducing the benefits payment card were progressing. Now that this project has been cancelled, we look to the Agency to tackle instrument of payment fraud with vigour". (Note 6)

During the year the agency sought to recover overpayments of £530 million, had written-off £77 million and had 285,000 cases awaiting investigation. It would seem to the writer that the recovery of overpaid benefits, whether through error or fraud, would be difficult, and the agency did indeed identify that recovery of benefit overpayment was ninth in the pecking order behind, for example, debts to the Water and Electricity Boards.

A total of £3.131 billion has been added to the summary at the end of this chapter.

SOURCE

PAC Report: *Appropriation Accounts 1997/98 Class XII, Vote I (Central Government Administered Social Security Benefits and Other Payments)*, HC103, 13 January 2000

NOTES

1 PAC Report, p2/7
2 ibid, p3/4
3 ibid, p3/4
4 ibid, p4/7
5 ibid, p5/7
6 ibid, p3/4

03 04 05

Tackling Benefit Fraud: DSS Appropriation Accounts

The 1998/99 accounts were examined by the Public Accounts Committee (PAC) in January 2000 and the committee's frustration at the lack of progress was reflected in the report. The accounts were again qualified, for the 11th year in a row, because the level of benefit fraud continued to give cause for concern, principally on Income Support and Jobseeker's Allowance, but also because of the level of payment fraud and the fraudulent encashment of instruments of payment.

Some background to Income Support was given in Section 03 04 04. The report noted that the National Insurance Recording System, NIRS2, gave cause for concern and it became impossible to finalise benefit payments, leading to distribution on an interim or emergency basis, which inevitably led to underpayments and overpayments as the level of entitlement could not been confirmed. (Note 1) Underpayments of benefits were always made good in favour of the claimant or through other benefit streams, and the agency remained legally entitled to recover overpayments. The level of official error during the year was £637 million. (Note 2)

Jobseeker's Allowance was also dealt with in Section 03 04 04. The estimated figure for error was £245 million, which was a substantial increase on the previous year. Peter Mathison, the former Chief Executive of the Benefits Agency, gave evidence that the main contributing factor for the increased number had been the political initiatives known as the New Deal, as well as various other Welfare to Work initiatives. Experienced staff had been transferred onto these projects, leaving young and inexperienced staff to deal with the administration of Jobseeker's Allowance, resulting in an increase in official error. One of the main reasons why error occurred is that the inexperienced staff did not insist on the jobseeker producing his/her signed jobseeker's agreement.

The PAC had already identified the complexity of the rules and regulations as a main cause of error, and had the opportunity of asking Mr Mathison about whether any progress had been made to simplify the system. He acknowledged the complexity in the system and "noted that there were 33 volumes of guidance on Income Support and 45 volumes on Jobseeker's Allowance". (Note 3) He, however, could not give comfort to the committee that the rules would be simplified, and having already suggested that the agency might be able to reduce the level of 10% in monetary value, the NAO acknowledged that "in his view it would be difficult to get the monetary level to below 2.5%". (Note 4) The problems of the department were not helped by the continuing difficulties with the technology programme: the delays to NIRS2; cancellation of the Benefit Payment Card; and the cancellation of the Debt Accounting and Management Project.

The level of benefit fraud, as opposed to error, in the Income Support and Jobseeker's Allowance programmes was £1.53 billion. The department ended their existing anti-fraud programme in March 1999 and replaced it with the Programme Protection Strategy (PPS), where the emphasis changed from chasing existing fraud, to preventing fraud entering the system. The PPS was given a target of reducing fraud and error by 30% by March 2007.

Losses due to the fraudulent encashment of instruments of payment amounted to £103 million. The cancellation of the Benefit Payment Card dictated that the department sought alternative means of protecting the taxpayer in the transitional period before the introduction of a fool-proof system, and it was suggested that barcode scanners might bridge the gap.

The PAC report estimated that losses from fraud in Child Benefit totalled £184 million for the period, and whilst previously the department had suggested that the main reason for such a high fraud figure was the parents' insistence that their children were in full-time education, the NAO conceded that the greatest difficulty arose from tracking people moving between separated parents.

The agency wrote-off £25.8 million worth of overpayments, which they felt could not be collected; £89.6 million in respect of an easement package (Note 5) in respect of Income Support; and a further £9.6 million in respect of benefits charged to the National Insurance Fund account.

The total level of fraud and error in the benefit system was £2.824 billion, which will be added to the summary at the end of this chapter.

SOURCES

PAC Report: *Appropriation Accounts 1998/99 (Class XII, Vote 1): Central Government Administered Social Security Benefits and other Payments*, HC521, 11 August 2000

NAO Report: *Appropriation Accounts 1998/99 (Class XII, Vote 1): Central Government Administered Social Security Benefits and other Payments*, HC11, 21 January 2000

NOTES

1 NAO Report, R18
2 ibid, R9
3 PAC Report, p2/7
4 ibid
5 NAO Report, R24

03 04 06

Tackling Benefit Fraud: DSS Appropriation Accounts

The accounts were again qualified and did not offer figures for instrument of payment or Child Benefit, nor did it detail write-offs for non-collection of overpayments.

They confirmed that the Government Statistical Service was now calculating the level of fraud and error, and was evaluating the use of a common sample using Area Benefit Reviews provided by the Benefits Agency, and data supplied by Quality Support Teams. The objective was to bring both measurement systems onto a common footing and to provide more accurate statistics. The NAO had suggested to the department that high suspicion cases, where investigations fell short of obtaining absolute proof to establish that fraud, should be examined in more detail before the overall estimates of fraud were finalised, giving the final figure more credibility. The department made the change in procedure.

As mentioned earlier, claimants for Income Support had to be working fewer than 16 hours a week, but the other requirement that combined savings or capital should be below £8,000 was changed – the new figure was £16,000. The level of fraud and error in Income Support was £890 million for 1999/2000 and again the NAO stressed the complexity of the benefit: "In 1999/2000, as in previous years, the Agency had to deal with millions of changes in circumstances, some of which were not reported by the claimant when they should have been. All of this contributes greatly to the level of error, including customer error, present within Income Support expenditure." (Note 1)

Job Seeker's Allowance was administered jointly by the Benefits Agency and the Employment Service. The Benefits Agency was responsible for those aspects of the claim relating to assessment and payment, whilst the Employment Service were responsible, through their network of Jobcentres, for the labour market aspects of the claim, including actively seeking and identifying availability for work conditions. The level of fraud and error detailed in the report was £420 million, and again the report mentioned the complexity of regulations governing awards, combined with the requirement for claimants to demonstrate that they are actively available for seeking work.

The total added to the summary at the end of this chapter for these two benefits is £1.31 billion.

SOURCE

NAO Report: *Department of Social Security Appropriation Accounts 1999/2000 Volume 12: Class XII*, HC25-XII, 16 February 2001

NOTE

1   NAO Report, R3

03 04 07

Tackling Benefit Fraud: DSS Resource Accounts

The department was renamed the Department for Works and Pensions (DWP) in June 2001. The accounts were again qualified: "I have qualified my opinion because of significant levels of estimated fraud and error in benefit awards, for which I have qualified the Department's appropriation account for the past 12 years, and significantly uncertainties over certain debtors and creditors balances in the balance sheet." (Note 1)

The uncertainty related to a significant amount of £1.7 billion which was not accounted for correctly. The NAO commented, "As a result of weaknesses in the Department's audit trails mainly arising from deficiencies in accounting systems, there were serious limitations in the evidence available to support my audit of certain significant debtor and creditor balances. There is, therefore, significant uncertainty over the accuracy, existence and completeness of these amounts, which total about £1.7 billion". (Note 2) The NAO did not offer a view of how the deficiency was treated in the accounts nor did it suggest that the move from appropriation accounts to resource accounts was in any way significant.

Inadequate information technology continued to be a barrier to improving performance, and the DWP had invested in a new system which would amalgamate the existing 20 separate IT systems – but not until 2006, meaning that the department would continue to rely heavily on clerical intervention. The PAC was not optimistic about the introduction of the new system: "The scale of the Department's legacy systems and track record of IT failure, and the recent deferment of a system for the Child Support Agency does not auger well." (Note 3) The report makes a case for the improvement of staff quality by offering higher salaries, but the evidence of a wide variance in performance between the 118 districts would suggest that locality and management had a large part to play in the performance of each office. The PAC took the approach that the experience of staff and the organisation of their workload would lead to improved performance and noticed that, even in difficult areas like London and other major cities, some local offices had secured performance improvements in recent years.

The PAC was caustic about the DWP's inability to offer estimates in all areas except housing: "Until they have robust estimates for all benefits, it is difficult to measure their performance in reducing the substantial drain on public funds." (Note 4) However, the Office for National Statistics now provided information and recorded that for this year the level of fraud and error in Income Support was £900 million and in Jobseeker's Allowance was £300 million.

The NAO recorded that £92 million worth of fraud and error was overpaid in respect of Incapacity Benefit and that £77 million was lost across all benefits as a result of the fraudulent encashment of order books and giro cheques. (Note 5) They also noted that the department had created a provision of £172 million in the accounts in respect of overpayments to customers: the debtor balance recorded in the general ledger did not agree with the combined balances from each of the field recovery systems leading to the provision. (Note 6) The NAO also had concern about the accuracy of the figures for overpayment debt and the department estimated that £230 million would have to be provided for. (Note 7)

The total added to the summary at the end of this chapter is £3.471 billion.

SOURCES

PAC Report: *Fraud and Error in Income Support*, HC 595, 11 September 2002

NAO Report: *Department of Social Security: Resource Account 2000/01*, 31 January 2002

National Statistics/Department for Work and Pensions 2002

NOTES

1 NAO Report, p3
2 ibid, p5
3 PAC Report, p2/4
4 ibid, p5
5 NAO Report, p4

6 ibid, p14

7 ibid, p15

03 04 08

Tackling Benefit Fraud

The NAO and the PAC reported on this matter during 2003. They recognised improvements over the previous years and recognised that the management information they received was more meaningful. The impression given is that the department recognised the seriousness of the situation and were taking steps to minimise the damage.

Definitions for fraud and error were offered. Fraud included all cases where the following three conditions applied: the basic conditions for receipt of benefit for the rate of benefit in payment had not been met; the claimant could reasonably be expected to be aware of the effect on entitlement; and benefit reduces as a result of the review. Customer error occurred when the information a customer provided was inaccurate or incomplete, or they failed to report a change in circumstance but without fraudulent attempt. Official error occurred when the benefit had been paid incorrectly due to inaction, delay or a mistaken assessment by the DWP, the Local Authority or HMRC.

The department was able to identify that one in 11 claims was fraudulent for Income Support with the main area of disingenuousness being failure to disclose that a 'lone' parent was living with a partner, and/or failing to disclose earnings from work, and/or failure to disclose other sources of income – the figure for pensioners was one in 31. The department carried out interventions in over 1 million new claims or in claims which they felt showed a high risk of fraud and/or error. The interventions resulted in one in six claims been altered – usually downwards. The department also encouraged tipoffs, reviewed cases and did computer checks in the period under review and accepted 390,000 cases for investigation, of which 161,000 resulted in an adjustment to payment.

The department was now more active in imposing sanctions. Fraudsters obtaining less than £400 were given a caution and asked to repay the amount. For amounts between £400 and £1,500 the fraudster would be asked to repay the amount plus a penalty of 30%, whilst those defrauding the department of over £1,500 faced prosecution. Some 12,340 cases were recommended for prosecution and the conviction rate was 98%, with 654 fraudsters imprisoned in 2001/02. They also invested in an extra 500 staff to support their anti-fraud activity, which delighted the PAC: "The Department spent about £100 million a year directly for investigation and employed more than 5,100 investigators and support staff." (Note 1) The amount overpaid dropped to £530 million. (Note 2)

Jobseeker's Allowance also reduced to £170 million. (Note 3) This discipline benefited from the anti-fraud activity already mentioned above, and extra training, which helped the 50,000 staff at Jobcentre Plus to identify potential fraudsters, was productive. Official and claimant error cost the taxpayer £350 million.

The Office for National Statistics also identified a further £800 million was lost through fraud in other benefits, i.e. Incapacity Benefit, Disability Living Allowance, Retirement Pension and Child Benefit. The schedule itemising this loss (Note 4) did not offer a breakdown of individual costs. The same schedule also identified that instrument of payment fraud for this period was £80 million. (Note 5)

The total which will be added to the summary at the end of this chapter is £1.93 billion.

SOURCES

PAC Report: *Tackling Benefit Fraud*, HC488, 4 July 2003

NAO Report: *Tackling Benefit Fraud*, HC393, 13 February 2003

National Statistics/Department for Work and Pensions 2003

NOTES

1. NAO Report, p20
2. ibid, p13
3. ibid
4. ibid
5. ibid

03 04 09

Ministry of Defence: Devonport Submarine Facilities

The Public Accounts Committee (PAC) found that the Ministry of Defence took a 'hands off' approach to the management of this project, despite having reservations about the prime contractor during the procurement procedure. They required the contractor to fulfil three pre-contract award evaluations that should have highlighted the need for subsequent close monitoring which did not happen. This decision was to cost the taxpayer dearly.

The saga has its genesis in 1997 with the sale of the Royal Dockyards at Rosyth and Devonport – the latter to Devonport Management Ltd (DML). A decision had been made by the MoD to concentrate all submarine refit work at Devonport, where DML had provided refit repair work to the dockyards without competition since 1987 using a Government Owned Contractor Operator (GOCO) arrangement.

In 1993 the MoD decided that the sale of Devonport would be of benefit and invited tenders – only one tender was received from the incumbent, DML. At the same time invitations were issued to upgrade the dockyard facilities to cope with nuclear submarines, a project identified as D154. The negotiations to purchase the Devonport facility and to upgrade the facility continued with DML, who were the only company involved. To facilitate the sale, which was valued at £97 million in March 1996, a sales price was agreed of £40.25 million, but the MoD allowed DML to take on to the balance sheet an evaluation of £73.25 million for the assets, which boosted DML's asset base. The pension fund surplus of £63 million was also passed to DML. The NAO noted that the sale of Devonport and the negotiation about D154 were inextricably linked. An unsolicited bid from a competitor was rejected. In March 1997, the contract for D154 was awarded to DML at an estimated cost of £236 million.

In 1997, the estimate rose to £315 million, and after recognising that VAT and DML's fees had been ignored, the figure was again revised upwards to £417 million. The agreement with DML was structured on the basis of a reducing fee, i.e. the fee would decrease if DML's costs exceeded their own estimates of the most likely outcome, and reduce to nothing should the maximum contract cost £410 million or above. It is against this background that we examine the construction of the new submarine facilities at Devonport.

The NAO estimated that the likely outcome for the construction would be £933 million, (Note 1) and the report identified four main reasons why the costs should be at such a high level: the costs of the regulatory and other bodies had been underestimated; there were delays in starting the project; there were problems with subcontractors; and there was a wilful lack of supervision by the MoD.

There were three organisations involved with the inspection and installation of the nuclear facilities: the Nuclear Installation Inspectorate; the department's Naval Nuclear Regulatory Panel; and a firm of independent nuclear consultants employed by the MoD at a cost of £14 million. It had been established that the Inspectorate would be the regulator. An argument was submitted by DML, suggesting that this was one of the reasons for the extra costs associated with the delay, but the NAO report pointed out that there was never doubt about the status of the Nuclear Installations Inspectorate. The latter declined the opportunity of working with the MoD's project sponsor and worked mainly with DML until 1999 when the Inspectorate required that the MoD and the Naval Nuclear Regulatory Panel should become more closely involved. The NAO report commented that "DML had assumed that the inspectorate would not be closely involved in the detailed regulation of the facility", (Note 2) which seems naive when DML had no previous experience of such a major project; when the MoD were extremely hesitant about rewarding DML the contract in the first place; and when the MoD had suggested that the department had learned from the Trident experience and was also aware of the more stringently applied nuclear safety standards as a result of the delays in the Rosyth dock facilities. The MoD had two histories to learn from, but seemingly chose not to pass their knowledge to DML.

DML started work in March 1998 and later that year submitted the set of safety cases to the Installation Inspectorate, which were rejected as inadequate, leading to the withholding of approval for the start of the construction of the Vanguard facilities. (Note 3) However, DML had already started construction work but had to undertake expensive reworking, sometimes involving the design and construction of additional requirements. DML were eager to meet the 2002 deadline, not least because the refitting of the Vanguard would mean guaranteed refitting turnover of £200 million-£250 million. The PAC report said, "The design of the facilities was evolving at the same time as they were being constructed and one lesson is that it would have been better to complete the design and the safer the case up front before committing to construction". (Note 4) DML were under commercial pressure to finish the construction phase of the docks but the Nuclear Regulatory body had a duty to meet its obligations and the two ambitions were incompatible.

As well as the lack of clarity about the requirements of the Nuclear Inspectorate, the MoD compounded the situation by being tardy in providing data for DML's design work and preparation of safety cases. This information dealt with the design of the nuclear reactor decontamination system and the MoD accepted that the late supply of the data was responsible for 23 weeks of delay in completing the work. Of particular significance was the completion of the Vanguard dock to accommodate the refit of *HMS Vanguard* in 2002. The decontamination data was supplied by Rolls-Royce against a specification provided by the MoD.

Problems were also experienced with subcontractors. The MoD had accepted that DML was the prime contractor and that they were working on a fixed fee basis, so the lower the cost the more profit they retained. This did not seem to be reflected in their negotiations with their subcontractors. "Significant extra costs arose because of poor scheduling of installation activities. Also, the changes to design drawings caused much reworking and poor control and incorrect component specifications resulted in it taking longer than planned to flush out and clean the building's pipework systems." (Note 5) All in all the MoD estimated that poor performance by DML and its subcontractors increased the cost by between £50 and £65 million.

The final reason for the delays and subsequent massive overrun in cost was a lack of supervision by the MoD over the entire project. The MoD had identified that DML were not capable, even before the contract was placed, and were also aware of the stringent requirements of the Nuclear Inspectorate from their previous experiences at Rosyth. They ignored and/or discounted an opportunist bid by the owners of Rosyth on the basis that having two separate docks implied competition, but by doing so left themselves without a negotiating position with DML.

The MoD did not place the contract to build the facilities until 1997, even though the decision to proceed had been taken in 1993, creating a timescale for completion that was extremely tight and removing any opportunity for time to evaluate and research other options when change of procedure was suggested. The MoD had no access to DML's cost forecasts – they did have access to DML's spent data – but only became aware of the gigantic cost increases when DML began to submit a series of claims in 1999. A quick survey revealed that by December 2000 DML had spent a total of £730 million against a contract of £410 million. Not surprisingly, the PAC report stated that "the Department is now taking a more hands on approach to the project management and exercising close scrutiny". (Note 6)

The NAO avoided specific criticism of the MoD's management of this project, but the PAC were more critical. The increase over the original estimate of £236 million was £697 million and this sum will be added to the summary at the end of this chapter.

SOURCES

PAC Report: *Ministry of Defence: The Construction of Nuclear Submarine Facilities at Devonport*, HC 636, 10 September 2003

NAO Report: *The Construction of Nuclear Submarines Facilities at Devonport*, HC 90, 6 December 2002

NOTES

1 NAO Report, p1
2 ibid, p4
3 Due for completion by 2002.
4 PAC Report, p6
5 NAO Report, p3
6 PAC Report, p9

03 04 10

Ministry of Defence: Resource Accounts

This was the fourth set of resource accounts produced by the Ministry of Defence (MoD). The National Audit Office (NAO) again qualified the accounts but recognised that the MoD had made strenuous efforts to secure improvement, but also felt that the accounts were still not robust enough to support as a true and fair opinion.

Five main areas were examined: the downwards adjustment of £1.128 billion of Royal Air Force (RAF) consumable stock and capital spares; the £118 million written-off because of the cancelled Defence Stores Management Solution; the total losses and special payments associated with the Constructive Loss (Note 1); the cancellation of the Joint Tactical Information System (JTIDS) for the Sea Harrier; and write-off of the JP233 anti-personnel landmine.

In the previous year the NAO noted that the MoD had problems with its inventory system which had not been designed to provide stock accounting data for resource type accounting. The NAO noted that the air force continued to generate data that could not be totally supported. Each month the system compared opening and closing values with the movements generated by the stock system, and whilst this reflected the stock inventory there was no supporting audit trail. The NAO referred to the procedure as an auto-balance procedure and in the 12 months under review the procedure generated a net credit to the operating cost statement of some £1.128 billion. The Defence Logistics Organisation (DLO) had examined some of the larger transactions and identified three main contributors to the problem: firstly, spurious transactions were generated when both the definition of quantity and the unit price changed simultaneously; the system recorded items on repair as negative stockholding; and when the items on repair were returned there were regarded as new items. The NAO felt that the auto-balance procedure needed investigation.

A loss of £118 million was crystallised when the MoD decided to suspend the Defence Stores Management Solution. Originally intended to provide a common inventory system across the DLO, it started life using existing software, Indus Passport, but soon found that essential changes were necessary to meet DLO requirements. A budget of £133.6 million was approved in June 2000 for the development and production of a new system, but by November 2001 serious doubts were emerging at executive board level about the technical viability of a single all-encompassing application. Alternative methods of funding were considered to keep the project alive but "in the event, it concluded that the Defence Stores Management

The Elephant in the Room

Solution did not command sufficient priority pending the outcome of the 2002 spending review". (Note 2) The project was suspended and contracts with suppliers were terminated and settled. Total expenditure had been £130.5 million, but the MoD retained hardware worth £12.2 million, creating a write-off figure of £118.3 million.

The reporting of constructive loss was required under resource accounting requirements. The MoD had the right to write-off expenditure as a loss or a special payment after appraisal of all the facts, but was also required to report the matter to parliament at the earliest opportunity. In this period the MoD reported losses of £131 million and special written-off payments of £129 million. This report also identified a further £1.015 billion of constructive loss incurred in previous years but not previously reported. (Note 3)

The Royal Air Force used a secure electronic countermeasure resistant high-capacity tactical datalink system called the Joint Tactical Information Distribution System (JTIDS), as did other NATO air forces. A project was established to upgrade the Sea Harriers' radar and to integrate the JTIDS terminals with existing avionic systems. The department decided in February 2002 to withdraw the Sea Harrier from service by early 2006 and in light of this the department terminated the development and production contracts for JTIDS, incurring a loss of £77.7 million in doing so. (Note 4)

In May 1997 the UK government announced a complete ban on the use of anti-personnel mines. This decision involved the write-off of stocks of JP233 landmines at the cost of £985 million, which included decommissioning. (Note 5)

The total added to the summary at the end of this chapter will be £3.583 billion.

SOURCE

NAO Report: *Ministry of Defence: Departmental Resource Accounts*, 30 October 2003

NOTES

1 NAO Report: "HM Treasury Government Accounting defines a constructive loss as one where, for example, services are correctly ordered, delivered or provided, and are paid for as being in conformity

with the order but which owing to a change of policy or similar reason prove not to be needed or to be less useful than when the order was placed." p13

2   NAO Report, p13
3   ibid, p13
4   ibid, p12
5   ibid, p12/13

03 04 11

The Libra Project

"The Libra Project is one of the worst IT projects I have ever seen. It may also be the shabbiest PFI project ever." (Note 1) Edward Leigh, Chairman of the Public Accounts Committee said that the Lord Chancellor's Department, despite throwing money at the problem, did not yet have a working national system, and that Fujitsu had performed badly, but had 'run rings' around department officials

An earlier NAO report identified that IT systems used by magistrates' courts were inadequate and that many of the 42 local magistrates' courts were using different systems and had entirely different working practices. Information could not be shared within the courts, and electronic transfers to other enforcement agencies such as the Police or Probation Service was, at best, piecemeal.

The Lord Chancellor's Department therefore decided to improve and support the efficiency of existing systems, rather than redesign business processes in parallel with the development of a new IT system, notwithstanding that "the Department recognises that the design of a business process model should normally come before seeking an IT solution". (Note 2) The department told the NAO that the magistrates' courts committee's priority was to have their ageing IT systems replaced and that "whilst they recognised the need and the advantages of a national standard IT system, they insisted that their local management independence should be maintained". (Note 3)

The Home Office appointed Price Waterhouse to develop a national system. This contract was terminated in August 1992 when the responsibility for the courts passed to the Lord Chancellor's office. It was cancelled on the grounds that the work done was substandard and had not been delivered as expected by the contract. The Home Office had paid £5 million for this work which the department sought to retrieve in total, without success. They did retrieve £1.4 million, but Price Waterhouse held on to £3.6 million.

In 1994 the department had another stab at solving the problem and this time tried to develop a system called the Magistrates' Courts Standard System (MASS) using several key suppliers, (Note 4) and hoped that this would lead to a robust product that would meet the needs of individual committees. The policy was that the committees would have to use the dedicated MASS software, but could choose from any one of three hardware suppliers. Two years later the software became available, but had not been tested and an independent review showed the department's strategy was so flawed that the existing contract was cancelled at a cost of £6.8 million. However, simultaneously, the department were negotiating a PFI agreement with one of the MASS suppliers, ICL, and in October 1996 initiated a procurement process with that company. During the procurement negotiation procedures the department spent £893,700 on legal, financial and technical consultants to provide advice, which no doubt later could be used to confirm the efficacy of any decisions taken. The NAO report struggled to justify why only one contact was approached during the procurement process and commented without irony, "The Department choose... to approach a number of IT providers informally to assess potential interest". (Note 5) One could interpret this as a use of the old boys' network, because ICL were not only the chosen supplier for the MASS scheme but also the chosen supplier for the disastrous Benefit Card Project. (Note 6)

ICL's initial bid was for £146 million and covered an 11-year period. ICL would develop the MASS software, having already evaluated the product pre-contract and found it satisfactory. However, three months after the contract was signed, ICL changed its mind and decided that the MASS software would not work. It advised the department that its bid had increased by £38 million to allow it to proceed with the development of a new software product. Both the NAO and the PAC were astonished to learn that, despite this being one of the first PFI projects, the department were not given a copy of the ICL financial model to justify the original bid nor indeed, the subsequent alteration. Treasury advice at that time suggested that the financial model did not need to be examined "if the bidder was funding the project from internal sources". (Note 7) A UNISON report about the project noted that "no quantitative baseline data is available for risk and risk premiums because the private company did not release their financial model to the Department or the NAO", (Note 8) and "consultants were employed to compare the cost of the revised contract and an estimate of what the contract 'should cost' but their calculations excluded 'interest, risk and profit' and these data are not published". (Note 9) The department accepted the new contract offered by ICL and justified the increase of £38 million as introducing incentive payments and agreeing higher caseload charges which then would lead to earlier delivery. The details do not stand up to scrutiny, with the incentive payments, for example, being paid if ICL started on time and finished on time. The PAC summary commented that "where contractors are not delivering what is required of them, Departments should be prepared to terminate contracts". (Note 10)

Running parallel with these negotiations in the late part of 1998, ICL were seeking a solution to their problems with the Benefit Card Project (see 01 02 06). The DSS had halted the development of the card, but ICL were allowed to establish new contracts with the Post Office and with the Lord Chancellor's Department. The PAC felt that the two deals were a covert form of bailout for the private sector: "The impression remains of an essentially political deal to ensure that ICL has a substantial contract with the PO at prices which seem to have been largely determined in advance of the contractual negotiation, as a means, however inadequate, of making up some of the £180 million written off by ICL's 1998/1999 accounts." (Note 11) It would be hard to believe that the awarding of the MASS contract and its subsequent immediate revision was unconnected with the problems experienced by ICL with the Post Office project.

The PAC theory placed ICL in a strong position, as the realisation that PFI did not mean transfer of risk to the private sector and that the taxpayer was still available as a source of funding for any contract beginning to sour. The Libra contract, as it is now known, did begin to sour and ICL came to the negotiating table in October 1999 when they discovered that their cash flow forecast showed a deficit of £39 million over the life of the contract. The department did not invoke their right to cancel the contract but increased the contract value. This time the department had access to ICL's financial model, but that did not stop ICL coming back to the negotiating table, showing that they would possibly incur a £200 million loss if the project was continued.

This resulted in another new contract worth £390 million for ICL and new contractor STL. The PAC noted that some senior people at ICL had lost their jobs as a result of this fiasco but no one within the department seemed to suffer: "Some people have been transferred elsewhere but no one has lost their job as a result of the work they had been doing on the project in contrast to the approach taken by ICL." (Note 12) The PAC were also highly critical of the performance of the Accounting Officer, Sir Hayden Phillips, who "told us that he had been less forthcoming than he might have been at the Committees hearing on June 24, 2002, as some of the matters under consideration were commercially confidential... where a Department feels as it cannot put evidence in the public domain on the grounds of commercial confidentiality, it should make the position clear and that the committee can consider whether to take evidence in secret". (Note 13)

The new owners of ICL, Fujitsu, twice threatened to withdraw unless it was paid more money. It realised the department had no contingency plan to bring into operation if the contract had been cancelled and also noted that the department had failed to carry out any credible independent check about whether the initial bid was realistic. A total of £257 million, representing the differential between the initial bid and the cost to date, plus the original losses associated with instigation of this concept, is added to the summary at the end of this chapter.

SOURCES

PAC Report: *New IT Systems for Magistrates' Courts: The Libra Project*, HC434, 11 November 2003

NAO Report: *New IT Systems for Magistrates' Courts: The Libra Project*, HC32, 29 January 2003

Pollock, Allyson and Price, David: *Public Risk for Private Gain? Case Study 1: New IT Systems for Magistrates' Courts: The Libra Project.* UNISON

Private Eye, Edition 1032, July 2001

NOTES

1 Collins, Tony, *Computer Weekly*, undated

2 NAO Report, p2

3 ibid, p10

4 The nominated suppliers were Admiral for systems and training development, F1 for software support and ICL, Digital and Bull for hardware.

5 NAO Report, p13

6 See Section 01 02 06.

7 PAC Report, p2 of 4

8 UNISON, p2

9 ibid

10 PAC Report, p2 of 3

11 ibid

12 ibid, p2/1

13 ibid, p2/2

03 04 12

Ministry of Defence: The Apache Helicopter

When the Ministry of Defence (MoD) entered into a PFI agreement (Note 1) with Westland and Boeing to provide training for their new Apache helicopters, it would have seemed sensible to synchronise the start of that contract with the arrival of the aircraft. However, this did not happen and a large number of helicopters were held in reserve for four years at an estimated cost of £6 million.

The MoD procured 67 Apache attack helicopters from Westland Helicopter Ltd for a total of £3 billion. In addition, they negotiated a PFI contract with Aviation Trading International Ltd (ATIL), a joint venture between Boeing and Westland, to provide training for pilots, ground crew and maintenance staff. Deliveries of the aircraft began in 2001 and it was anticipated that the full programme of both deliveries and training would be completed by 2007. Any project this size, even with a generous contingency allowance, would attract problems leading to additional cost, and the Apache helicopter programme was no exception.

One of the initial problems was that the Full Mission Simulator (FMS) to be supplied by ATIL was delayed and, accordingly, about 40 aircraft delivered on schedule had to be mothballed in Shropshire between July 2002 and January 2006. A range of capital works at Dishforth in Yorkshire and Wattisham in Suffolk was approved. Described as hangars for storage and improved security requirements, the budgeted cost was exceeded by £8.1 million. (Note 2)

£34 million was wasted due to the delayed installation of the FMS. The MoD had paid ATIL for maintenance courses which could not run in the period from August 2000 to March 2002, but ATIL still rejected a claim from the MoD for a refund of some £8 million of these costs. The other £26 million of maintenance training was not pursued "because the delays in pilot training meant that the helicopters were not being flown as regularly as expected and did not need as much maintenance". (Note 3) Indeed, the aircraft were nicely cocooned in the air-conditioned hangars in Shrewsbury.

It was always assumed that the Apache would support maritime operations – a capability defined as the Littoral Manoeuvre, i.e. sea-to-land operations. However, the MoD did not identify to Westland, or itself, the navy's full requirements, so an additional £30 million to provide eight suitably configured aircraft for Littoral Manoeuvre had not been included in the original contract. (Note 4) The cost of appropriate training for amphibious operations was not disclosed.

The Apache's predecessor, the Lynx, operated with a Tube-launched, Optically-tracked, Wire-guided (TOW) missile system and these TOW missiles needed life extension to 2005 to allow 24 Lynx helicopters to continue operation until that time. Solving the FMS problem became critical, as the TOW missile life could not be extended beyond 2005. A cost of £13.9 million was approved to modify the TOW missiles. (Note 5) The delay of the FMS also meant that whilst most of the pilot training was deferred, a degree of training did take place in America at a cost of £3.5 million, which was outlined in a note provided to the PAC by the MoD. (Note 6)

The delay in the delivery of the FMS also impacted on a unique procurement arrangement with Westland. Rather than the traditional method of procuring spares to match the delivery of the helicopters, the MoD decided to enter into a £120 million contract to provide core spares for the first 30 months following delivery of the aircraft, with Westland required to provide the spares within 48 hours of request. The price was based on the assumption that the aircraft would fly 15,500 hours in the 30-month period, but in the event it flew approximately 5,000 hours, so the need for spares was significantly reduced. Jon Trickett, MP for Wakefield, identified the ludicrous nature of the contract with Westland. On the one hand Westland had a contract worth £120 million with the MoD to provide spares; on the other hand it was a partner in ATIL who had caused the delay by their inability to provide the FMS on schedule. Mr Trickett's questioning of Sir Kevin Tebbit KCB, CMG, Permanent Secretary at the MoD (Note 7) flustered that civil servant to such a degree that Sir Kevin commented, "If I may say so, you're being an unreasonably hostile questioner". (Note 8) It is difficult to draw a conclusion about how much of the £120 million had been lost or wasted, but Sir Kevin does acknowledge that only one third of the projected flying hours were actually used, leading to the conclusion that two thirds of the £120 million contract had been lost or wasted – £80 million.

The forecast cost for the aircraft was £71 million above budget due to a range of factors, including higher modification costs and the increased costs of trials and these costs have been noted in Section 02 03 16. A total of £166 million has been added to the summary at the end of this chapter.

SOURCES

PAC Report: *Ministry of Defence: Building an Air Manoeuvre Capability: The Introduction of the Apache Helicopter*, HC533, 18 November 2003

NAO Report: *Ministry of Defence: Building an Air Manoeuvre Capability: The Introduction of the Apache Helicopter*

NOTES

1 For more detail about the Private Finance Initiative (PFI) see Introduction.

2 NAO Report, p22

3 PAC Report, p6

4 NAO Report, p4

5 PAC Report: Supplementary memorandum submitted by the MoD, item 3, q171, para 3

6 ibid

7   PAC Report, qs35-66

8   PAC Report, q55

03 04 13

NATS

Some might say that the sale of the National Air Traffic Services (NATS) was engineered to relieve a cash flow issue in the Department of Transport. In return for £50 million, a consortium of airlines became the owners of 50% of a national asset worth £758 million, but the asset gained debt of £733 million.

NATS had a monopoly to provide air traffic control facilities for aircraft flying over the United Kingdom and, with its Irish equivalent, the north-east Atlantic. In 1997, when a new Labour government assumed power, they decided to accept the previous expenditure totals, decided by a Conservative government, for the Department of Transport, (Note 1) and those totals included an assumption of a £500 million capital receipt from the sale of NATS. It was on this premise that the already agreed sale of NATS was actioned. A further attraction for the department, and presumably the Treasury, was that the movement of NATS out of the department would offer NATS scope to raise capital for development. NATS had estimated in 1997 that it needed £100 million per year of capital investment for each of the following ten years to allow for increased capacity. The department appointed their lead advisers, Credit Suisse First Boston (CSFB) in summer 1998, initially on a monthly fee of £220,000 for an 18-month period. (Note 2) The department accepted CSFB's position that it was not their practice to provide records to enable payment on the basis of actual time spent. CSFB were appointed even though their fees were 16% higher than their nearest competitor, but the department did have a stand-down clause which allowed them to retain CSFB at nil payment for up to a total of six months if there was little or no work for them to do. CSFB did not 'stand down' for 33 consecutive months. The contract cost the department £7.326 million instead of £3.996 million.

In the March to May period of 2000, CSFB marketed the opportunity to purchase NATS to a range of investors, and initially identified nine potential investors, of whom three submitted formal offers, i.e. The Airline Group,

Nimbus and Novares. The Airline Group was a consortium of airlines that utilised NATS and the shareholders were IAG (the holding company for British Airways, BMI and IBERIA), Virgin Airways, TUI, Thomas Cook, Monarch Airlines and easyJet. (Note 3) Nimbus and the Airline Group were the two shortlisted companies, and in March 2001 submitted their final offers, with a decision announced on 27 March 2001 that the Airline Group had been the successful bidder. David Morrison's excellent polemic (Note 4) argued that the Airline Group had a direct conflict of interest with NATS: "In their core business they have a financial interest in low air traffic control charges, whilst NATS have an interest in pushing them up in order to maximise revenues." He suggested that the investment was a defensive measure to prevent any other body gaining an interest in NATS – the Airline Group accepted that they would not benefit as a traditional shareholder, and indeed the argument was emphasised by easyJet who wrote-off their £7 million investment.

Having signed the Public Private Partnership (PPP) with the Airline Group, the department were then advised two months later that, because of a downturn in traffic and an underestimate of staff costs, the Airline Group could no longer finance their original offer of £845 million, but would offer £758 million which, coincidently, was some £87 million below the department's expectation, but fortunately £8 million above the Nimbus offer. According to Rachel Lomax, Permanent Secretary at the Department for Transport, when questioned by PAC member David Rendel, MP for Newbury, who asked if the government had been gazumped, replied, "We prudently took account of what was happening in the outside world and I think we would have been criticised if we had not… We did take account of the fact that the world was changing and that the world economy was slowing, that foot and mouth was hitting the North Atlantic trade quite severely and that those were good reasons for allowing the Airline Group to revise its forecast down. Even so, it remained higher than the Nimbus Group and the Nimbus Group voluntarily decided that they did not want to adjust their bid". (Note 5)

The financing of the deal provided some clues about the motivation of government. The shareholders provided £50 million capital and NATS self-financed the remaining £733 million by commercially raising capital supported by the assets of NATS – not the assets of the new owners nor the use of the government's National Loans Fund. The Chairman of NATS, Sir

Roy McNulty, wrote to the government on June 11 and June 15, 2001, describing the proposed financial scenario as unworkable, and pointed out that, as a result of the financial structure, NATS's debt would be £350 million higher and also wrote that "the success of the PPP would be judged against whether these things happen in practice, not against the specific level of proceeds (to the Treasury) achieved in the short-term". (Note 6)

The CAA also objected and wrote to the Transport Select Committee: "The CAA has profound reservations about the proposed high debt financing of NERL (NATS en route service), its subsequent ability to meet its obligations under the loan facility and its ability to fund its development programme if it is buffeted by plausible adverse shocks." (Note 7) Why was NATS itself and its regulatory body so disturbed by the financial structure created to sell the service? They quite rightly identified that money raised commercially would be more expensive than money raised from the National Loans Fund, but their major disquiet was that most of the money raised would be used to repay money due to the Treasury. The PAC report into the affair stated that "the Department and Treasury took £758 million out of NATS in sales proceeds leaving the company burdened with over twice as much debt as it carried before PPP". (Note 8) This report concluded that "the maximisation of sale proceeds seems to have taken precedence over the financial robustness of NATS", (Note 9) whilst also commenting that "the Airline Group acquired a 46% share, a majority on the board and operational control of NATS despite having paid only one sixteenth of the purchase price", (Note 10) and "the Airline Group declined to provide NATS with further financial support. Leaving only the government shareholders to meet such financial requirements is difficult to reconcile with the concept of risk sharing in public/private partnerships". (Note 11)

Government received £758 million from the sale of its shares, of which £330 million was used to repay the National Loans Fund, leaving £428 million for the Treasury. Angela Eagle, MP for Wallasey, questioning Brian Glicksman, Treasury Officer of Accounts, at a PAC witness hearing on 18 November 2002, identified that the £500 million capital receipt was in the budget of the previous government and "there was a big hole in the expenditure on the income for the Department which necessitated raising monies in order to fill that hole", (Note 12) to which Mr Glicksman, after some civil service type prevarication dryly replied, "A capital receipt would have enabled the plans to be reconciled, yes". (Note 13)

With pressure to produce funds, and despite the strong unease of the chairmen of both NATS and the CAA, the department pressed ahead. The plan left NATS woefully short of working capital, with the reduction of fees for five years agreed during negotiations. NATS was in a financially sensitive state moving forward. They may, however, have succeeded before the terrorist attacks in New York in September 2001 led to a severe reduction of intercontinental travel between North America and Europe, with obvious implications for NATS. Costs were cut and the new control centre for Scotland was postponed and creditors were paid more slowly.

In March 2002 the government and NATS' lending banks made available a £60 million short-term six-month loan facility to allow NATS to source a new equity investor. The shareholding at this stage was the Airline Group with 46%, NATS employees with 5% and the government with the remaining 49%. The Airline Group declined to provide more equity, assessing correctly that government could not afford to let NATS fail and would be obliged to resolve the situation. An agreement was eventually reached with the British Airports Authority (BAA) who ran a number of strategic airports, including Heathrow, to buy 4% of the shares held by the Airline Group for a consideration of £65 million, which again emphasised the significant bargain achieved by the Airline Group, who purchased 46% for some £50 million. As a responsible shareholder, government matched the £65 million invested by BAA, giving NATS some breathing space whilst trans-Atlantic traffic recovered to its previous levels.

The government therefore lost £87 million, which, with determined negotiation, should have been demanded from the Airline Group as a substantial premium. £87 million will therefore be added to the summary at the end of this chapter as well as unbudgeted legal fees of £3.3 million. Readers will note that, even in the early part of the 21st century, government was selling assets to fund their current account.

SOURCES

PAC Report: *The Public Private Partnership for National Air Traffic Services*, HC80, 9 December 2003

Transport, Local Government and the Regions Committee: *National Air Traffic Services' Finances*, HC 789, 17 July 2002

NAO Report: *The Public Private Partnership for National Air Traffic Services*, HC 1096, 24 July 2002

Morrison, David: *Why NATS' Debt was Doubled*, Labour and Trade Union Review, October 2002

UNISON: *Public Risk for Private Gain: National Air Traffic Services*

NOTES

1 PAC Report, Minutes of Evidence, ev 4, q4
2 NAO Report, p23
3 ibid, p21
4 Morrison, David, p9
5 PAC Report, Minutes of Evidence, q59
6 Morrison, David, p11
7 Transport, Local Government and the Regions Committee, p7
8 PAC Report, p4
9 ibid, p6
10 ibid
11 ibid
12 PAC Report, Minutes of Evidence, ev10, q82
13 ibid, q85

SUMMARY: CHAPTER FOUR – 2003

03 04 00	The 2001 Outbreak of Foot and Mouth Disease	£3.030 bn
03 04 01	Individual Learning Accounts	£0.097 bn
03 04 02	NHS (England) Summarised Accounts	£0.968 bn
03 04 03	Ministry of Defence: Reducing Stocks	N/A
03 04 04	Tackling Benefit Fraud	£3.131 bn
03 04 05	Tackling Benefit Fraud: DSS Appropriation Accounts	£2.824 bn
03 04 06	Tackling Benefit Fraud: DSS Appropriation Accounts	£1.310 bn
03 04 07	Tackling Benefit Fraud: DSS Resource Accounts	£3.471 bn
03 04 08	Tackling Benefit Fraud	£1.930 bn
03 04 09	Ministry of Defence: Devonport Submarine Facilities	£0.697 bn
03 04 10	Ministry of Defence: Resource Accounts	£3.583 bn
03 04 11	The Libra Project	£0.257 bn
03 04 12	Ministry of Defence: The Apache Helicopter	£0.167 bn
03 04 13	NATS	£0.090 bn
	Total	£21.534 bn
	Total adjusted for inflation to December 2014	£27.585 bn

INDEX: CHAPTER FIVE – 2004

04 05 00   Fraud and the Inland Revenue
04 05 01   Wembley and the Lottery Grant
04 05 02   NHS (England) Summarised Accounts 2002/03
04 05 03   GCHQ: New Accommodation Programme
04 05 04   NIRS2 and the National Insurance Fund
04 05 05   Tax Credits, PAYE Records and the Construction Industry
04 05 06   NIRS2 Contract Extension
04 05 07   Inland Revenue: Tax Credits
04 05 08   Inland Revenue: Tax Credits and Tax Debt Management
04 05 09   Inland Revenue: Tax Credits
04 05 10   The Recovery of Debt
04 05 11   Housing Benefit: Tackling Benefit Fraud
04 05 12   Housing Benefit Fraud
04 05 13   Fraud and Error in Housing Benefit
04 05 14   Losses on Alcohol Duty
04 05 15   The Rocques Report
04 05 16   Value Added Tax: Missing Trader Fraud
04 05 17   Value Added Tax: VAT and IT
04 05 18   Value Added Tax: Tackling Vat Fraud
04 05 19   Ministry of Defence: Major Projects Report

"The invention of the teenager was a mistake. Once you identify a period of life in which people get to stay out late but don't have to pay taxes – naturally, no one wants to live any other way."

> Judith Martin, journalist, a.k.a. Miss Manners (b.1938)

"When a new source of taxation is found it never means, in practice, that the old source is abandoned. It merely means that the politicians have two ways of milking the taxpayer where they had one before."

> H L Mencken, journalist and satirist (1880 -1956)

04 05 00

Fraud and the Inland Revenue

"The Revenue do not see estimating the shadow economy as a priority because they have not identified any reliable and practical techniques to assess the scale of unknown activity in the shadow economy and its effect on the tax gap, partly because aggregate measures will include non-taxable activity." (Note 1)

The Inland Revenue collected tax from 29 million taxpayers with a yield of £214 billion in direct tax and National Insurance, of which Income Tax provided £103 billion, National Insurance provided £65.3 billion, Corporation Tax provided £32 billion and the remainder came from Stamp Duty, Capital Gains Tax, Inheritance Tax and Petroleum Revenue Tax. The department spent £428 million on investigations and enquiries to tackle non-compliance and the total number of serious fraud investigations instigated was 400, of which 60 were prosecuted. With these statistics, the Revenue was subliminally advising professionals and their clients that they lacked the resources to tackle seriously the issue of compliance and non-compliance within the shadow/informal economy.

The shadow/informal economy existed in many guises, including false accounting; individuals and businesses not registered for tax and unknown to the revenue; employees registered for tax who also worked for third parties for cash; use of diverted cash to pay top-up wages; contrived liquidations to avoid tax liabilities; use of diverting cash to pay cash top-ups to subcontractors and theft or false use of exemption certificates; self-employed traders putting cash into a back pocket and knowingly underreporting sales and the concealment of substantial amounts of income. The list is not exhaustive. In view of the shadowy nature of most of these transactions it is not surprising that the Revenue was unable to provide figures for the shadow/informal economy and establish the level of the tax gap.

However, the Revenue did make some progress in establishing some figures for Income Tax Self-Assessment as a result of a programme of random enquiries initiated for the three-year period from 1996 onwards, which became available in 2001. "The Revenue estimated that in total one third of taxpayers had not complied, which they believed to be a reasonably accurate estimate." (Note 2) The results were consistent from year to year based on a statistical sample of 6,000 returns out of the nine million returns each year. The PAC noted that a fourfold increase in the sample would give a significantly better estimate, but this was not initiated because of cost constraints. Whilst the results fluctuated from year to year, the PAC noted that the latest estimates indicated £2.5 billion to be at risk, roughly equivalent to 5% of the tax that should have resulted. A small proportion of taxpayers were responsible for the majority of the value of tax at risk, i.e. 15% of cases examined account for 89% of the total tax at risk. (Note 3)

The results also indicated that non-compliance was most common among sole traders and partnerships, confirming areas the Revenue had previously regarded as high risk. The random enquiry programmes helped the Revenue to understand better the compliance risks, so it was planned to introduce the programme for Corporation Tax, PAYE and National Insurance contributions. The Revenue had some success with tackling 'pension busting' fraud, i.e. where fraudulent early liberation of an individual's pension funds avoided the payment of tax. "In all, an estimated total of between £80 million to £100 million of pension funds have been liberated, entailing an estimated tax lost to the Revenue of approximately £35 million which recovery has been sought." (Note 4) The Revenue had some success with tackling the abuse of offshore accounts and structures and expected to produce around 450 cases of tax fraud, with an estimated recovery of £90 million. At the date of the NAO report £5.1 million had been recovered.

The PAC report into the matter did not examine aggressively the inability of the Revenue to establish accurate figures or a plan for recovery. Indeed, unusually, the witness meeting was almost clubbable. £2.5 billion a year for six years, plus the £35 million at risk from 'pension busting', and £85 million from offshore account evasion, a total of £15.12 billion, will be added to the summary at the end of this chapter.

SOURCES

PAC Report: *Tackling Fraud against the Inland Revenue*, HC62, 13 January 2004

NAO Report: *Tackling Fraud against the Inland Revenue*, HC 429, 28 February 2003

NOTES

1 NAO Report, p8
2 PAC Report, p7/8
3 NAO Report, p20
4 ibid, p48

04 05 01

Wembley and the Lottery Grant

There was a great deal of uncertainty about the handling of the £120 million worth of lottery funds, at the time the largest grant ever made by Sport England, awarded to assist in the creation of a new national stadium at Wembley.

One issue was that the £120 million was used in 1999 to purchase the old stadium at Wembley before the Football Association subsidiary, Wembley National Stadium Ltd (WNSL), had agreed access to financing to allow construction of the new stadium to proceed. The second issue was that Sport England allowed WNSL to demolish the old stadium, and in the process reduced the valuation to £30 million. Sport England's financial security package comprised a legal charge on the assets acquired with the lottery grant, but in allowing the demolition of the old Wembley had reduced their security to £30 million. It is somewhat ironic that Sport England took a charge on property for which they had provided funds.

The idea for a national stadium was promoted by Sport England, who envisaged a national home for three sports: football, rugby league and athletics. A national competition in 1996 considered proposals from Bradford, Birmingham, Coventry and Wembley, and the latter was chosen as the preferred site with the target completion date of 2002 and an anticipated total budget of £320 million. Sport England, as a distributor of lottery funding, would provide £120 million and the remainder would be sourced commercially. By March 1999 the majority of the lottery funding had been transferred to fund the acquisition of the existing Wembley Stadium and business.

By December 2000 WNSL found that the commercial financing needed would not be forthcoming and there was a possibility that the project would not proceed. Sport England was entitled to recover the lottery grant, but the Football Association/WNSL did not have sufficient resources to repay the money. Sport England had a legal charge over the assets and yet did not seem to have appreciated that the closure of the old Wembley Stadium, one of the prime assets, would further diminish the likelihood of retrieving the lottery grant. The strange decision to close Wembley Stadium in 2000, thus ensuring that events would have to be staged elsewhere, could be regarded as corporate blackmail.

In December 2000 it was agreed by Sport England that WNSL be allowed to amend the lottery funding agreement to remove athletics. £20 million was to be repaid in instalments over a five-year period beginning that month, but when the first repayment date passed without money been returned to Sport England, and with the revised lottery funding agreement unsigned, athletics was restored to the plans for the stadium.

By June 2001 the Football Association's request for further public funding for the project led to a report by Patrick Carter which examined the project, and in November 2001 recommended that if the project was to succeed, the government and Sport England had to be seen to support the project, both in principle and in terms of any financial commitment. Consequently, Sport England contributed a further £20 million and the London Development Agency contributed £21 million of taxpayers' money. Sport England became aware of concerns about the aspects of management and oversight of the procurement process carried out by WNSL, and commissioned a report by David James CBE to look into the matter. He confirmed the existence of serious concerns relating to the tendering process and the resulting contractual arrangements, but found no evidence of criminal intent or impropriety. The project cost had now risen to £757 million. The stadium eventually opened in 2007.

The Department for Culture, Media and Sport (DCMS) report into the matter was scathing: "We repeat that Sport England's protection of the £120 million, the largest single lottery grant ever awarded to a sporting project, entirely fails to meet the standards to be expected of such a public body. We believe that Sport England's performance has been deficient to the point of dereliction." (Note 1) A total of £161 million is added to the summary at the end of this chapter on the basis of the inefficient use of Lottery Funds and the subsequent awards of £41 million which allowed the Football Association to proceed.

SOURCES

PAC Report: *The English National Stadium Project at Wembley*, HC254, 10 February 2004

DCMS Select Committee Report: *Wembley Stadium Project: Into Injury Time*, July 2002

NAO Report: *The English National Stadium Project at Wembley*, HC699, 6 June 2003

NOTE

1 The DCMS Select Committee Report, p6 of 6, para 17

04 05 02

NHS (England) Summarised Accounts 2002/03

From 1 April 2002, the NHS Litigation Authority (the Authority) took full responsibility for managing clinical negligence claims within the NHS, on behalf of primary care trusts and NHS trusts, to ensure conformity and consistency in the handling of such claims. New claims in the year were 10,582 and the files were closed on 6,037 existing claims. Whilst the Authority paid out £446 million pounds in cash for all clinical negligence schemes during the year, they also made provision of £640 million for expected claims.

Whilst the spin doctors suggested a healthy situation for fraud, reporting for instance that pharmaceutical fraud had been reduced by £70 million, in truth this report allocated just three paragraphs to the issue. The report forlornly recorded, "I asked the NHS Counter Fraud Service to consider what additional steps could be taken to obtain an overall estimate of fraud across the NHS as a matter of priority. The Department has informed that the system to measure fraud locally at Strategic Health Authority and Primary Care Trust level is being developed. This will firstly concentrate on identifying the estimated fraud within payroll expenditure and then move on to other significant areas of expenditure". (Note 1) Note the emphasis on the future tense about developing a measurement of fraud. It would seem that even the NAO were cowed by the aura surrounding the NHS.

The unavailability of accurate information about fraud continued until the CFSMS was subsumed by NHS Business Services and rebranded as NHS

Protect on April 1 2011. A report by Jim Gee, previously the Accounting Officer for CFSMS, suggested that fraud in the NHS could be as high as £7 billion, (Note 2) whilst the UK's National Fraud Authority (NFA) indicator for 2013 suggested that fraud was closer to £229 million. Mr Gee's figures were based on an analysis of fraud using data from other countries with similar healthcare structures. If the NFA figures were correct it would seem that the NHS was up to five times better than the rest of the world in preventing and detecting fraud.

There are no figures available for fraud in this report so the total added to the summary at the end of this chapter is £640 million provided for in respect of clinical negligence.

SOURCES

NAO Report: *NHS (England) Summarised Accounts 2002/03*, HC505-1, 28 April 2004

NHS Report: *The Counter Fraud and Security Management Service Annual Accounts 2004/05*

Gee, Jim and Button, Mark: *The Financial Cost of Healthcare Fraud 2014*, 25 March 2014

NOTES

1 NAO Report, p28
2 *The Financial Cost of Healthcare Fraud BDO*, Press Release p1/2

04 05 03

GCHQ: New Accommodation Programme

GCHQ either forgot to factor in the cost of moving their computer systems when they consolidated their accommodation in Cheltenham into one unit or they used the opportunity to upgrade their systems. Either way, the cost went from £20 million advised to the board, to £450 million without ministerial approval or the tedious procedure of signing a contract.

In another spooky coincidence GCHQ included an uplift of 24% to reflect possible increases in building costs when compiling a comparison between a PFI and a public sector arrangement: during the 21-month period when the successful bidder was given preferred status, the bid increased by 21%, giving a final figure just £3 million short of the figure offered by one of the other competing bidders. The 24% uplift, advised by the Treasury, ensured that the PFI arrangement was the more competitive one.

GCHQ had occupied over 50 buildings at two sites in Cheltenham, and in 1997 the decision was taken to relocate to a single site within a ten-mile radius of the city. The preferred bidder, IAS, was approved in September 1998 and a contract was signed 21 months later to provide new, fully serviced accommodation for a period of 30 years. The building was completed and occupied in 2003.

Because of the nature of its activities GCHQ retained responsibility for moving its technical capability into the new building, and in 1997 advised its board that the cost would be £20 million despite internal papers showing that the technical transition costs would be £41 million. In 1998, a review identified that the technical transition costs would be £60 million, but after the establishment of a new technical review team in October 1999 another review established that the cost would be £450 million. It was at this stage that GCHQ sought assurance that the Treasury would support the cost of technical transition, but the Treasury said costs were too high. (Note 1) The Treasury did agree to provide additional funding of £216 million but insisted that GCHQ solve the issue about the remainder, which they did by delaying the transfer of staff and keeping one site open until 2012 at a cost of £43 million.

Jon Trickett, MP for Hemsworth, suggested to Sir David Omand KCB, "I am just suggesting that there is an ideological predisposition, probably in the Treasury, to PFI, for whatever reason, and the figures, time and time again, Chairman, as we have seen, had been used in a particular way, which is due to a particular result". (Note 2) This suspicion seems to be confirmed by the final comparison between the PFI bid and the public sector comparator. (Note 3) The IAS deal showed that their final bid cost some £71 million less than the public sector comparator, whose figure included a total of £156 million for risk adjustment, i.e. a possible cost overrun of 24%. Without this additional figure, which no doubt became known to IAS, the public sector comparator would have been £85 million cheaper and would have been difficult to justify as a PFI arrangement. (Note 4) The PAC critically said, "It seemed to us that the Public Sector Comparator figures could be used to demonstrate any result required. Such uncertain figures risk clouding the issue of value for money and could cloak a predisposition to go in for PFI". (Note 5)

GCHQ's inefficiency meant that the Treasury had to support the agency to an additional £216 million and also meant that GCHQ incurred an additional cost of £43 million associated with keeping one of its sites open to 2012, which when added to the increased bid of £85 million by IAS during the post-preferred bid status and the signing of contracts means that £344 million will be added to the summary at the end of this chapter.

SOURCES

PAC Report: *Government Communications Headquarters (GCHQ): New Accommodation Programme*, HC65, 15 June 2004

NAO Report: *Government Communications Headquarters (GCHQ): New Accommodation Programme*, HC955, 16 July 2003

NOTES

1 NAO Report, p18
2 PAC Report, ev9, q59
3 NAO Report, p12, fig 5
4 ibid, p25, fig 12
5 PAC Report, p12

It is necessary to look at a five-year period and a broader base of reports to allow an analysis of the Tax Credit Scheme introduced in 1999. The problems experienced because of the inefficient introduction of NIRS2 hampered the smooth introduction of tax credits, so that is also examined, as is the contract extension for NIRS2. Also examined is the creation of the Inland Revenue Debt Management Service (DMS).

04 05 04

NIRS2 and the National Insurance Fund

Materiality is relative. Someone given £100 and losing 5p will regard the latter as immaterial. However, it beggars belief that mandarins could regard the loss of £32 million as immaterial, but that's exactly what they did when considering this fund. The NAO report into the matter noted that "the value of losses in Retirement Pension and Widows Benefit amounted to £32 million. This loss is not material in the context of the expenditure of £37,705 million on these particular benefits". (Note 1) A Morrisons, a Ryanair, a Ford or a Unilever would do their utmost to ensure that a loss of £32 million was avoided, but if not avoided would make every effort to effect both recovery and future avoidance. The sheer size of government finance and the size of the tax take has created an environment where £32 million is regarded as immaterial. One of the recurring problems, still relevant now, was the inability of government to specify and implement information technology which allowed them control. This section therefore deals with the problems associated with the NIRS2 scheme.

NIRS2 was first conceived in May 1995 when Andersen Consulting, later to become Accenture, was awarded a contract to develop and operate a new computer system which would accommodate the business and legislative changes associated with the Pensions Reform Act 1995. The contract was awarded in the year of the legislation. Andersen identified significant risks to the successful delivery of the original implementation plan and accordingly agreed a phased partial implementation with the Department of Social Security (DSS), targeted for 1998. Because of the delay, the effects for the Benefits Agency were horrific – the DSS were unable to correctly calculate contributory benefits and many benefit awards were made on an interim or emergency basis, which helped contribute to the fraud and error which occurred. Claimants were inconvenienced and the Contributions Agency were unable to make full payment of National Insurance rebates to members of contracted-out schemes, which led to a loss of state earnings pension benefits to those customers.

By July 1999, the Public Accounts Committee (PAC) had issued a critical report suggesting that the two parties involved in this marriage, i.e. Andersen Consulting and the Contributions Agency had not demonstrated a "shared understanding of what was meant by the delivery of the NIRS2 system". (Note 2) HMRC had by this time taken responsibility for National Insurance contributions and also took ownership of the NIRS2 project. The PAC suggested to them that they should resolve the issue of who was responsible for the problems of NIRS2, and if they found the fault lay with Andersen they should take steps to recover all costs clearly due, as failure to do so would result in the risk transferred to Andersen under the PFI agreement being transferred back to the public sector. HMRC instigated an independent report from PA Consulting which reported favourably about the design of the system, but noted that HMRC needed to develop strong management controls of future development and operation of the system whilst also needing to be more proactive in managing future system requirements.

At that time there were still 4.5 million contributors from previous years which needed entry onto the system. The aim was to reach an acceptable level of operation by April 2000, but the NAO felt it would be October 2001 before normal working could be resumed. As a result of the investigation Andersen made a compensation payment of £4.1 million to the government, whilst at the same time negotiating an extension of the contract despite the fiasco of the implementation of the scheme. Treasury Minister Dawn Primarolo told parliament: "It would not be sensible or cost-effective to seek further compensation from Andersen Consulting beyond the amount of £4.1 million which is paid for delays in 1997 and 1998. I'm satisfied that taking action against Andersen Consulting would prejudice the partnership relationship now established between it and the Inland Revenue." (Note 3) The Treasury was asked by *Private Eye* about the level of compensation that should have been claimed for this disaster and were told, "We cannot give you that figure". (Note 4)

The figure for fraud and error has been dealt with elsewhere, so this report only deals with the costs incurred as a result of the difficulties with the NIRS2 system. One contingency plan was the operation of a fax-back service between the Contributions Agency and the Benefits Agency which cost £292,000. The total cost of paying the backlogs was £14.1 million and it was additionally estimated that overpayments of £1.1 million were made because of the delays. When it became clear that the National Insurance rebates in respect of the 1997/98 tax year were going to be paid late it was decided to give individuals an amount in recognition of this delay, and by 1 November 1999 £34.95 million had been paid out. In addition, £127,000 was paid out in compensation for unreasonable delays and 200,000 payments of £10 each were made to claimants of contributory benefits who had experienced unreasonable delay. A total of £50.6 million will be added to the summary at the end of this section.

SOURCES

PAC Report: *Report by the Comptroller and Auditor General: National Insurance Fund Account 1998/99*, HC350, 9 August 2000

PAC Report: *Improving the Delivery of Government IT Projects*, HC65, 5 January 2000

NAO Report: *National Insurance Fund Account 1998/99*, HC146, 1 March 2000

NAO Report: *National Insurance Fund Account 1999/2000*, HC446, 4 May 2001

Private Eye, Edition 1001, 5 May 2000

Pollock, Allyson and Price, David: *Public Risk for Private Gain*, Unison, undated

NOTES

1 NAO Report 1999/2000, R2

2 ibid, 1998/99

3 *Private Eye*, p26

4 ibid

04 05 05

Inland Revenue: Tax Credits, PAYE Records and the Construction Industry

The press release introducing these accounts presciently quoted the Comptroller and Auditor General, Sir John Bourn, "New schemes, such as tax credits, have, in general, gone smoothly, but the Department should ensure that action is taken to manage risks which have emerged during the implementation of some projects". (Note 1) Tax Credits were to become one such scheme which would, in time, become a major source of embarrassment for government.

In his 1998 Budget, Gordon Brown, the Chancellor of the Exchequer, announced the creation of tax credits, designed to enable working families and disabled people to receive financial assistance through the tax system, rather than through social security benefits. Initially, payments would be made directly by the Inland Revenue, but also via the recipients' employers from April 2000. In the first six months examined by this report, £1.033 billion was paid out by the Inland Revenue.

The report noted that the changes had increased the number of applicants entitled to support and were providing generally a larger level of award than the previous system. The report noted that "in March 2000, the Inland Revenue was paying working families' tax credits awards averaging £72 a week to 1,057,000 applicants, compared to some 817,000 family credit awards averaging £63 a week by the Benefits Agency in August 1999". (Note 2) The report did not query why the average payment had increased by over 14%, but the department did carry out quality assurance work on awards and calculated that errors of £13.4 million may have been made in the period to 31 March 2000. (Note 3)

The report also noted that the department made an error of £22 million (Note 4) when, because of the difficulties in processing employers' end of year returns, they erased the PAYE tax records of 1 million people without knowing whether the correct amount of tax had been paid in 1997/98. This was the first year in which data processed by the NIRS2 was interfaced with the PAYE computer system (COP) and a number of difficulties convinced the Inland Revenue to eradicate the records on the basis that it believed that the extension of processing 1997/98 information would further delay the processing of 1998/99 and 1999/2000 data.

The administration of tax for the construction industry had always been difficult, and in 1972 the Inland Revenue introduced the Construction Industry Tax Deduction Scheme whereby self-employed–contractors either received payments from the contractor net of tax or could obtain an exemption certificate. This allowed the contractor to pay his subcontractors gross, with any tax due being paid by the latter at a later date. The department estimated that abuse of the system was costing the Exchequer in excess of £100 million each year through non-declaration of taxable income and from false claims for repayment of tax deducted at source. The arrangements were therefore strengthened by the introduction of a registration card for subcontractors who were not entitled to be paid without deduction of tax at source; tighter rules governing the entitlement of individuals to a tax certificate; a requirement for contractors to send vouchers giving payments made under the scheme to the Inland Revenue each month; and new powers for the Inland Revenue to penalise contractors for using unregistered subcontractors.

The strengthening of the regulations convinced 100,000 subcontractors to register for their first time, but only 1.4 million vouchers were returned by January 2000 against an expectation of six million. 30% of the vouchers were referred for investigation because of potential errors or other anomalies, and the Inland Revenue's administration was not helped when their computer partner, EDS, stockpiled post without opening it – once opened they discovered it contained 2,600 cheques with a value of £3 million. Nevertheless, the department awarded EDS an ex-gratia payment of £800,000. (Note 5) Whilst the strengthening of the rules and regulations regarding subcontractors in the construction industry had its difficulties, the Inland Revenue still estimated that an additional £280 million in tax and National Insurance contributions were received as a direct result of the new regulations, thereby suggesting that their own estimates of an annual £100 million loss were understated.

Fraud and error of £13.4 million for tax credits; losses of £22 million because of the erasure of PAYE tax records; £280 million uncollected by the Revenue in previous years; an ex-gratia payment of £800,000 to EDS makes a total of £316.2 million, which will be added to the summary at the end of this section.

SOURCES

PAC Report: *Report on Inland Revenue Appropriation Account 1999/2000*, HC421, 20 August 2001

NAO Report: *Appropriation Accounts 1999/2000, Volume 16: Class XVI Departments of the Chancellor of the Exchequer: Inland Revenue*, HC25-XVI, 9 February 2001

NOTES

1   NAO Report, press release, p1
2   ibid, R16
3   ibid, R20
4   PAC Report, p4/8
5   The payment was justified on the basis that productivity levels were

lower than expected and the department felt they could not subject EDS to financial losses in the first year of co-operation.

04 05 06

NIRS2 Contract Extension

The fallibility, and the costs associated with that fallibility, of the NIRS2 system did not deter HMRC from negotiating an extension to its contract with Andersen Consulting (now known as Accenture). The original PFI contract had been for ten years and was worth £75 million, which required Andersen to undertake development work as well as replacing the original system; to transfer data from the original system to NIRS2; to develop the system to implement the legislative changes which would arise from the Pensions Act 1995; and to operate the system until the contract ended in 2004. New Labour became government in 1997 and in the following two years introduced six legislative changes, which was a test of the preparedness of the Civil Service and their IT contractors.

The DSS were aware of the proposed new legislation but the NAO noted that "although the former Department of Social Security assessed the implications of individual changes to Pensions and National Insurance legislation, at the point when responsibility for the system was transferred to the Inland Revenue, neither Department was in a position to determine their aggregate impact on NIRS2". (Note 1) It is perhaps unfortunate that the IT implications were not totally considered when the Inland Revenue was merged with HMRC.

Consideration was given to cancellation of the contract but the cost of cancelling was estimated at £44 million, although analysis of that figure (Note 2) suggests that the department sought a rationale to continue discussions with Accenture about a new contract. A PA Consulting report had concluded that NIRS2 was a reliable and robust platform and this, when considering integration of the Inland Revenue into the HMRC structure, did mean that the department could avoid sourcing a completely new supplier. The PAC were critical in their report, stating that "the price agreed appears to be very generous for a non-competitive contract, when in practice the Inland Revenue had little option but to use Accenture because of the high break cost of the original contract". (Note 3) There was also the consideration of timescale, which was not available to process the full procurement routine.

NIRS2 was a large and complex system designed to support the administration of the National Insurance scheme, and held details of some 65 million individual national contribution records. The department held 100 million contributions in a suspense file, i.e. a file where information provided by employers did not match the relevant contributor's records. The individual figures were small, but collectively were significant, and with pressure to solve the problem it can be understood why the decision to continue the contract with Accenture was attractive.

The extended contract was valued between £70 and £144 million, and in the second year of the new extension the Accenture margin increased to 44.5%, even after returning 9.5% to the Inland Revenue as part of a 'super profit' claw-back arrangement. The Inland Revenue had to provide for £15.3 million in their accounts to recover compensation that arose from overpayment of age-related payments in 1999/2000. They accepted that pension scheme members may have been adversely affected and suffered a loss to their pension fund, and they therefore agreed in October 2003 some principles by which they would accept claims. They also paid out £85.72 million, over a five-year period, to compensate those individuals contracted out of the State Earnings Related Pensions Scheme (SERPS) and also had the find an additional £67.9 million following the decision to create an integrated recovery programme to resolve difficulties following the implementation of NIRS2.

The total taken to the summary at the end of this section is £168.9 million.

SOURCES

PAC Report: *The National Insurance Recording System (NIRS2)*, 7 August 2002

NAO Report: *NIRS2: Contract Extension*, HC355, 14 November 2001

National Insurance Fund Account 2002/03, HC159, 22 January 2004

NOTES

1 NAO Report, Press Release 53/01, 14 November 2001
2 ibid

3   ibid, p14

04 05 07

Inland Revenue: Tax Credits

There was unease at the NAO about the reluctance of the Inland Revenue to allow access to employers who paid tax credits on behalf of the government. The matter was aired at a Public Accounts Committee (PAC) when Jon Trickett, Labour MP for Hemsworth, asked, "Am I correct in saying that effectively what would be regarded as Government expenditure has been transferred from DWP, or DSS as it was, through to Inland Revenue?" (Note 1) Sir John Bourn, Comptroller and Auditor General, replied, "What would have accounted as public expenditure, no longer counts as public expenditure, but it is public expenditure". (Note 2) And so continued the battle between the NAO and the Inland Revenue.

During their consideration of the Tax Credits Bill 1999, the PAC asked whether the NAO, in their role as auditors, would have access to employers who were distributing government money, thus allowing confirmation that tax credit payments were being handled correctly. Government indicated that adding the NAO to the many inspectors already authorised to visit employers would be an additional burden on the employers, and instead suggested that the NAO should verify their figures by examining the Inland Revenue's compliance reports. The NAO were unhappy about this and argued that the tax credits form of payment using employers as a conduit needed an external auditor who should have access to the books and records of the organisation which processed payments.

In the first year of payments, 1999/2000, the NAO recommended that the Inland Revenue should provide management accounting information as a matter of routine. In 2001/02 the department was unable to provide details of award notifications sent to employers and were unable to reconcile their figures with payments made by employers. They cited a number of reasons for their inability to reconcile the figures: employer payroll cycles did not coincide with the tax year; there were errors by employers in completing their returns; and there were errors keying data into the departmental systems. The NAO also noted the difficulty it had about obtaining satisfactory information about visits to employers by the department's compliance teams. There was uncertainty about the number of visits, which included cases were tax credits had been paid and checked. The NAO commented, "In addition, a lack of detailed data meant that the Department could not estimate the level at which employers had paid Tax Credit incorrectly". (Note 3)

Richard Bacon, Conservative MP for South Norfolk, questioned Sir John about the matter and asked, "Are you saying that without these rights of access, it is not possible for you to fully do your duty to Parliament in respect of these expenditures?" (Note 4) Sir John replied, "I do not want to say that all my work in this field would be totally undermined. What I am saying is that the external auditor requires rights of direct access and that he or she determines upon their employment". (Note 5) Mr Bacon asked further, "If this committee were to recommend that [you have access] you would not have too much difficulty in agreeing with that recommendation", (Note 6) and the reply came, "I should have no difficulty at all". (Note 7) The Chairman of the Committee added his weight to the NAO campaign by suggesting to Sir John, "You might even assist us in writing the report". (Note 8)

This report noted that at March 2001, over 1.2 million individuals were receiving an average of just under £80 a week in tax credit, of which £1.41 billion was routed via employers and was funded mainly from PAYE tax deducted from other employees. The department conceded to the PAC that they "have not been able to estimate how many people are eligible for Tax Credits". (Note 9) In the absence of any more detailed information from the department, the NAO estimated that £27.2 million (Note 10) may have been overpaid to tax credit applicants and it is that sum which will be added to the summary at the end of this section.

SOURCES

PAC Report: *Inland Revenue: Tax Credits*, HC866, 6 November 2002

NAO Report: *Inland Revenue Appropriation Accounts 2000/01*, 31 January 2002

NOTES

1   PAC Report, ev13, note 103

2   ibid

3 ibid, p9

4 ibid, ev 19, q156

5 ibid

6 ibid, q157

7 ibid

8 ibid

9 ibid, p6

10 NAO Report, R12

04 05 08

Inland Revenue: Tax Credits and Tax Debt Management

The 2001/02 accounts for the Inland Revenue disclosed that tax credit awards were probably overpaid by £53 million. (Note 1) They also noted that in the same year the department had been unable to evaluate the level of error in tax credit payments routed through employers, so in early 2000 the NAO carried out an investigation to identify instances where the information provided by the employer did not match the awards made by the department. They reached the conclusion that any discrepancy that arose was generally from error or the complexity of reconciling records. The PAC, however, noted that "the Department had not sought to quantify the level of fraud evasion and avoidance, whereas HM Customs and Excise have published estimates of fraud including some £358 million lost to the hidden economy, in their annual report". (Note 2) It was also noted that from April 2003 the existing tax credit schemes, first introduced in 1999, would be replaced

The Inland Revenue carried out an exercise to estimate the degree of non-compliance by applicants for tax credits during the year 2000/01 but were only able to provide the NAO with the results of the exercise in August 2003 – five months after the original tax credit scheme had finished. The department estimated that some 10-14% of tax credit payments may have been overpayments due to applicant non-compliance, which represented between £510 and £710 million for the year. The main reasons for the errors were: understated declared income; understated or undeclared capital; or an undeclared partner. Whilst the department argued that some changes were made which would reduce the figures for the following two years, the Comptroller said, "I have seen no evidence to demonstrate that these changes will have produced a significant reduction in the rate of error. I have therefore concluded that the probable rate of error in 2002/03 remains unacceptably high, leading me to qualify my audit opinion on the trust statement accounts for 2002/03 in respect of the tax credit payments". (Note 3) The NAO recorded that a total of £17.8 billion had been spent on the tax credit schemes which began in 1999 and ended on 6 April 2003, so the probable loss, using 12% as a median figure, was £2.136 billion.

The department noted that applicants with Children's Tax Credit were not required to verify that the child existed and there was no requirement for the applicant to provide a child benefit reference, if available. The department therefore carried out a survey that sought to match the child benefit details with information provided by the applicant to the DWP. The result was an estimate that there was some £21 million overpaid across the 2.4 million applications centrally processed. (Note 4) A further 2.2 million applications processed at local tax offices were not examined and, accepting the accuracy of the centrally processed applications, this would mean a further £20 million had been overpaid at local tax offices.

The accounts also reported on the work of the Receivables Management Service (RMS) which was created on 1 April 2001 to combine the collection of taxes and debt management services. RMS inherited a backlog of legacy debt, totalling £619 million, and managed to collect £59 million, whilst writing off £105 million as uncollectable. (Note 5) However, it was also noted that £27.3 billion of legacy debt, which was under appeal by the taxpayer before 1996/97 and was regarded as 'stood over', was likely to be cancelled as not due. Whilst 'stood over', the tax assessed is not collectable and cannot be recovered – in essence the department was writing off £27.3 billion to allow the RMS to start with a clean balance sheet.

A total of £29.629 billion, representing error, fraud and legacy debt write-off in the Revenue's accounts, will be added to the summary at the end of this section.

SOURCES

PAC Report: *Inland Revenue: Tax Credits and Tax Debt Management*, HC332, 2 July 2003

NAO Report: *Comptroller and Auditor General's Standard Report on the Accounts of the Inland Revenue 2001/02*, 8 November 2002

NAO Report: *Inland Revenue: Standard Report 2002/03*, 6 November 2003

NOTES

1 NAO Report, p64
2 ibid, p66
3 ibid, p74
4 ibid, p71
5 ibid, p71

04 05 09

Inland Revenue: Tax Credits

"When the new tax credit schemes went live for payment in April 2003, problems with the IT systems resulted in several hundred thousand claimants receiving payments after they fell due, while the department were unable to reconcile payments made with the amounts authorised." (Note 1)

The IT contractor, EDS, did not achieve a stable system until ten weeks of live operations had passed, and in July the department engaged consultants to conduct a review to provide independent assessment about the problems. It is probably not unsurprising that the consortium, which included EDS, competing for the department's overall IT service provision was not selected as a preferred bidder. In mitigation, EDS emphasised that the project was one of the most challenging that government had ever undertaken and that the timetable had been compressed. There was a six-week delay while the rules for calculating tax credits were finalised and the 19-week system training window had been cut significantly. In particular, the volume testing timetable was cut from 12 weeks to 4 weeks.

The June 2003 PAC report said that the Inland Revenue would need to demonstrate more sophisticated risk management structures for these new tax credit systems, aiming for minimisation of error and fraud. The 2000 PAC report, however, stated that "the Department has yet to demonstrate any reduction in error of fraud. The Department do not have a target error rate for New Tax Credits. They recognise they will never get error rates down to zero and fraud is endemic in benefits". (Note 2) Sir Nicholas Montague, giving evidence on behalf of the Inland Revenue to the committee, agreed that error and fraud were endemic in benefits but also suggested that he "would be very disappointed if one does not see an immediate halving of error rates for new Tax Credits". (Note 3)

The new tax credits scheme was estimated to cost £16 billion in 2003/04 and the PAC suggested that "as the procedures were not changed significantly in subsequent years, it is reasonable to assume overpayments continued on broadly the same scale", (Note 4) i.e. the level of overpayments was between 10 and 14% by value. The loss to the taxpayer through fraud and error is therefore estimated at £1.9 billion. Some of the costs incurred as a result of the IT failure were advised and £37 million was written-off in respect of overpayments to households where the overpayment was less than £300; £10 million was incurred in extra administrative costs; and a further £11 million was written off as official error. (Note 5) The total therefore added to the summary at the end of this section will be £1.978 billion.

SOURCES

PAC Report: *Inland Revenue: Tax Credits*, HC89, 22 April 2004

NAO Report: *Comptroller and Auditor General's Standard Report 2003/04*, 1 October 2004

NOTES

1 PAC Report, p5
2 ibid, p8
3 ibid, ev2, qs12/13
4 ibid, p3
5 NAO Report, p124

04 05 10

The Recovery of Debt

This was the first assessment by the PAC of the Receivables Management Service (RMS) which had been created in 2001 to combine the collection of tax and debt management services for the Inland Revenue. This collection of debt was dispersed across the department, which created inconsistencies in the pursuit of debt and a lack of common goals and objectives.

The new service provided a 'start to finish' debt management function and consisted of three receivable telephone centres; 150 local recovery offices with 11 associated group offices; three specialist offices dealing with insolvencies; and the accounting and payment service. A total of 7,000 staff were employed, i.e. about 10% of the department's total employees. They were taxed with the collection of three types of debt: self-assessment debt; assessed debts; and that collected on behalf of the department by employers and other third parties including PAYE, National Insurance contributions and Student Loan deductions.

The issue of writing-off £27.3 billion worth of legacy debt has already been dealt with in section 04 05 08. Modern legacy debt totalled £619 million and the RMS managed to collect £59 million in the first year of operation, but wrote-off £159 million pounds as uncollectable. (Note 1) In the period under review the RMS collected a further £61.5 million and wrote-off a further £99 million, leaving a total modern legacy debt of £294 million. (Note 2) These figures exclude amounts written-off because of bankruptcy liquidation, on the basis that these matters were generally outside the control of the debt collector. The department wrote-off a further £286 million worth of debt on the following basis: that the debts were not worth further pursuit; that the taxpayer was no longer at the address given; that the taxpayer had moved abroad; and that the debt was doubtful. £275 million worth of National Insurance contributions were also written-off in the year to March 2003.

The PAC report concentrated on areas where it was felt that relatively minor changes, such as accepting credit cards for payment; seeking additional powers to enforce debt; using telephone centres more frequently; using other departments' records to find taxpayers; offering accurate information on its website and leaflets in different languages would allow the department to achieve similar debt clearance rates to the utility sector, where the debt clearance rate was 90% within 90 days, whilst the department's rate was 59% within 90 days.

A total of £660 million has been added to the summary at the end of this section representing modern legacy debt, National Insurance debt and general debt written-off during the period.

SOURCES

PAC Report: *The Recovery of Debt by the Inland Revenue*, HC584, 25 November 2004

NAO Report: *The Recovery of Debt by the Inland Revenue*, HC363, 22 March 2004

NOTES

1   See Section 04 05 08

2   NAO Report, p22

Housing Benefit

The Department for Work and Pensions (DWP) was responsible for policy, regulation and the rate of housing benefit paid to people living in rented accommodation who were out of work or on low incomes, while 408 local authorities were responsible for the delivery of the benefit. When the PAC examined the issue of fraud and error in housing benefits they had to do so in the knowledge that estimates to measure the level of fraud and error had not been provided since 1997/98.

04 05 11

Tackling Benefit Fraud

The issue of fraud and error in housing benefit was not examined in the department's resource accounts for 2000/01 and 2001/02. The NAO identified deficiencies in the accounting systems operated by the department and had again qualified the accounts.

They did not begin to measure housing benefit loss on a continuous basis or on the same basis as Income Support and Jobseeker's Allowance until 2001. And when they did start to analyse the level of fraud and error they encountered problems with data collection; had an imprecise mechanism for gathering data; lacked full engagement with the local authorities who dispersed the benefits; and had a biased sample. They did not carry out a pilot study which might have allowed them to avoid these problems. £3.2

million was spent on this measurement exercise but the results were felt to be so inaccurate that they could neither be published nor be used to establish a baseline estimate of fraud and error.

The PAC noted that local authorities were deficient in the performance of housing benefit administration and anti-fraud work, and also acknowledged that the department, despite repeated commitments over the years to address the problem, had not done so. They suggested that if the local authorities were not able to deliver the benefit without substantial loss to the taxpayer, the department should consider alternative methods of delivery. The department felt that driving up the level of prosecutions and other sanctions available to local authorities was one way of reducing losses, but also felt that an incentive scheme to motivate local authorities to tackle fraud through changes was also appropriate. They created joint working units to tackle a continuing problem of working relationships at a local level, with the ambition of establishing why fraud was only prosecuted in 2% of detected fraud, whilst the figure for other detected fraud was 7%.

Since the mid-1990s the department operated a subsidy scheme to encourage anti-fraud work by local authorities. However, the NAO noted that the scheme had significant flaws – it contained perverse incentives that encouraged inflated claims of savings achieved from detection and did little to encourage authorities to prevent or deter fraud. Over time these schemes were modified and in April 2002 a new incentive scheme, which reduced the threshold for success, overcame the deficiencies, so that 75% of local authorities were theoretically able to earn subsidy from the scheme. Only 15% of local authorities chose to operate the new scheme and the threshold targets were further reduced. Even so, take-up was not substantial. Besides a lack of empathy with local authorities, the NAO noted the department "made the Housing Benefit scheme increasingly complex for local authorities and difficult to administer". (Note 1) The PAC had noted in previous reports that complexity was a major problem facing housing benefit. Government agreed and saw the need to both raise standards of administration and simplify the system. However, the Audit Commission reported that "the Government's many further changes to Housing Benefit administration were designed to control expenditure or to tackle fraud, rather than to simplify the system, despite simplification also having a contributing role in reducing the risk of fraud". (Note 2)

Both the PAC and NAO reports were critical about the lack of detailed information, but the NAO suggested that the estimate of fraud per year was £500 million based on an extrapolation of data collected in 1997/98, and that this estimate was an upper limit of what loss for fraud might be. (Note 3)

A total of £1.5 billion, based on three years from 1999, will be added to the total at the end of this section.

SOURCES

PAC Report: *Tackling Benefit Fraud*, HC488, 4 July 2003

NAO Report: *Tackling Benefit Fraud*, HC393, 13 February 2003

NAO Report: *Department of Social Security Resource Accounts 2000/01*, 31 January 2002

NAO Report: *Department for Work and Pensions Resource Accounts 2001/02*, 7 February 2003

NOTES

1 NAO Report, p44
2 ibid
3 ibid, p13, fig1

04 05 12

Housing Benefit Fraud

As the DWP had a target to reduce losses in housing benefit by 25% before 2006, it was important that the department had an accurate estimate of the level of fraud and error. The first estimate had been calculated in 1996 and the PAC found it unacceptable that the department did not begin to measure loss "on the same basis as Income Support and Jobseeker's Allowance until April, 2001". (Note 1)

The NAO commented: "Housing Benefit is another area where levels of fraud and error are a concern. The first results of a new continuous Housing Benefit Review to measure fraud and error published in December 2003 indicated that around £750 million (6.2%) of Housing Benefit expenditure is estimated to have been overpaid by local authorities on behalf of the

Department in 2002/03 due to fraud and error." (Note 2) The necessity of providing accurate information had first been mooted in 1996.

A total of £750 million has been added to the total at the end of this section.

SOURCE

NAO Report: *Department for Work and Pensions Resource Accounts 2002/03*, 12 December 2003

NOTES

1 NAO Report, p17
2 NAO Report, para 7

04 05 13

Fraud and Error in Housing Benefit

It would appear that the authorities had lost confidence in the ability of the department to produce an accurate estimate of the level of fraud and error in housing benefit, and the task was delegated to the Office for National Statistics who, in their 2002-2005 review of the matter, concluded that the level of fraud and error was £680 million for 2003/04.

The total taken to the summary at the end of this section is £680 million.

SOURCE

DWP/National Statistics Report: *Fraud and Error in Housing Benefit April 2002 to September 2005*

On 1 June 2000, Richard Broadbent, the then Chairman of HM Customs and Excise, and until recently the Chairman of Tesco plc, informed the Paymaster General, Dawn Primarolo, that a series of excise diversion frauds between 1994 and 1998 appeared to have been mishandled. Although Customs became aware of the threat of outward excise diversion frauds as early as 1994, they did not take effective action to curtail these frauds until 1998. It is against this background that losses to the taxpayer from fraud on alcohol duty are examined.

04 05 14

Losses on Alcohol Duty

The creation of the single European Market in January 1993 brought with it the removal of restrictions on the movement of goods between member states. The immediate reaction of the Treasury was to remove all regular Customs presence from bonded warehouses in the UK, without an alternative strategy in place. The decision to remove the Customs presence coincided with a drive by the Treasury to reduce headcount for Customs and Excise by some 4,188 personnel. However, the decision was welcomed by the more entrepreneurial members of the alcohol trade, who quickly identified ways and means of avoiding the payment of duty. It is estimated that in 1993/94 the level of alcohol duty evasion was £200,000.

To understand how alcohol duty evasion fraud worked it helps to understand the single market. Member states were required to operate a system of duty suspension in order to facilitate the alcohol trade. Traders and warehouse keepers were allowed to produce, process and move goods without payment of duty, which only became payable when the goods were released for consumption. Alcohol could therefore be stored at either one of the 1,100 excise warehouses in the UK approved by Customs, or one of the approximately 20,000 warehouses within the European Community, and duty would only become payable when the goods were released by the warehouse keeper, i.e. whisky produced in Scotland could move into a bonded warehouse in England and on to a bonded warehouse in France and would not be liable for duty until the French warehouse keeper had delivered the goods to the consumer market.

The removal of the Customs personnel from the bonded warehouses in the UK no doubt acted as an invitation to the more unethical entrepreneurs, who almost immediately tested the situation to see whether goods could be diverted to the domestic or international market without the tiresome obligation of paying duty. The Public Accounts Committee (PAC) was alert to the implications and sought comfort: "In February 1994, Customs told the Committee of Public Accounts, in evidence on the Comptroller and Auditor General's Report on the Department's 1992/93 accounts, that there was at that time no sign of increased fraud, as a result of the new single market arrangements", (Note 1) and were reassured that the department was watching very carefully for new types of fraud arising as a result of the single market. However, even as they gave evidence, the fraudsters were active and duty evasion had grown from £200,000 to £46.3 million by the end of March 1995.

The first serious investigation was mounted in 1995, as criminals acquired increasingly large consignments of alcohol intended for export and diverted them into the domestic market, and this investigation resulted in the identification of some £19 million worth of revenue evaded. The facts were presented to the Chairman of Customs and Excise in December 1995, which begs the question about why government were not told until 2000, after Customs and Excise had decided to withdraw the guarantee scheme they operated for warehouses. The guarantee had been compulsory pre-1993 for all intra-European movements of duty-suspended alcohol and had been intended to cover the occasional or minor loss and was not intended to underwrite organised diversion. However, it acted as a minor deterrent and its abolition made life easier for the criminal fraternity.

On an operational level, Customs and Excise decided to let suspected fraudsters move suspect consignments from excise warehouses under observation – a tactic referred to as 'letting loads run' – on the basis that this would lead to evidence which would help the conviction of the suspected fraudster. Duty evasion had in the meantime moved from £46.3 million in 1995 to £137 million in 1996, (Note 2) and Customs and Excise, to support the 'letting loads run' tactic, decided to give warehouse keepers indemnity against liability for duty on consignments which left the warehouse. The warehouse keeper's cooperation was essential, both in alerting Customs to fraudulent or potentially fraudulent consignments, and also in letting the suspect consignments leave the warehouse under surveillance. The implication was that the warehouse keeper was liable for the duty if the consignment which left his warehouse was misdirected. Some warehouse keepers were given written indemnities, whilst other warehouse keepers were given verbal or implied indemnities. It has transpired that 53% of the revenue evaded was indemnified. Meanwhile, duty evasion had moved on from £137 million in 1996 to £334.8 million in 1997. (Note 3)

Customs and Excise were aware that the problem existed but were unsure of the scale. They entered into cooperation agreements with other member states of the community to create an early warning system, and created IMPEX (Import/Export) groups throughout the UK to address the problem.

Duty evasion grew less dramatically, and by 2000 had reduced to £13.4 million. (Note 4)

The NAO report into the matter nonetheless accepted losses of £668 million between 1993 and 2000 where alcohol destined for export had been fraudulently diverted to the UK market without the payment of excise duty or VAT, and £216 million revenue lost from diversion into overseas markets where duty would have been due in the country of import had the goods not been fraudulently diverted. A total of £884 million is therefore added to the summary at the end of this section.

SOURCES

PAC Report: *Losses to the Revenue from Frauds on Alcohol Duty*, HC331-1, 20 May 2002

NAO Report: *HM Customs and Excise Appropriation Accounts 1999/2000*, HC25-XII, 9 February 2001

NAO Report: *Losses to the Revenue from Frauds on Alcohol Duty*, HC178, 19 July 2001

NOTES

1 PAC Report, p4/8
2 NAO Report, HC178, p15, figure 4
3 ibid
4 ibid

04 05 15

The Rocques Report

In July 2001 the government published an independent report by John Roques into the causes of fraud, and recommended action to be taken forward by Customs.

A pre-Budget report identified that the problem of alcohol diversion and resulting fraud had not decreased to the levels estimated in previous reports, and indeed had shown a steep rise since 1999/2000. This fraud was particularly attractive to criminals, as the illicit product had not been subject to duty in the UK or elsewhere, and was sold at or near legitimate duty-paid prices. It was difficult to differentiate illicit product from legitimate product at the retail stage, making this type of fraud both highly profitable and relatively uncomplicated. Alcohol frauds were undertaken by both large organised crime syndicates and small-scale operators. There were three main types of excise diversion fraud: inward excise diversion, where the duty-suspended goods from the EU diverted into the UK market without payment of UK duty; outward excise diversion, where duty-suspended goods ostensibly for export were diverted into the UK home market; and inland excise diversion, where duty-suspended goods moving within the UK were diverted directly into the UK market.

Customs work on managing the risk of alcohol fraud was given lower priority against that given to tobacco and oil evasion, based on a relative assessment of the risk to revenue posed by each sector and resourcing constraints. This decision may have been helped by the difficulty in establishing the level of revenue loss and the size of the illicit market.

Estimates for fraud were provided by the Customs' Analysis Division, which considered the total UK consumption figure for spirits and subtracted the legitimate UK alcohol market to arrive at a figure for the illicit market. Examination differed for the three main categories, but for 2001/02 the Analysis Division estimated that a total of £700 million had been lost. (Note 1) A PAC report recorded that "there is significant uncertainty about any estimates of spirits fraud based upon current methodologies and data sources", (Note 2) and also noted that the fraud estimates produced by both Customs and the Scotch Whisky Association "can hardly be reliable when they result in such widely different estimates. Discussions continue between the Office for National Statistics, Customs and the Scotch Whisky Association to reconcile the differing estimates". (Note 3) This uncertainty suggested that the reported figures for fraud for 1998/99 of £12.6 million and £13.4 million in 1999/2000 had been grossly understated.

A total of £1.75 billion, calculated as £700 million for 2001/02 (Note 4), £450 million for 2002/03 (Note 5) and £600 million for 2003/04 (Note 6), is therefore added to the summary at the end of this section.

SOURCES

PAC Report: *HM Customs and Excise Standard Report*, HC284, 22 July 2004

NAO Report: *Standard Report 2003/04*, 17 March 2004

NAO Report: *HM Customs and Excise: Standard Report 2002/03*, 18 December 2003

NAO Report: *Customs and Excise Appropriation Accounts 2000/01*, 13 February 2002

NOTES

1 NAO Report 2002/03, p31
2 PAC Report, p4
3 ibid, p8
4 PAC Report, p5
5 ibid, q15
6 ibid

Value Added Tax

Value Added Tax (VAT) is collected by HM Revenue and Customs and is a tax on consumption. First introduced in 1973 at a single rate of 10% on most goods and services, the tax is currently 20% with some goods zero-rated and some goods charged at a reduced rate. The tax is optional insofar as it is only paid when goods are purchased. The seller collects the tax on behalf of government but has to register once taxable turnover has reached £79,000. Traders may choose to register even if their turnover is less than that amount. Traders must account for VAT at the appropriate rate on all taxable supplies, but can offset any VAT paid on purchases related to those supplies. The net amount of VAT due has to be remitted to Customs (or claimed back if more VAT has been paid on inputs then collected on sales) when the trader submits their VAT returns. This report examines the collection of VAT from 1999 onwards.

04 05 16

Missing Trader Fraud

These accounts recorded that "the Department has not yet completed their assessment of fraud in VAT, which is Customs' largest tax stream, representing 50% of total receipts". (Note 1) Customs estimated a total of £6.8 billion had not been collected as a result of fraud, (Note 2) but admitted that only one aspect of VAT fraud, i.e. missing trader intra-community fraud had been examined in detail. Their estimates were that losses to the Exchequer for missing trader fraud were £1.9 billion and £2.1 billion in 1999/2000 and 2000/01 respectively. (Note 3)

Missing trader fraud involves fraudsters obtaining VAT registration to acquire goods VAT-free from member states of the European Union. Having sold the goods onwards at VAT-inclusive prices they then disappeared without paying the VAT paid by their customers. The fraudsters disappear by the time the tax authorities follow-up the registrations as part of their regular checking activities – hence the missing trader description. There are a number of refinements including 'carousel' fraud, where the goods that have been sold on in the UK are then sold again through a series of transactions to another member state, and the goods then re-enter the UK; acquisition fraud where the fraudster obtains a VAT number for the purpose of purchasing goods VAT-free from another member state – the goods are then supplied on to the UK at a VAT-inclusive price, but the fraudster goes missing without paying the VAT; repayment fraud where fraudsters register for VAT, make false claims for repayment from Customs, and then abscond; suppression fraud where traders understate the proportion of sales or inflate their claims to input tax to reduce their VAT liability; and the shadow/informal economy fraud where a company above the VAT registration threshold deliberately does not register for VAT.

The department had a total of 1.6 million traders registered at the end of March 2001, but felt that their computer system, LORDS, had weaknesses that could affect the accuracy of the information held. The system "also had poor logical security and it cannot produce transaction logs, audit logs or printouts of access rights". (Note 4) The Departmental Trader Register (DTR) was unavailable for periods of time between February and June 2001 owing to technical problems and, when available, response times were poor. Understandably, Customs intended to replace LORDS with a system that would meet their demands, but the NAO noted that there had already been slippage in the implementation timetable.

The estimated loss for fraud and error for the two-year period 1999-2001 was £4 billion, calculated on missing trader fraud of £1.9 billion in

1999/2000 and £2.1 billion in 2000/01 and these sums will be added to the summary at the end of the section.

SOURCE

HM Customs and Excise Appropriation Accounts 2000/01, 13 February 2002

NOTES

1 NAO Report, R2
2 ibid
3 ibid, R17
4 ibid, R16

04 05 17

VAT and IT

Three quarters of a million traders had not been visited by Customs staff in the ten years prior to this report and, of these traders, approximately two thirds had not had their VAT position assessed in detail. It will not therefore come as a surprise to find that, during 2001/02, Customs identified underpayments of £2.5 billion in VAT and excise through their assurance work.

Customs made assessments of tax liabilities by comparing the trader's VAT return for the month with till rolls and other records. They also observed traders who rarely gave receipts, and produced estimates which could be used to approach other, similar, traders in the area with assessments of their VAT liability. This activity identified underpayments of £2.5 billion in VAT and excise in 2001/02. Despite this success Customs made considerable organisational changes during the year, creating a Large Business Group which concentrated on the top 1,000 revenue payers and revamped the Regional Business Service, which collected VAT from companies not in the Large Business Group, as well as collecting from SMEs. In November 2002 Customs produced a VAT compliance strategy and published estimates of the possible extent of fraud and evasion for VAT, totalling £8.6 billion. (Note 1)

The importance of IT technology to the collection of VAT cannot be overemphasised. The department operated dedicated systems for specific needs. A decision to replace the LORDS IT system was reviewed and it was decided to continue to operate the system until it was replaced as part of the Customs e-Business programme, despite reservations previously expressed about the system. The Departmental Trader Register (DTR) holds the permanent record for each trader. The system could not cope with demand, so it was decided to introduce a single system in phases in April 2001 and November 2001. DTR suffered significant amounts of downtime and was unavailable for five months.

The Database for Investigation And Management Of New and existing Debt (DIAMOND) was affected by the unavailability of DTR, which affected response time for users and unavailability for about 6% of total staff time. Another major operational problem for Customs was the lack of a full interface between DIAMOND and the VAT Information System Inter-Office Network (VISION), which meant that receipts of revenue from traders were not always updated automatically onto DIAMOND. The NAO identified £300 million recorded on VISION which could not be traced to DIAMOND, (Note 2) which suggested that staff at the Debt Management Unit had not been notified of certain debts. It would seem that Customs IT problems added to the department's difficulties in collecting VAT.

The total of £8.6 billion identified by Customs in their November 2002 report will be added to the summary at the end of this section.

SOURCES

PAC Report: *The Operations of HM Customs and Excise in 2001/02*, HC398, 12 June 2003

NAO Standard Report 2001/02

NOTES

1 PAC Report, p7
2 NAO Report, p38

04 05 18

Tackling VAT Fraud

Customs achieved 69 convictions for VAT fraud in 2002/03. They had 1,050 Large Business Group traders and 1.7 million smaller traders. They had 161 intelligence staff responsible for monitoring duty collection, but this resource was reduced from 16% of what was available to 13% on the basis that the tobacco fraud area needed greater attention, a fact recorded in the PAC report: "The 13% of intelligence resources allocated to VAT was proportionately much less than its share of the tax receipts involved." (Note 1)

The sheer scale of VAT fraud and error was now becoming apparent to Customs and Excise. They calculated the tax gap by comparing the total level of expenditure in the economy that theoretically would be liable for VAT with the actual level of VAT receipts, mainly using data from the Office of National Statistics, and assumed that the difference represented the total revenue loss. For 2002 and 2003 they also relied on operational and intelligence data to produce estimates of losses from specific areas of activity, and using these procedures Customs estimated that the tax gap in 2002/03 was £11.9 billion. The latter figure was a staggering 15.7% of total VAT receipts.

There were four main areas of concern: missing trader fraud; tax avoidance schemes; trader non-compliance; and the informal/shadow economy.

Missing trader fraud had become more sophisticated, with the variant referred to as carousel fraud involving usually high-priced but small high-density computer components or mobile telephones which passed between a number of companies and jurisdictions. Customs and Excise would pay VAT refunds to companies in a chain without corresponding income, one of two companies would disappear and Customs and Excise would be left with the debt. The estimate for this type of fraud was £2.26 billion.

Depending on implementation, some VAT avoidance schemes were not illegal, but Customs did not consider it acceptable for businesses to use schemes that were artificial and had no other business purpose other than to save VAT. The Treasury in 2003 tackled this area of avoidance and closed various loopholes and required businesses with a turnover of £600,000 plus to disclose use of VAT avoidance schemes to appear on a register. Customs, however, estimated the loss as £3.05 billion. (Note 2)

Customs also estimated that around £500 million was lost from about 125,000 to 218,000 traders who failed to register for VAT. Customs identified 3,600 traders by liaising with the Inland Revenue and the Department for Work and Pensions and sharing information. Customs also identified net additional liabilities of £1.06 billion from large businesses and £2.6 billion from small and medium-sized traders in the year.

The PAC report suggested that the department was complacent about VAT collection. The Chairman, Edward Leigh, set the tone for the meeting by asking the department, "You are not complacent?" (Note 3) Gerry Steinberg, MP for the City of Durham, said, "I think that for a Department that is, frankly, not collecting £20 billion, your attitude is very complacent. We would not be having this debate today if you had collected that £20 billion because all of the public sector would change in terms of finance". (Note 4) The committee was also surprised at the lack of investigations of professionals: "Despite the thousands of under declarations of VAT discovered each year Customs reported the accountant or other professional involved to their professional body on four occasions." (Note 5)

The impression given is that the department was getting to grips with the financial implications of fraud and error as far as VAT was concerned. A total of £11.9 billion VAT was lost in 2002/03 as a result of error, avoidance and fraud. The NAO standard report for 2003/04 suggested that the tax loss was 12.9%, (Note 6) which has been calculated at £9.1 billion. A total of £21 billion is added to the summary at the end of this section.

SOURCES

PAC Report: *Tackling VAT Fraud*, HC512, 29 July 2004

NAO Report: *Tackling VAT Fraud*, HC357, 3 March 2004

NAO Report: *HM Customs and Excise: Standard Report 2002/03*

HMRC Measuring Tax Gaps 2011

NOTES

1 PAC Report, p10
2 ibid, p11
3 ibid, ev 1, q3
4 ibid, ev 5, q44
5 ibid, p5, para 7
6 NAO Report 2003/04, p131

04 05 19

Ministry of Defence: Major Projects Report

This was a bad year for the MoD. Only two of their pre-Main Gate projects moved into Main Gate status; the NAO report highlighted that costs had increased by £3.1 billion; the tensions between the department and one of its major suppliers, BAE, was exposed at a Public Accounts Committee (PAC) meeting; and one of their projects, the Support Vehicle Project, was strongly criticised for being behind time and ahead of cost, caused, the NAO believed, by the MoD's decision to ignore the SMART Acquisition Process.

The tensions between the MoD and a main supplier, BAE Systems, were exposed by the comments of Sir Raymond Lygo, Chief Executive of British Aerospace in the 1980s, who said that "the company consistently underbid for contracts knowing that they could recover the true cost when the project was underway". (Note 1) Mike Turner, the Chief Executive of BAE Systems, stated that the company did not knowingly underbid for contracts, whilst Sir Kevin Tebbit KCB, CMC added that "even if underbidding had been prevalent during the era of cost plus contracting 20 years ago, the Department now had a sophisticated system to understand the price base of bids, and said he was absolutely certain that underbidding was not taking place today", (Note 2) which suggests that underbidding occurred 20 years earlier.

The NAO report was critical of the MoD's decision to introduce, into the demonstrate and manufacture phase, the Support Vehicle Project. The NAO was and is very committed to the SMART Acquisition Process as it provides much-needed assessment of projects before they arrive at Main Gate, and by doing so reduces the risk of cost overruns and time slippage. The NAO had in previous years documented how well the MoD had observed the SMART Acquisition Programme and how, in doing so, the department was meeting its objectives and was bringing into line fraught procurement policies, so a departure from the process caused the NAO much angst. They commented, "In the event, the Department's and industry's understanding of the requirement was immature and has resulted in programme slippage through an extended competitive phase". (Note 3)

The Brimstone Project was first mentioned in the Major Projects report for 2000, and had moved into serious difficulty in budgetary terms. The anti-armour weapon was planned for use on Tornado, Harrier and Typhoon aircraft and was scheduled to replace the BL755 cluster bomb. The contract, managed by MBDA, was running 31 months late, and technical difficulties, inflation and accounting adjustments added £139 million to the cost.

The Astor Programme saved £11 million during the year, which will be reflected in the total of the summary at the end of this section

The Astute class submarine had been in Main Gate for a number of years but not under the microscope, as its budget seemed controlled. The original contract was placed with GEC-Marconi in 1997 for three units. GEC and Marconi demerged in 1999 and the latter joined with British Aerospace to create BAE Systems. Despite this consolidation and the internal turbulence caused, the MoD admitted that "between 1997 and 2002 the Department did not explicitly monitor the integration of designs via the computer-aided design tool and did not include the use of the tool as a separate item on its risk register". (Note 4) This, despite the fact that one of the fundamentals of the contract was to use computer aided design (CAD) to achieve improved quality through efficiency. BAE Systems, after the takeover of Marconi, downsized the workforce at Barrow-in-Furness whilst still working on other shipbuilding programmes, the Landing Platform Dark replacement programme and the Auxiliary Oiler. The seriousness of the situation became apparent in late 2001, by which time the programme has slipped by 43 months and was £886 million over the original estimate. BAE Systems were required to make a £250 million contribution to the cost of the programme and the contracts with the American Electric Boat shipyard. The NAO recorded the variation as £984 million, which will be added to the summary at the end of this section.

The Bowman Project to provide the armed services with 48,000 radios of varying types began life in 1988 with a company called ACSL Ltd, at an estimated cost of £130 million. It took the MoD 12 years to realise that ACSL was not able to provide the equipment as specified, and they initiated another contract with Canadian company CDC for £2.073 billion. A total of £276 million was spent with ACSL Ltd, of which £206 million was recognised in a previous report. £70 million will therefore be added to the summary at the end of this section.

The Nimrod maritime reconnaissance and attack aircraft, designated MRA4, was intended to replace the existing Nimrod MK, with enhanced anti-submarine and anti-surface warfare capability. The contract for 21 aircraft was given to BAE Systems in 1996 on a fixed-price basis, but by 1998 the company informed the MoD that they were unlikely to meet contract timescales, which led to negotiations in May 1999, in February 2002 and finally in February 2003. The contract was reduced to 18 aircraft and BAE Systems made provision in their accounts for a contribution of £800 million. The 2003 agreement led to the curtailment of any work beyond the first three aircraft. Sir Raymond also changed the basis of the contract from a fixed-price contract to a Target Cost Incentive fee basis. The forecasted overrun was £394 million, with an additional cost of £194 million as a result of the slippage of the delivery date, so the total added to the summary at the end of this section will be £588 million.

The Eurofighter, now renamed Typhoon, was managed by the NATO Eurofighter Tornado Management Agency (NETMA) on behalf of the partners in the project, i.e. Germany, Italy, Spain and the UK. By 2014, four aircraft completed their maiden flights, albeit some 54 months late. Because variation against budget was £1.037 billion, the necessity to run on with the Tornado and Jaguar aircraft because of the delivery delays cost £47 million extra. On the positive side, £165 million was saved by redefinitions, and accordingly £1.084 billion will be added to the summary at the end of this section.

The MRAV armoured vehicle was a joint French/German/Dutch/UK venture to build a modern and flexible range of armoured utility vehicles. The MoD withdrew from the programme in 2003 at a cost of £30 million.

The total added to the summary at the end of this chapter is £2.875 billion.

SOURCES

PAC Report: *Ministry of Defence: Major Projects Report 2003*, HC383, 21 October 2004

NAO Report: *Ministry of Defence Major Projects Report 2003*, HC195, 23 January 2004

NOTES

1   PAC Report, p12

2   ibid

3   NAO Report, p2

4   ibid, p28

SUMMARY: CHAPTER FIVE – 2004

04 05 00	Fraud and the Inland Revenue	£15.120 bn
04 05 01	Wembley and the Lottery Grant	£0.161 bn
04 05 02	NHS (England) Summarised Accounts 2002/03	£0.640 bn
04 05 03	GCHQ: New Accommodation Programme	£0.344 bn
04 05 04	NIRS2 and the National Insurance Fund	£0.051 bn
04 05 05	Tax Credits, PAYE Records and the Construction Industry	£0.316 bn
04 05 06	NIRS2 Contract Extension	£0.169 bn
04 05 07	Inland Revenue: Tax Credits	£0.027 bn
04 05 08	Inland Revenue: Tax Credits and Tax Debt Management	£29.629 bn
04 05 09	Inland Revenue: Tax Credits	£1.978 bn
04 05 10	The Recovery of Debt	£0.660 bn
04 05 11	Housing Benefit: Tackling Benefit Fraud	£1.500 bn
04 05 12	Housing Benefit Fraud	£0.750 bn
04 05 13	Fraud and Error in Housing Benefit	£0.680 bn
04 05 14	Losses on Alcohol Duty	£0.884 bn
04 05 15	The Rocques Report	£1.750 bn
04 05 16	Value Added Tax: Missing Trader Fraud	£4.000 bn
04 05 17	Value Added Tax: VAT and IT	£8.600 bn
04 05 18	Value Added Tax: Tackling Vat Fraud	£21.000 bn
04 05 19	Ministry of Defence: Major Projects Report	£2.875 bn
	Total	£91.134 bn
	Total adjusted for inflation to December 2014	£115.557 bn

SUMMARY: GOVERNMENT WASTE BY CALENDER YEAR

2000	Section 00 01 00 to 00 01 18	£27.284 bn
2001	Section 01 02 00 to 00 02 12	£18.992 bn
2002	Section 02 03 00 to 00 03 15	£44.724 bn
2003	Section 03 04 01 to 03 04 14	£27.585 bn
2004	Section 04 05 00 to 04 05 19	£115.557 bn
Total		**£234.142 bn**

SUMMARY: GOVERNMENT WASTE BY DEPARTMENT

1	HMRC	£133.948 bn
2	Department for Works and Pensions	£35.223 bn
3	Department of Defence	£31.240 bn
4	Department of Health	£14.129 bn
5	HM Treasury	£9.859 bn
6	Department for Environment, Food and Rural Affairs	£4.032 bn
7	Home Office	£2.580 bn
8	Department for Culture, Media and Sport	£2.034 bn
9	Department for Transport	£0.573 bn
10	Ministry of Justice	£0.380 bn
11	Department for Education	£0.142 bn
12	Department for Communities and Local Government	£0.002 bn
Total		**£234.142 bn**

"In quiet and untroubled times it seems to every administrator that it is only by his efforts that whole population under his rule is kept going, and in this consciousness of being indispensable every administrator finds the chief reward of his labour and efforts. While the sea of history remains calm the ruler-administrator in his frail bark, holding on with a boat hook to the ship of the people and himself moving, naturally imagines that his efforts move the ship he is holding on to. But as soon as a storm arises and the sea begins to heave and the ship to move, such a delusion is no longer possible. The ship moves independently with its own enormous motion, the boat hook no longer reaches the moving vessel, and suddenly the administrator, instead of appearing a ruler and a source of power, becomes an insignificant, useless, feeble man."

Tolstoy, Leo, War and Peace, 1868/69

CONCLUSION

The summary on Page 234 identifies that over £234 billion was wasted by government through fraud, error and inefficiency, and suggests that taxes collected were not used effectively. The sheer size of the figure, approximately 14% of the national debt, invites the reader to question its accuracy, and indeed if the figure is finite. The writer cannot give a definitive answer to these questions as a number of inhibitors have to be considered.

A primary inhibitor was the lack of information available in the reports about certain categories. The impression given was that government was not aware of the level of fraud, error or inefficiency in some specific departments in the earlier years of the decade.

Housing benefit was just one example where, even by 2003, the department seemed unable to give the National Audit Office (NAO) an accurate figure about the level of fraud etc., so the compilation of figures was eventually handed to the Office for National Statistics. Similarly, the Treasury could not or did not offer definitive figures to the NAO when tax credits were first introduced in 1999 and suggested that the fraud figure was in the order of £2-3 million a year. In fact, the figure for fraud, error and inefficiency was later identified as about £600 million a year. Customs and Excise did not get to grips with alcohol smuggling until 2002/03, some eight years after the removal of restrictions on the movement of goods within the European market, and in 2004 were still negotiating with spirit manufacturers about which set of fraud figures were more accurate.

These examples, and there are others, suggest that government was playing catch up with establishing the level of waste in the system rather than being proactive in the eradication of waste etc.

What did not help was a decision to change the accounting requirement from appropriation to resource accounts. With appropriation accounts the various departments of state operated on a cash basis, i.e. were given an appropriation for the year with the brief to work within budget. One weakness of such an accounting procedure is that it removes from the department a motivation to underspend, as the following year's budget was established on the previous year's expenditure. Resource accounting moved the departments into line with business in the UK and departments had to accrue liabilities on their balance sheet for equipment for which payment was scheduled over a number of years, e.g. the Admiralty, having bought Apache helicopters and arranged to pay for them over a ten-year period, would have to accrue appropriate finance. The early years of this report notes a number of departments where difficulties with the transition skewed some of the figures available.

The figures may also be skewed by a lack of resources available to the writer. Whilst writing this conclusion it was noted that a computer failure at Swanwick caused delays at Heathrow and other airports, and a press report suggested that when it was initially delivered it was six years late and hundreds of millions of pounds over budget. Whilst this book does report on the National Air Traffic sale (Section 03 04 14), publication deadlines did not allow research and completion of the report into the reported overspend at Swanwick. No doubt there will be other examples for this period that have been missed, but hopefully, with experience, the identification of fraud, error and inefficiency will improve. There is also the facility to include any unidentified projects in Volume 3, covering the period from 2005 to 2009, as well as the ability to correct any errors.

The NAO, on the other hand, has a staff of 850 people who produced 493 reports at a cost of £170,000 per report. Admittedly, the latter figure is a very crude figure based on the resources available to the NAO divided by the number of reports they produced, whilst ignoring their other activities, but it does give some indication of the resources available.

The government of the period under review sought to be a reforming one, and whilst it later lost its direction, on the one hand by taking the country to war in Iraq, and on the other hand by improving pay in the public sector for political purposes, it nevertheless achieved some success in the measurement of fraud, error and inefficiency in the system. Identification of the problem at least offered the hope that the problem could be solved or eradicated.

No doubt some people will immediately assume that our politicians are at fault for this unhappy state of affairs. They are, after all, our elected representatives and are sent to Westminster to, amongst other duties, ensure that the taxes collected on behalf of government are suitably distributed, and that taxpayers' money does not find its way to fraudsters or is spent inefficiently. The political base has some 650 MPs at Westminster, 760 bodies in the House of Lords, 129 Scottish MSPs in Edinburgh, 108 members of the Legislative Assembly in Northern Ireland and 60 members in the National Assembly for Wales as well as 751 MEPs in Brussels or Strasbourg. The naive would assume that, as devolution was established in Wales, Scotland and Northern Ireland, the base of MPs at Westminster would reduce but that's not the case. Similarly, there is an assumption that, as Brussels and/or Strasbourg takes over more of our legislative activities, then the need for so many people at Westminster and the Lords will also reduce, but again that is not true.

The psyche of the politician does not allow for cost control or any type of reduction and likes to boast about government spend rather than restraint and, like most bureaucracies, seeks to grow. Politicians are transitory, fight to get into parliament and, having arrived at Westminster, spend the first period trying to understand the workings of the House and the Civil Service. A second period is spent trying to promote the ideals upon which they were elected and the last period of their stay in the House is spent working on their re-election programme. They live in a bubble and are cocooned by spin doctors, lobbyists and special advisers; media reaction is more important than constituent contact. More and more MPs have little experience of working outside the political bubble. Over 30% of Conservative and Liberal Democrat MPs have an Oxbridge education, mostly studying politics, philosophy and economics (PPE). The figure for Labour is 25%.

They regard themselves as underpaid but still have a basic compensation package which is three times the average wage, have generous secretarial and travel allowances and various other perks. Indeed, an MP costs £118,000 a year. They have not recognised the damage done to the brand by the expense scandal of some years ago when a significantly large number of MPs decided to fiddle their expenses to compensate for their basic package. MPs now approach a trapdoor, involving an increase in basic pay which will attract further opprobrium from the voting public and will also allow the Civil Service, quangos, the judiciary and other public sector workers to argue that if money is available for MPs then it should be available for other public sector employees. They hide behind the suggestion that this increase in salary was independently assessed and approved, knowing full well that no one is independent of their paymaster, and in this case the paymaster is the taxpayer.

Upon their arrival at Westminster politicians inherit a civil service which exists to interpret, action and administer legislation, which the politician decides, on a utilitarian basis, is good for the country. All too often the legislation is assessed after conversations with the media, spin doctors and special advisers. The incoming government also inherits a programme initiated by the previous government and has to decide quickly whether or not to continue with the legislation proposed or to cancel – sometimes at significant cost.

Civil servants see themselves in a different light. They offer the continuity necessary when government changes but very rarely make a recommendation about a course of action. They offer a number of options to their political masters and, if they feel one particular course of action is more attractive than another, that course of action will be presented in a way that convinces the minister that he is making his own decision about the project. The Senior Civil Service (SCS) believes it runs Britain. Indeed, a leaked document circulated amongst SCS members and passed to Cabinet by Francis Maude (Conservative Cabinet Office Minister in the 2010 to 2015 coalition government) said that the criteria for choosing permanent secretaries who run Whitehall departments included the ability to tolerate "high levels of ambiguity and uncertainty and rapid change – and at times irrational political demands", (Note 1) as well as the "ability to manage trade-offs and pivot between serving and leading... Being shrewd about what needs to be sacrificed, what cost and what the implications might be". (Note 2) Mr Maude, in a letter which accompanied the report to Cabinet wrote that "the civil service exists 'not to serve the long-term aims of the department' but the priorities of the government of the day, while retaining the ability to serve a future government". (Note 3)

The image of a civil servant is someone working for government receiving lower than average pay but having employment for life and a reasonable pension upon retirement. In 2000 there were 461,000 civil servants, (Note 4) but that figure had been reduced to 407,000 (Note 5) by the end of 2014. Fifty per cent of the latter are employed by executive agencies or other non-departmental public bodies (NDPBs). The easy-to-define image has also changed, as there is uncertainty about employment for life, with government eager to reduce the size of the state, and some salary packages at the upper level of the SCS are now as attractive as those in the private sector.

The SCS is the elite of the civil service, and the crème de la crème of the elite are the 40 Permanent Secretaries, 130 Under Secretaries and 650 Deputy Secretaries. (Note 6) These are the generalists. (Note 7) Likely to be have been educated at Oxbridge or at a Russell Group University, having achieved a good degree, the generalist would move between departments on average every two years on the basis that frequency of movement was crucial if the generalist was "to develop specialism – his knowledge and experience of the working of the government machine". (Note 8) Note that the specialism is knowledge of the working of government. If success was not available within the highest ranks of the service a generalist could always find a niche within a department or transfer to one of the many quangos, (Note 9) created from the 1980s onwards, or to one of the 1,148 semi-autonomous public bodies connected to UK central government. (Note 10) Permanent and Under Secretaries are responsible for their departments and responsible for the interface between those departments and the hundred or so ministers of government. They have responsibility but little accountability, as demonstrated by the 78 reports examined for this exercise. But there should be accountability.

Senior civil servants have a confidence which is sometimes mistaken for arrogance buoyed by the fact that, despite the onslaught of major reforms since the 1970s, they still managed to create potential employment prospects in quangos, executive agencies and Europe. They feel undervalued and unloved and look with envy at their equals in Europe who are quoted and feted at every top table. The President of the European Commission, now Jean Paul Juncker, formerly Jose Manual Barroso, is very much the public face of the EC, but is responsible for controlling the 23,000 European civil servants – not the European Parliament.

Civil servants know they lack the experience of managing large-scale organisations, and indeed, Gus O'Donnell, former Head of the Civil Service, explained, "We don't do project management". (Note 11) John Cassels, a permanent secretary in the Cabinet Office said, "The Civil Service is bad at implementation and always has been, because clever chaps can think up policies all the time, but find it dreary to apply them. We have never been good at doing that. We are always making mistakes". (Note 12) And yet project management is exactly what's required if you're going to build a Millennium Dome, a Channel Tunnel rail link or invest in the new Wembley Stadium. This thought process perhaps explains why in most PFI projects, which required a comparison between a project built by the private sector or one built by the public sector, invariably the public sector price would include a risk element which could be as high as 25%, whilst the private sector price did not include such a penalty. In effect, the Civil Service were saying that if we run the project then it will go over budget. Some people might think that the risk element added to the public sector price would more often than not make the private sector price cheaper and ensure that the project became a PFI budget, both off the government balance sheet and also off the responsibility list for the Civil Service.

The same mind process now dictates that a budget is no longer a budget, but is an indication of price which allows the buyer to reach preferred bidder stage and then start the proper negotiation with the supplier. An excruciating example of this was the 2012 Olympics, when a budget was established of £2.5 billion, against the better judgement of the then Chancellor, Gordon Brown, and this sum was duly submitted to the IOC in Singapore. On that basis the Olympics came to London in 2012, but in the period between the bid and the opening ceremony the cost escalated to £9.5 billion, and if Premiership football team West Ham United's ability to get the rights to the stadium for £15 million, plus annual rental, is a measurement of performance by the London Legacy Development Committee, then the £9.5 billion will be exceeded. The spin doctors had the chutzpah to circulate a note pointing out how wonderful it was that government had operated within budget – the £9.5 billion budget! The civil service need to revisit the definition of budget and, if they can't find enough money to finance a project, then that project should not go ahead.

Some of the reports examined are value for money (VfM) reports originated by the Public Accounts Committee (PAC), whilst others are statutory reports prepared by the National Audit Office (NAO). VfM reports are examined by the PAC and, in a lengthy procedure, call as a witness any civil servant or indeed supplier they feel can answer questions not fully exposed by the NAO report. The politicians involved are asked to put aside their own political influences – generally without success. Examination of civil servants and other witnesses can be brusque and demanding, and on occasions requests are made for supplementary information. The civil servants appearing before the committee are always of a senior level and handle themselves with the style expected of such senior personnel. However, in looking at the 78 reports it is noticeable that a large number of civil servants who appeared before the committee were new to the position and that the previous incumbent, who was perhaps responsible for whatever disaster had occurred, had moved on to another department. Having heard the evidence and deliberated, the PAC would then approve a report for circulation to interested personnel. One of the more familiar clichés from a number of reports was that there were lessons to be learned and that this report was a basis upon which civil servants could learn and avoid the same problem occurring again. Alas, what really happened was that the report was filed and the people who provided evidence to the committee assessed whether their performance had been sufficiently buoyant and that they were not too obtrusive.

Section 02 03 00 identified that tobacco smuggling cost the taxpayer about £3.5 million in 1999/2000 and the PAC recommended a course of action to eradicate the problem. A BBC report on 14 June 14 2014 highlighted that tobacco smuggling was still a major issue and was still costing the taxpayer about £2.4 billion a year, so the problem had not been solved and is still ongoing some 14 years later. The Civil Service answer to the problem was to introduce, over a two-year period, 12 X-ray scanners, even though they had 43 approved points of entry. The smugglers naturally booked their ferry tickets to ports without scanners.

Similarly, the very first project looked at in this book was the Case Work Programme, (00 01 00) which examined IT technology, which would make the processing of applications from people who wish to apply for citizenship, seek asylum or extend their stay more efficient. A report in *The Telegraph* on 29 October 2014 recorded that the Home Office had now initiated their third attempt at providing the necessary technology. Immigration is a major political issue and it would seem after 15 years that the Civil Service were still not in a position to provide their front-line troops with the necessary technology to ensure that everyone in the country is here legally.

Reform of the Civil Service is fundamental if the losses to fraud, error and inefficiency are to be reduced to the bare minimum. Part of that reform must include the realisation that materiality is not an excuse for avoiding investigation of loss. The NAO itself is guilty of falling into this trap, suggesting a sum of £32 million becomes immaterial and not worth investigating as it's less than 1% of a total budget. There is not a business in the land who would accept such a scenario, and the Civil Service and government have to adopt the same approach.

Disraeli wrote in his novel *Endymion* about civil servants that "the relations between a minister and secretary are, or at least should be, amongst the finest that can subsist between two individuals. Except the married state, there is none in which so great a confidence is involved, in which more forbearance ought to be exercised, or more sympathy or to exist". (Note 13) Somewhere between Disraeli and Harold Wilson the relationship deteriorated, and all subsequent Prime Ministers to different degrees have acknowledged the need for reform

Harold Wilson's government originated the Fulton Report about the Civil Service and one of its main recommendations when it was published in 1968 was that the cult of the generalist was obsolete and that civil servants should become more specialist. The job of implementing those recommendations was given to Sir William Armstrong, at the time Head of the Home Civil Service, who proceeded to implement the changes that suited the Civil Service and obfuscated about those changes which did not suit. Peter Kellner and Lord Crowther-Hunt, authors of *The Civil Servants*, suggest that Armstrong defeated Fulton, and by proxy the government, and noted that whilst the majority of the 158 recommendations made by Fulton were implemented, "Those reforms at the heart of Fulton to make the Civil Service more professional and accountable were either ditched or fudged, even though Fulton ostensibly had Government support". (Note 14) In March 1978, a government White Paper about the Civil Service said about the Fulton Report, "The acceptance... resulted in a number of radical changes in the organisation and management of the civil service". But the radical changes were peripheral and the main recommendations were ignored.

The 1979 government of Margaret Thatcher convinced Derek Rayner, joint Managing Director at Marks & Spencer, to organise a drive against waste and inefficiency. Rayner made his name introducing innovative management techniques, fostering enterprise and employees, driving down costs and bringing in improved financial management at Marks & Spencer and his role was to try to bring about the same in Whitehall as head of the Efficiency Unit. Thatcher had a critical view of the Civil Service as a bureaucracy and had a determination to bring about cuts to the overall number of civil servants and quangos. Rayner had mixed results. He discovered along the way that if a permanent secretary took a grip on what was happening there could be genuine action, but if the scrutiny (Note 15) was delegated it was less likely to be implemented fully and successfully. A NAO report calculated that, by 1983, when Rayner left, 155 scrutinies had been conducted, and savings of £170 million had been achieved with the potential of another £100 million.

In 1988, the Next Steps Report was published in an attempt to understand why the scrutiny philosophy was not delivering longer term change. Their main recommendation was a need for an arm's-length agency to take on the role of delivery, thereby focusing on the job to be done but ensuring that the lines for accountability and responsibility for these bodies was crucial. The report had an uneasy birth but, by 1988/89, the initiative caught alight and, a decade after the report, three quarters of civil servants were employed by agencies.

When Margaret Thatcher was dramatically deposed in 1992, John Major became Prime Minister and accepted the Next Steps formula, as it agreed with his own philosophy about increased transparency and accountability through the Citizens' Charter programme. The Civil Service 'bought' into the Next Steps philosophy as it offered new opportunities and increased the base of bureaucrats.

Tony Blair's appointment as popular Prime Minister in 1997 initially led to a number of reports about Civil Service reform. New Labour realised there was a problem with the Civil Service but the problem was not one which they expected. To quote Blair, "The problem with them... was inertia. They tended to surrender, whether to vested interests, to the status quo or to the safest way to manage things – which all meant: do nothing". (Note 16) Sir Michael Lyons (Note 17) published his report on 15 March 2004, recommending that 20,000 civil servants should be moved out of London, whilst Sir Peter Gershon (Note 18) presented his report to Cabinet with a suggestion that 84,000 Civil Service jobs might be cut. Gordon Brown took the opportunity of reducing the Civil Service head count by just over 70,000 people.

David Walker of *The Guardian* suggested in an article in June 2014 that Whitehall leaders have agreed a Faustian pact with government for the last

12 months of the present parliament. Walker suggests, "Civil Service leaders struck an unholy bargain with Cameron and his ministers. You can shrink us, you can shave our pay and perks... But as long as you don't touch our amateurism and lack of accountability, we won't protest even when your policies are impossible". (Note 19) Walker continues, "Whitehall's line is that rail contracts, Universal Credit, student loans and other organisations failures in recent years were one offs. But however ropey the policies, we cannot just blame the politicians. Take Universal Credit – the Civil Service must have thought it could be delivered because the Work and Pensions permanent secretary never asked for a 'letter of direction'". (Note 20) Walker continues: "Pick up virtually any recent report from the National Audit Office, parliamentary committees or the IfG. Together they describe an anachronistic system, one that has failed to keep up. As outsourcing is burgeoned, Whitehall simply has not acquired the capacity to write contracts that stretch contractors including third sector providers. As the G4S and Serco examples show, officials seem to have given up on monitoring performance. Whitehall simply lacks the commercial skills; civil servants don't understand 'systems' (including arm's-length bodies and local government); they have not adopted technology." (Note 21)

This book was conceived when the writer first read about the very public spat between John Prescott and his civil servants about who was to blame for the £1 billion FiReControl fiasco. Politicians are not blameless and have ducked the responsibility of holding the Civil Service and other bodies they control to account. They have the power but not the time nor inclination to act. The senior members of the Civil Service walk the corridors of power and regard themselves as the facilitators who empower all that happens in Britain today.

The evidence of this book shows that they are out of touch, incompetent and in dereliction of their duty to taxpayers. This volume has looked at the period from 2000 to 2004, and the indications are that the waste figure is exaggerated by a lack of knowledge about the true condition of the financial accounts and also by the change in accounting policy which required large write-offs at the beginning of the period studied.

It would seem to the writer that a project examined by the PAC because of failure should not end with the politicians analysing how successful they were in the media battle or the administrators congratulating themselves on well-written reports and a reasonable result on the witness stand. A number of MPs on the PAC committee and the administrators responsible for the gaffe should be given a special purposes vehicle (SPV) with six or seven external directors who command equal status with, and who should outnumber, the MPs and the administrators. The management board of the SPV should be given two to three years to eradicate the problem which they have just examined and given a package which will reward all members of the board, including MPs and civil servants, substantially if they achieve the necessary result. Failure would not be an option. Only eradication of the root of the problem will solve this long-term issue of government waste.

The issue of government waste needs urgent attention. The government coffers are empty and, whilst there may be upfront costs to eradicate waste, the other option of again increasing taxes is less palatable both to the taxed and the Treasury. The next volume of this series will appear in 2017 and will hopefully identify a reduction in the level of waste.

NOTES

1 Sylvester, Rachael: *The Times*, 8 July 2014, p23

2 ibid

3 ibid

4 Stanley, Martin: Manchester University 1824, December 2014

5 ibid

6 Crowther-Hunt, Lord and Kellner, Peter: *The Civil Servants*, p33 (see Bibliography)

7 ibid. "The concept of the generalist was, and is, most evident in the pre-Fulton Administrative Class... The members of this class number just 2500: almost all the direct entrance were graduates; their job was to examine policy options and prepare advice for ministers; they were responsible for the administration and control of government departments." p33

8 ibid, p33

9 Maer, Lucinda: House of Commons Library, 31 January 2011. Standard Note 05609

10 James, O., Moseley, O., Petrovsky, N. and Boyne, G: *Agentification in the UK*, pp1-22

11 Sampson, Anthony: *Who Runs this Place?* p129 (see Bibliography)

12 ibid, p127

13 Sampson, Anthony: *Who Runs This Place?* p115 (see Bibliography)

14 Crowther-Hunt, Lord and Kellner, Peter: *The Civil Servants*, p98 (see Bibliography)

15 Scrutiny: See Haddon, Catherine: *Reforming the Civil Service Institute for Government*

16 Blair, Tony: *A Journey*, p205 (see Bibliography)

17 Lyons, Sir Michael: *Public Sector Relocation Review*, 2004

18 Gershon, Sir Peter: *Gershon Efficiency Review*, 2005

19 Walker, David: *The Guardian*, 10 June 2014

20 A Letter of Direction is usually sought by a Civil Servant when he/she thinks the matter under consideration will create a problem at a later date.

21 Walker, David: *The Guardian*, 10 June 2014

BIBLIOGRAPHY

Armitage, Sir Arthur. *Committee on Political Activities of Civil Servants*. London, 1978. Her Majesty's Stationary Office.

Bacon, Richard and Hope, Christopher. *Conundrum*. London, 2013. Backbite Publishing Ltd.

Barnett, Joel. *Inside the Treasury*. London, 1982. Andre Deutsch.

Bayley, Stephen. *Labour Camp*. London, 1998. BT Batsford Ltd.

Blair, Tony. *A Journey*. London, 2004. Harper Collins.

Blunkett, David. *The Blunkett Tapes*. London, 2004. Bloomsbury.

Bootle, Roger. *The Trouble with Europe*. London, 2014. Nicholas Brealey Publishing.

Bower, Tom. *Gordon Brown*. London, 2004. Harper Collins.

Brooks, Richard. *The Great Tax Robbery*. London, 2013. OneWorld Publications Ltd.

Brown, Colin. *Fighting Talk*. London, 1997. Simon and Schuster Ltd.

Cable, Vince. *Free Radical*. London, 2009. Atlantic Books

Cameron, Sue. *The Cheating Classes*. London, 2002. Simon and Schuster Ltd.

Campbell, Alaistair and Stott, Richard (eds). *The Blair Years. The Alaistair Campbell Diaries*. London, 2007. Hutchinson.

Carswell, Douglas. *The End of Politics*. London, 2012. Backbite Publishing Ltd.

Chapman, Leslie. *Your Disobedient Servant*. London, 1978. Chatto and Windus.

Chisholm, John. *The Qinetiq Question*. London, 2011. Amazon.

Clark, Alan. *Diaries*. London, 1994. Orion Books Ltd.

Colombi, David. *The Probation Service and Information Technology*. Aldershot, 1994. Avebury.

Cook, Robin. *The Point of Departure*. London, 2003. Simon and Schuster UK Ltd.

Craig, David and Brooks, David. *Plundering the Public Sector*. London, 2006. Constable and Robinson Ltd.

Craig, David and Elliott, Matthew. *Fleeced*. London, 2009. Constable and Robinson Ltd.

Crewe, Ivor and King, Anthony. *The Blunders of our Governments*. London, 2013. OneWorld Publications.

Crowther-Hunt, Lord and Kellner, Peter. *The Civil Servants*. London, 1981. McDonald Futura Publishers.

Elliott, Matthew and Rotherham, Lee. *The Bumper Book of Government Waste*. Petersfield, 2006. Harriman House Ltd.

Elliott, Matthew and Rotherham, Lee. *The Bumper Book of Government Waste*. Petersfield, 2007. Harriman House Ltd.

Dowding, Keith. *The Civil Service*. London, 1995. Routledge.

Garrett, John. *Managing the Civil Service*. London, 1980. William Heineman.

Giddens, Anthony. *Where Now for New Labour?* Cambridge, 2002. Polity Press.

Gould, Philip. *The Unfinished Revolution*. London, 1998. Little, Brown and Company (UK).

Hancock, Matthew and Zahani, Nadhim. *Masters of Nothing*. London, 2010. Biteback Publishing Ltd.

Healy, Denis. *The Time of my Life*. London, 1989. Michael Joseph.

Henderson, Nicholas. *Mandarin*. London, 1994. Weidenfeld and Nicholson.

Hennessy, Peter. *Whitehall*. London, 1989. Martin Secker and Warburg Ltd.

Jay, Anthony. *Confessions of a Reformed BBC Producer*. London, 2007. Will Stop Centre for Policy Studies.

Jones, Owen. *The Establishment*. London, 2014. Allen Lane.

Kaufman, Gerald. *How to be a Minister*. London, 1980. Sidgwick and Jackson Limited.

Keegan, William. *Mr Lawson's Gamble*. Sevenoaks, 1989. Hodder and Stroughton Ltd.

Kwarteng Kwasi, Patel Priti, Raab Dominic, Skidmore Chris, Truss Liz. *After the Coalition*. London, 2011. Backbite Publishing Ltd.

Lawson, Nigel. *The View from Number 11*. London, 1992. The Bantam Press.

Lewis, Michael. *Liar's Poker*. London, 1989. Hodder and Stroughton.

Livingstone, Ken. *You Can't Say*. London, 2011. Faber and Faber Ltd.

Lloyd, John. *What the Media are Doing to our Politics*. London, 2004. Constable and Robinson Ltd.

MacIntyre, Donald. *Mandelson and the Making of New Labour*. London, 2000. Harper Collins.

Mc Bride, Damien. *Power Trip*. London, 2013. Biteback Publishing Ltd.

Meyer, Christopher. *DC Confidential*. London, 2005. Weidenfeld and Nicholson.

Mullin, Chris. *A View from the Foothills*. London, 2009. Profile Books Limited.

Mullin, Chris. *Decline and Fall*. London, 2010. Profile Books Ltd.

Mullin, Chris. *A Walking Part*. London, 2011. Profile Books Ltd

Myddlelton, D.R. *They Meant Well: Government Project Disasters, (2007). Institute of Economic Affairs Monographs*. Hobart. Paper number 160.

Oborne, Peter. *The Triumph of the Political Class*. London 2007. Simon and Schuster Ltd.

O'Callaghan, Sean. *The Informer*. London, 1998. Transworld Publishers Ltd.

O' Toole, Fintan. *Ship of Fools*. London, 2009. Faber and Faber Ltd.

O' Toole, Fintan. *Enough is Enough*. London, 2010. Faber and Faber Ltd.

Parkinson, Cyril Northcote. *Parkinson's Law on the Pursuit of Progress*. Harmondsworth, 1973. Penguin.

Paxman, Jeremy. *Friends in High Places*. Harmondsworth, 1991. Penguin.

Petherick, Simon (ed). *The Essential Civil Servant*. London, 1994. Robert Hale Limited.

Peston, Robert. *Who Runs Britain?: and Who's to Blame for the Econmic Mess We're in*. London, 2008. Hodder and Stroughton Ltd.

Price, Lance. *The Spin Doctor's Diary*. London, 2005. Hodder and Stroughton Ltd.

Rawnsley, Andrew. *Servants of the People*. London, 2000. Hamish Hamilton Ltd.

Rawnsley, Andrew. *The End of the Party*. London, 2010. Viking.

Robinson, Geoffrey. *The Unconventional Minister*. London, 2000. Michael Joseph.

Routledge, Paul. *Gordon Brown*. London, 1998. Simon and Schuster Ltd.

Sampson, Anthony. *The Changing Anatomy of Britain*. Sevenoaks, 1982. Hodder and Stroughton Ltd.

Sampson, Anthony. *Who Runs this Place?* London, 2004. John Murray.

Scott, Derek. *Off Whitehall*. London, 2004. I.B Tauris and Company Limited.

Seddon, John. *The Whitehall Effect*. Axminster, 2014. Triarchy Press.

Sinclair, Iain. *Sorry Meniscus*. London, 1999. Profile Books Ltd.

Todd, Selina. *The People*. London, 2014. John Murray.

Williams, Shirley. *Climbing the Bookshelves*. London, 2009. Virago Press.

Wilson, Rob. *Five Days to Power*. London, 2010. Biteback Publishing Ltd.

PRINTED AND BOUND BY:

Copytech (UK) Limited trading as Printondemand-worldwide,
9 Culley Court, Bakewell Road, Orton Southgate. Peterborough,
PE2 6XD, United Kingdom.